T5-BPY-357

THOMAS AQUINAS AND HIS LEGACY

STUDIES IN PHILOSOPHY
AND THE HISTORY OF PHILOSOPHY

General Editor: Jude P. Dougherty

Studies in Philosophy
and the History of Philosophy   Volume 28

Thomas Aquinas
and His Legacy

edited by David M. Gallagher

THE CATHOLIC UNIVERSITY OF AMERICA PRESS
Washington, D.C.

B
765
,T54
T46
1994

Copyright © 1994
The Catholic University of America Press
All rights reserved
Printed in the United States of America

The paper used in this publication meets the minimum requirements of
American National Standards for Information Science—
Permanence of Paper for Printed Library materials,
ANSI Z39.48–1984.

∞

LIBRARY OF CONGRESS CATALOGING-IN-PUBLICATION DATA
Thomas Aquinas and his legacy / edited by David M. Gallagher.
     p.   cm. — (Studies in philosophy and the history of
philosophy ; v. 28)
   Includes bibliographical references and index.
    1. Thomas, Aquinas, Saint, 1225?–1274. 2. Thomas, Aquinas, Saint,
1225?–1274—Influence—Philosophers, Modern. 3. Philosophers,
Modern. 4. Neo-Scholasticism. I. Gallagher, David M., 1956– .
II. Series.
B21.S78 vol. 28
[B765.T54]
189′.4—dc20
93-25825
ISBN 0-8132-0790-8 (alk. paper)

Contents

Abbreviations

The following abbreviations will be used in referring to the works of Thomas Aquinas. Unless otherwise noted, all quotations and citations are from the editions listed.

ST	*Summa theologiae*, Leonine edition (*Sancti Thomae de Aquino opera omnia*, Rome, 1882–), vols. 4–11.
SCG	*Summa contra gentiles*, Leonine, vols. 13–15.
In Sent.	*Scriptum super libros Sententiarum*, ed. P. Mandonnet and M. Moos (Paris: P. Lethielleux, 1929–47), 4 vols.
De veritate	*Quaestiones disputatae de veritate*, Leonine, vol. 22.
De malo	*Quaestiones disputatae de malo*, Leonine, vol. 23.
De potentia	*Quaestiones disputatae de potentia*, in *Quaestiones disputatae*, vol. 2, ed. P. Bazzi, M. Calcaterra, T. S. Centi, E. Odetto, P. M. Pession (Turin-Rome: Marietti, 1965).
De virt. in comm.	*Quaestio disputata de virtutibus in communi*, in *Quaestiones disputatae*, Marietti, vol. 2.
De anima	*Quaestio disputata de anima*, ed. J. H. Robb (Toronto: Pontifical Institute of Mediaeval Studies, 1968).
De spiritualibus	*Quaestio disputata de spiritualibus creaturis*, in *Quaestiones disputatae*, Marietti, vol. 2.
Quodlibet	*Quaestiones Quodlibetales*, ed. R. Spiazzi, 9th ed. (Turin: Marietti, 1956).
In Post. Anal.	*Expositio libri Posteriorum*, Leonine (2d ed.), vol. 1–1.
In Periherm.	*Expositio libri Peryermenias*, Leonine (2d ed.), vol. 1–2.
In Ethicorum	*Sententia libri Ethicorum*, Leonine, vol. 47.
In Politicorum	*Sententia libri Politicorum*, Leonine, vol. 48.
In Physicorum	*In octo libros Physicorum Aristotelis expositio*, ed. P. M. Maggiòli (Turin: Marietti, 1954).
In De caelo	*In libros Aristotelis De caelo et mundo expositio*, in *In Aristotelis libros De caelo et mundo, De generatione et corruptione, Meteorologicorum expositio*, ed. R. M. Spiazzi (Turin-Rome: Marietti, 1952).
In Metaph.	*In duodecim libros Metaphysicorum Aristotelis expositio*, ed. M.-R. Cathala and R. M. Spiazzi (Turin: Marietti, 1950).
In De anima	*Sentencia libri De anima*, Leonine, vol. 45–1.

In De Trinitate	*Expositio super librum Boethii De Trinitate*, ed. B. Decker (Leiden: E. J. Brill, 1965).
In De causis	*Super librum De causis expositio*, ed. H. D. Saffrey (Fribourg: Société Philosophique-Louvain: Éditions E. Nauwelaerts, 1954).
In div. nom.	*In librum Beati Dionysii De divinibus nominibus expositio*, ed. C. Pera (Turin-Rome: Marietti, 1950).
In Ioan.	*Super Evangelium S. Ioannis lectura*, ed. P. C. Cai, 5th ed. (Turin-Rome: Marietti, 1952).
Comp. theol.	*Compendium theologiae seu Brevis compilatio theologiae ad fratrem Raynaldum*, Leonine, vol. 42.
De regno	*De regno ad regem Cypri*, Leonine, vol. 42.
De ente	*De ente et essentia*, Leonine, vol. 43.
De unitate	*De unitate intellectus contra averroistas*, Leonine, vol. 43.

Introduction

I

To pursue philosophy within a tradition has, since the rise of the Enlightenment, been viewed with suspicion. *Sapere aude!* Tradition, it is thought, is merely the refuge of the faint-hearted who, fearful of the call to think for themselves, cling to the ready-made formulae handed down to them, like frightened children to their mother. Tradition leaves its followers unable and unwilling to seek new truths or entertain new thoughts. Within a tradition, every truth is an old truth, novelty is equated with falsehood. Thus the widespread notion that thinkers who explicitly embrace a tradition cannot be true philosophers, but are simply a species of historian, interested in their particular aspect of the past. They may present the old ideas to us anew; they may clarify them and render them accessible; nevertheless, in the final analysis, they are not pursuing truth itself, but only exposing what others have held to be true.

We should recognize that such an understanding of tradition's role in the intellectual life is not wholly inaccurate. There have always been and always will be those who cling to the past simply as past, those who view all innovation with suspicion, and those who would reduce all philosophy to mere scholarship. We should not, however, mistake the abuse for the use; *abusus non tollit usum.*

A philosophical tradition stands before its followers just as a teacher does before his students. Any authentic teacher aims to lead the students entrusted to him to truth, and while the paths his teaching may take are many and various, all tend to this one goal. Having himself already reached the goal, or, as is usually the case, having traveled at least some way down the path, the teacher can show the students the way along which they must walk. But of course, the present teacher has had his own teachers, and so they have had theirs; this chain of teachers stretches back into the past, at times into the distant and unknown past. These past teachers, however, do not remain only in the past. Even in the present they continue to teach, not now with their own voices, but in the living voices of their students—our teachers—as well as in the still pages of their writings. The doctrines of the whole ensemble both dead and living, those shared conceptions of the truth and the paths that lead to it, the agreement about which questions matter, the commonly accepted distinctions and concepts that serve to answer those questions, the agreement about the falsity or inadequacy of alternate answers; these constitute a tradition. This ensemble, both through its living followers and through the writings which it has generated, serves as a common teacher.

To ask, then, why one would seek to follow a tradition amounts at bottom to asking why one would seek a teacher. The reply is both a simple and a profound one: to learn something from someone who already knows it is much surer and quicker than to discover it entirely on one's own. Many basic facts of human life, both of knowledge and of practice, find here their root cause. Moreover, besides learning more quickly and more surely, we often learn from others what we by ourselves would never have learned. It took the genius of Newton and Leibniz to discover the calculus; now each year thousands of students of ordinary intelligence master it. For most people, in fact, not to be taught is not to learn at all.

The fact that one person can learn from another allows for the growth of both sciences and arts. The students who are taught can learn, in a fraction of the time, what many persons spent their lives to discover. In the time remaining to them, they can then push knowledge forward, and so each generation can begin a little higher than the previous. Thus, to enter into a tradition, whether it be in physics or biology or philosophy, enables one not only to enjoy the fruits of decades or even centuries of labor, but also to contribute to the wealth of human knowledge. Anyone who rejects tutelage inevitably consigns himself to intellectual poverty and sterility.

There must, of course, be those geniuses who can learn without being taught, who in fact stand as the original teachers, and yet, even here, the wholly self-taught are found only at the beginning. Once some knowledge has been gained, genius manifests itself not by ignoring teachers but by transcending them. There are new discoveries and additions to knowledge, refinements of existing knowledge, corrections of false knowledge: new leaves which hang from the old branches. It is from these geniuses, especially in philosophy, that traditions take their names. Hence we can properly speak of a Platonic tradition, an Aristotelian tradition, a Kantian tradition, and most certainly of a Thomistic tradition. All these thinkers began with what they received from their predecessors, but went beyond them to leave a more or less defined body of thought which bears their personal stamp and has shaped the thought of men for centuries.

But how is it possible to share in a tradition, to have one's thoughts shaped by that of earlier thinkers, without giving one's self over to intellectual servitude? Here, too, the answer lies in seeing tradition as a teacher. Authentic teachers never take themselves or their teaching as ends. Rather, the goal is that the student should come to the truth. But not only should the student acquire truth; he should also accept it as true because he himself *sees* it to be true. While it may occur, indeed often does occur, that a student accepts something as true only because he has been so taught, this is not the goal of an authentic teacher. Ideally the teacher brings the student to see the evidence, that is, to take something to be true by seeing it to be true and not because a teacher has taught it. Any other approach is mere dogmatism. The authentic teacher wants, in the end, to become superfluous, a scaffold used only to raise the building and not to bear its weight.

So too, the point of a tradition is never that its followers should accept it simply as "traditional." This unfortunately often occurs, and it is just this attitude which makes "tradition" synonymous with "dogmatism." Whenever someone is satisfied with accepting a view merely as "traditional" there is only "dead" tradition; such tradition no longer produces the fruit of true understanding. For a tradition to be living, for it truly to function as a tradition, its followers must never be satisfied to accept anything merely as "traditional." Rather, they must so enter into the tradition that they see the truth for themselves, independently of the fact that it has been taught to them. Here we have the true middle ground between the slavish adherence to tradition simply as what has been held and taught in the past, and the wholesale rejection of tradition. Here tradition serves intellectual freedom because it serves as a means to truth, and to truth grasped in the way most appropriate to free knowers: because it is *seen* by the knower to be true. The desire for truth so grasped gives rise to tradition in the first place, and it alone can vouchsafe a tradition's continuance and progress.

The intellectual labor of those who have accepted a tradition as their teacher falls into two broad areas: first, the concerns internal to the tradition, and second, the issues and questions that arise from outside. Among the tasks that are carried out internally, the most basic is that of assimilation. Each individual must carry out the painstaking task of understanding the various propositions and the arguments for them, thereby transforming what is initially accepted on the word of a teacher into what is seen to be true by evidence. Such assimilation is arduous and long, for one must trace the accumulated thoughts of those who themselves dedicated their whole lives to answering the most difficult of questions. Not surprisingly, few persons can complete the work of assimilation and almost all remain students to the end of their days. In the second place is the task of correcting and refining a tradition. Precisely in the light of evidence, one may see that what is taught is not in fact true and so introduce the necessary rectifications. At times one may recognize confusion, lack of clarity, missed distinctions. Here the work is to identify these and to introduce the distinctions which are their remedy. The final task is that of furthering a tradition, the sort of pure addition which is not a simple refinement, but an actual step forward toward a more profound understanding of the matter at hand. Here more than anywhere else, genius is required.

The furthering of a tradition often occurs under the pressure of questions and issues raised from outside the tradition, questions and issues which cannot be ignored simply because they have not arisen from within. It falls to "living" tradition to deal with challenges made to it by proponents of different and opposing traditions. Either these challenges must be met and repulsed as unfounded, or the received tradition must be modified to accommodate the truth of the opposed view. So too the tradition must welcome new truths as the knowledge of nature and of human affairs increases. Here again followers of the tradition, especially a living tradition, must be willing to accommodate the new by modifying the old. With each new set of historical circumstances new questions arise, especially concerning human affairs, and the resources of the tradition must be employed to understand the significance of such new circumstances and to guide the practical response they call forth.

As Alasdair MacIntyre has suggested, we might look to Thomas Aquinas as a sort of model for what it means to do philosophy within a tradition. It is hard to imagine anyone more eager than Thomas to learn from his predecessors. Such eagerness finds expression in the story told of him, that upon drawing near to the city of Paris one day and being asked by a companion if he would like to be lord of the city, he replied that he would rather have the homilies of Chrysostom on the gospel of St. Matthew. Moreover, as MacIntyre has pointed out, Aquinas was able to enter into several distinct traditions to such a degree that they were for him like "first languages," understood on their own terms and not by any "translation" into the framework of opposing traditions. It was precisely this capacity for assimilating traditions which permitted him to forge the synthesis of Aristotle, the Arabic commentators, Neoplatonism, and Augustinianism that is found in his corpus.

The melding of these apparently disparate traditions into an orderly and harmonious synthesis, a synthesis that transcends simple eclecticism, is one of Thomas's greatest works of genius. Within his thought the central themes of his teachers, far from being suppressed, find their place in a whole larger than any of them. Here there is a tireless work of refinement, an unending attempt to clarify the meaning of his predecessors, to remove confusions in their thought, to make explicit what they had only intimated.

Yet this work of synthesis and refinement was possible only because Thomas had his own unique contribution to make. Above all, this means his doctrine of the act of being, the *actus essendi*. The doctrine of *esse* pervades his work and lies at the bottom of his solution not only of metaphysical problems, but also of epistemological and even ethical questions, as for example, his characterization of a morally good act as one which enjoys its appropriate *plenitudo essendi*. Here, at the roots of his thought, we see most clearly that despite the respect for and appeals to authority which mark every page of Thomas's work, he was in no way bound to them; for the sake of truth he transcended the traditions handed down to him.

Thomas's synthesis of the prior traditions along with his unique contribution to that synthesis allowed him to hand down to his followers the teaching and tradition that bears his name. From his first followers like the Dominicans Thomas Sutton and John Quidort in the decades following Thomas's death, through the works of the great sixteenth- and seventeenth-century commentators such as Thomas of Vio, Sylvester of Ferrara, and John of St. Thomas, and into this century following the impulse given to Thomistic philosophy by Leo XIII's *Aeterni patris*, thinkers of all casts of mind and of all degrees of talent have chosen Aquinas and his students as their own teachers. Thomas has provided, and still provides, a comprehensive philosophical understanding of the world from which we can approach all the various questions peculiar to our own age and circumstances.

The essays which the present volume comprises can be taken as part of the ongoing effort to do philosophy under the tutelage of Aquinas, including both the work of assimilation as well as the application of the tradition to new questions. All these essays were originally given as papers in the 1990 Matchette Lecture Series of the School of Philosophy at The Catholic University of America. The first five can be taken as sharing in the work internal to the tradition, especially the work of assimilation, with each one attempting to elucidate some central theme of Thomas's philosophy. The second five essays are all concerned in one way or another with the application of Thomas's philosophy to issues and concerns that arise from thinkers who disagree with him or to new questions that arise from changing historical circumstances or from new discoveries within science and their applications. All the essays display the philosophical wealth that can be found in the works of Thomas and his legacy.

II

In chapter 1, *Kenneth Schmitz* describes the role of *esse*, the act of being, within Thomas's thought. He reviews the major currents of the last sixty years in the study of Thomas's metaphysics: first an emphasis on being as universal, then the recognition that being is always found in the concrete and the particular (Aimé Forest), then a realization of the role of participation (Cornelio Fabro, Louis-Bertrand Geiger), and finally an insistence on the primacy of *esse* (Etienne Gilson). *Esse*, as found in all existing things, is absolutely comprehensive and, as the act of all acts in any particular thing, is absolutely intensive. *Esse*, then, overcomes the dichotomy between universal and particular. Finally, Schmitz discusses the priority of *esse* to its co-principle. Although *essentia* is said to "have" *esse*, its capacity for *esse* is not prior to *esse*, but in fact only arises with the bestowal of *esse*.

Aquinas's solution to the age-old question of the ontological status of universals is the theme of *Jorge Gracia*'s essay in chapter 2. Gracia traces the development of the problem from Boethius, who posed the question in terms of existence in the mind versus existence outside the mind, to Avicenna, who posited a third mode of existence different from these, to Aquinas's *De ente et essentia*. Aquinas refuses to accept Boethius's formulation of the problem, and, framing the question in terms of *natures*, holds that natures in themselves have *no* particular mode of existence, nor even unity or multiplicity. The mode of being, as well as unity or multiplicity, belongs only *per accidens* to the nature taken in itself. In this way Thomas can explain how the nature exists both in and outside the mind and how it can be both one and many.

David Gallagher's essay in chapter 3 is an analysis of the precise nature of moral goodness in Aquinas's ethical thought. An initial exposition concerning the notion of the good (*bonum*) in general and its convertibility with being lays the groundwork for discussing moral goodness as the form of goodness found in voluntary actions, specifically, the goodness found in the will. Moral goodness is precisely the will's adherence to the proper rule in the activity of willing. Gallagher points out that moral goodness is an analogical notion which, while said primarily of the will, can also be properly used of moral virtues, moral law, and so forth. In a final discussion, he shows why it is in terms of their moral goodness that human beings are said to be good without qualification.

In "Aquinas on Moral Responsibility in the Pursuit of Knowledge" (chapter 4), *Gregory Reichberg* brings to light an important but somewhat neglected aspect of Thomas's ethical thought, namely, the moral dimension of speculative or theoretical knowing. In contrast to many modern conceptions of knowledge, Aquinas takes knowing as a *personal* act. As such it enjoys the voluntary character proper to all human acts, and is thus a *moral* activity. Truth, as a particular good, becomes the object of moral choice. Since the will governs the activity of knowing in its *exercise*, it is there, as opposed to the knowing's *specification*, that we discover the moral dimension. Thomas, in fact, proposes a specific moral virtue, *studiositas*, which governs the morally good use of speculative intellect.

In chapter 5, *Edward Mahoney* takes up the question of Thomas's critique of Averroes' doctrine of the unity of the intellect. His interest is to show how the arguments Thomas used in his well-known *Tractatus de unitate intellectus contra averroistas* were not first introduced in that work, but had already appeared in earlier works. Mahoney systematically reviews the critique of the unicity of the intellect as it is found in Thomas's major works. In doing so he demonstrates the consistency of Thomas's teaching throughout his career. He also brings out the wide range of arguments employed by Thomas, even including some based on the destructive consequences of the Averroistic position for the moral life.

The Thomistic understanding of perfection and its contrast with that of Charles Hartshorne is *Oliva Blanchette*'s theme in chapter 6. Blanchette shows how the meaning of the term "perfection" is found first in natural beings which are generated and gradually reach a fulfillment or perfection. This understanding is then extended—with modifications—to God, who is not generated. Perfection can also be predicated of the created universe as a whole insofar as there is nothing outside of it. Blanchette points out that Hartshorne applies to God the notion of perfection that Aquinas applied to the universe as a whole, and suggests that this application yields Hartshorne's particular understanding of the divine perfection.

Alejandro Llano (chapter 7) takes issue with Jaakko Hintikka and Simo Knuuttila, both for their assertion of the "principle of plenitude" according to which everything which is possible must be actualized, and for their claim that Aquinas invokes this principle in the proof for God's existence based on contingency (the *tertia via*). Llano shows that for Aquinas, as well as for Aristotle, "possibility" is an analogical term, used both of real being (*ens proprium*) and being as truth (*ens ut verum*). What is not possible in one sense can be possible in the other. Hintikka and Knuuttila understand possibility only as logical possibility, the possibility appropriate to being as truth, and so fail to see that things could be different from how they actually are, that is, that there could be real possibility. For Aquinas the ontological is prior to the logical and cannot be reduced to it.

Yves Simon and Jacques Maritain both looked to Aquinas for the basic principles on which they argued for the desirability of liberal democracy for modern states. In chapter 8, *John Hittinger* examines these arguments and the Thomistic texts to which they appeal. He asks whether Thomas meant by "democracy" what is currently meant, and whether Thomas would, like Simon and Maritain, hold that democracy is the best form of rule. Underlying this question is a deeper one, namely, whether the modern democratic spirit is consistent with the principles of Thomas's political philosophy.

William Wallace (chapter 9) applies some basic principles of the Aristotelian-Thomistic philosophy of nature, especially its explanation of the body/soul unity in terms of matter and form, to the ethical questions related to death and dying. Wallace suggests that the human body may continue to live after the death of the person, just as Thomas thought that the body, in its initial stages, was alive, but was not yet animated by a human soul. His distinction between personal (active) death and biological (passive) death would have direct bearing on many questions in medical ethics.

In the final chapter *Stephen Brown* describes Henry of Ghent's views on the relation of theology to the other speculative sciences. Henry's views reflect, to a large extent, his reaction to Aquinas's teaching on this subject. The chief theoretical issues center on the understanding of *subalternatio*. What did Aristotle mean by this term and how exactly does it apply to the relationships of the sciences to theology? Henry rejects Thomas's understanding of this point, and gives the term a wider meaning. In the end, he insists that all the sciences are ordered to theology and that one can rightly pursue them only if one explicitly recognizes this ordination.

D.M.G.

1

The Root and Branch of St. Thomas's Thought

KENNETH L. SCHMITZ

Over the past one hundred years a great deal of ink has been crafted concerning St. Thomas's thought. Thomistic metaphysics has usually held a place of honor in this Thomistic revival. This should not surprise us, since metaphysics stands in close relation to the credal confession of Christian faith that was so central in Thomas's thought and life. But it has stood that way for all the centuries since St. Thomas, whereas, over the past fifty years, there has been among Thomists an intense and overriding interest in Thomistic metaphysics. Now, it seems to me that this concentration *should* surprise us. For there have been past times when even those who did not care for metaphysics of any kind found other matters of interest in St. Thomas's *corpus*: matters of law and politics, of theology and biblical exegesis, of ethical and spiritual norms. Of course, no age can be completely aware of the grounds of its own interests, and ours is no exception. And so, too, we should not be surprised if this intense preoccupation with the most arcane part of philosophy should occasion surprise among those who come after us.

There can be no doubt that the metaphysics is there in St. Thomas's writings: it stands out from every page. But the fact that something is there is surely not a sure reason for supposing that we will pay attention to it. Why this all but exclusive concern for his metaphysics now? Is the current absorption with metaphysics among Thomists today due to the fact—alleged with some credibility by many—that our own age is *not* metaphysical? It is true that our age tends to scatter its intellectual energies in other directions—towards pragmatism and activism—or to suspend them—in positivism. Certainly we are suspicious of grand claims; for we have had enough of them since the seventeenth-century metaphysicians pressed their systems upon us. In contrast, philosophy with us seems to have taken the modest posture of analyzing analysis, of talking about talk and of deconstructing texts;

and for more rough and ready tastes, it has gone out onto the streets to lend its voice to the demand for one or another sort of revolutionary change. What, then, has the calm of metaphysics to do with all of this busy-ness?

And yet metaphysics is quietly alive, both among professional philosophers generally, and among Thomists in particular. It is no longer banished from the philosophical arena by the varieties of positivism that want to get on with more obvious matters, nor is it intimidated by the varieties of activism that want to get on with more practical projects. Indeed, metaphysics has become respectable enough in some quarters today so that it assumes in their eyes the face of the enemy.[1] During the last fifty years a surprising number of devotees has resolutely pursued the study of metaphysics; and the study of Thomism proves no exception to this fascination with the very root of things. What is more, among Thomists and other readers of St. Thomas, the principal focus has been upon a central doctrine in St. Thomas: the doctrine of *being*. In the great tradition of Aristotle, Thomas fashioned his metaphysics as a philosophy of *being:* the subject of the science was for him, as for Aristotle, the study of *being* precisely *as being: ens inquantum ens.*

There are, to be sure, those who insist that what is important in St. Thomas's writings is what is perennial in them. They take that perenniality to consist in what he learned from Aristotle. Or more exactly, they take what is *philosophically* significant in Thomism to be St. Thomas's endorsement of the same principles as those formulated by the Stagirite; and perhaps even in this or that instance, Thomas's clarification or betterment of the statement of one or another principle. These advocates of the perenniality of Thomism voice their greatest appreciation for St. Thomas's scientific and pedagogical methods and for his philosophy of nature. Indeed, one of their fears is that wishing to "save" Thomistic metaphysics, ardent metaphysicians might surrender the study of nature whole and entire to the positive sciences, thereby abandoning the Aristotelian philosophy of nature. It would be too much to say that metaphysics gets short shrift from these perennialists, but it is not too much to say that the center of *their* attention lies elsewhere.

---

1. I have in mind the attempts stemming from Martin Heidegger to overcome the "onto-theo-logical" complex, and of deconstructionists, such as Jacques Derrida, to displace "logocentrism." For my own views, see "From Anarchy to Principles: Deconstruction and the Resources of Christian Philosophy," *Communio* 16 (Spring 1989): 69–88; and "Postmodern or Modern-plus?" *Communio* 17 (Summer 1990): 152–66.

Now, this perennialist position is not without benefit. In such difficult and complex issues most of us are neither wholly in the truth—unfortunately; but, fortunately, neither are we wholly in error. These Thomists remind the more enthusiastic metaphysicians among us that we must not lose sight of other aspects or dimensions of St. Thomas's thought.[2]

For there is, indeed, a danger in the intensive stress of St. Thomas's metaphysics, the danger that we might reduce all of philosophy to metaphysics, then reduce metaphysics to the study of being, and finally reduce the notion of being to that of existence.[3] Is it inevitable that the metaphysics of St. Thomas be seen as an existential metaphysics? That his thought be "reduced" to an existential core? And is it inevitable that such a "reduction," such a "resolution," be an impoverishment? Well, as the Jesuit said, there are reductions, and then there are reductions . . .[4] The broad tradition of Thomas reminds us that there are issues into which St. Thomas poured much of his energy, issues that are not matters of metaphysics directly, though—to the extent that St. Thomas has succeeded in weaving a synthetic tapestry of thought—we have every right to expect that most of his discussions will bear at least some traces of his deepest philosophical conceptions.

Let me recall the most prominent features of this recent concentration upon the Thomistic metaphysics of being. Had we turned to the all-pervasive manuals used in most Catholic colleges more than fifty years ago, manuals which claimed to represent various versions of more or less Thomistic scholasticism, we would have learned from most of them that the pre-eminent characteristic of the central notion of *being*, the notion that gives definition to the science of metaphysics, is its *absolute universality*. This is, without a doubt, undeniable. Most manualist authors would have denied that *being* is a genus and that its universality is generic—they knew the Aristotelian-Thomistic ar-

2. I have in mind such reputable Thomists as Ralph McInerny; see, for instance, his recent *Boethius and Aquinas* (Washington, D.C.: The Catholic University of America Press, 1990), in which the author argues strenuously for the close continuity and even identity of St. Thomas's philosophical principles with those of Boethius and Aristotle.

3. See, for example, John Beach, "Another Look at the Thomism of Etienne Gilson," *The New Scholasticism* 50 (1981): 522–28, on the alleged reduction of all theoretical philosophy to metaphysics with the resultant neglect of the basic role of the philosophy of nature.

4. The neophyte is supposed to have asked his Jesuit teacher whether it was Jesuit practice to draw so many distinctions. To which the Jesuit replied: "Well, there are Jesuits . . . and then there are Jesuits."

guments against that thesis—but in practice the term functioned by virtue of its all-encompassing generality, more or less as the *summum genus*.

Perhaps the most massive shift in the approach to St. Thomas's metaphysics in the past fifty or sixty years, then, is the turn to the concrete.[5] The title of an influential study published almost sixty years ago points up the new direction. It is the work of Aimé Forest, *The Metaphysical Structure of the Concrete according to St. Thomas Aquinas.*[6] What the turn to the concrete brought about was a clearer realization of the paradoxical character of St. Thomas's central metaphysical term. It is here that Aristotle's sense of the diversity of things and the equivocity of *being* is transformed for St. Thomas into the analogous diversity of beings within the commonality of *being*. Now, the term *being* is here taken in its existential force; for as Thomas says many times, "[the term] *being* (*ens*) is drawn from the very act of existing (*actus essendi*)."[7] And so the term *being* (*ens*) is meant both to embrace and to penetrate the whole of reality, to be both absolutely comprehensive and absolutely intensive. He tells us that "nothing can be added to *esse* that is extraneous to it, since nothing is extraneous to it except nothing (*non-ens*)."[8] It is somehow root and branch of all that is; it takes up everything into its full amplitude, even to the singularities. Its commonality does not abstract from its singularities but penetrates them to their most intimate depths. Those depths are existential; and so again he tells us that the act of existing (*esse* in its verbal and primary sense) "is what is innermost in each and everything, and what is deepest in them all . . ."[9] *Esse*, then, is neither simply

5. See Helen James John, "The Emergence of the Act of Existing in Recent Thomism," *International Philosophical Quarterly* 2 (1962): 595–620, esp. 599.

6. Aimé Forest, *La structure métaphysique du concret selon saint Thomas d'Aquin* (Paris: J. Vrin, 1932).

7. *De veritate*, q. 1, a. 1, c.: "ens sumitur ab actu essendi" (Leonine, p. 5). See also: *In I Sent.*, d. 8, q. 1, a. 1, c. (Mandonnet, p. 195); *In I Sent.*, d. 25, q. 1, a. 4, obj. 2 and c. (Mandonnet, pp. 611–12); *In II Sent.*, d. 37, q. 1, a. 1, c. (Mandonnet, p. 944); and elsewhere. St. Thomas attributes the point to Avicenna, though he gives it a different meaning. Cf. SCG II, chap. 54: "et ipsum esse est quo substantia denominatur ens." (To avoid giving the substance a primordial and underived substantive status, one might translate the Latin thus: "and it is the very be-ing itself [*ipsum esse*] by which substance is called a being [*ens*]"; but English can tolerate only so much, and a truth can be lost by being made to look foolish.)

8. *De potentia*, q. 7, a. 2, ad 9 (Marietti, p. 192). This is the famous and oft-quoted text in which he underscores the unqualified importance of *esse*, beginning with the rare personal form of expression: "What I call *esse* is among all principles the most perfect . . ."

9. ST I, q. 8, a. 1, c.: "Esse autem est illud quod est magis intimum cuilibet, et quod

indeterminate nor simply determinate; it transcends the indeterminacy of potency and the limits of ordinary determinacy. It is the original *trans-determinacy* that surmounts the diversity within being even while it unites them in the community of being.

A second, complementary line of interpretation emerged in the 1930s. To those Thomists who saw in St. Thomas primarily another Aristotle, *Aristoteles redivivus christianus*, this second line of interpretation muddied the clear waters of any Thomistic Aristotelianism that claimed for Thomas a whole-cloth identification with Aristotle.[10] For this second line of interpretation claimed that there is a strong undercurrent of Neoplatonism in St. Thomas's thought.[11] In 1939 Cornelio Fabro published *The Metaphysical Notion of Participation according to St. Thomas Aquinas*,[12] and in 1942 Louis-Bertrand Geiger published *Participation in the Philosophy of St. Thomas Aquinas*.[13] Given St. Thomas's persistent attacks upon what he took to be the abstractionism and the univocity of Plato's philosophy, it should not surprise us that Thomas did not take over the doctrine of participation in the form that Plato had given it. Nor indeed, did it come down to him in that form. The sources of Thomas's "Platonism" are manifold. When it reached him—through the writings of Augustine, Boethius, and the Pseudo-Dionysius, and through the compendium of Proclus's *Elements* which Thomas knew under the title *The Book of Causes*, and also through the

---

profundius omnibus inest . . ." For a gathering of such texts see Joseph Owens, "Aquinas: Intimacy and Contingency of Existence," *American Catholic Philosophical Quarterly* 64 (1990): 261–64; also James Anderson, *Introduction to the Metaphysics of St. Thomas Aquinas* (Chicago: Regnery Gateway, 1953), 21–23.

10. See the argument against such identification in J. Owens, "Aquinas as Aristotelian Commentator," in *St. Thomas Aquinas 1274–1974: Commemorative Studies*, ed. Etienne Gilson (Toronto: Pontifical Institute of Mediaeval Studies, 1974), vol. 1, 213–38. For another view see G. Ducoin, "Saint Thomas, Commentateur d'Aristote," *Archives de Philosophie* 20 (1957): 240–71, 392–445.

11. Indeed, W. Norris Clarke, "The Limitation of Act by Potency: Aristotelianism or Neoplatonism," *The New Scholasticism* 26 (1952): 167–94, esp. 190–94, in a nuanced summary of the role of participation in Thomas, suggests that, while it may be more usual to speak of Thomas's thought as basically Aristotelian with a dash of Neoplatonism, one could as well say that Thomas was in some ways a Platonist specified by Aristotelianism. See also his "The Meaning of Participation in St. Thomas Aquinas," *Proceedings of the American Catholic Philosophical Association* 26 (1952): 147–57.

12. Cornelio Fabro, *La nozione metafisica di partecipazione secondo S. Tommaso d'Aquino* (Milan: Soc. Ed. 'Vita e Pensiero,' 1939); *Participation et causalité selon S. Thomas d'Aquin* (Louvain: Publications Universitaires and Paris: Béatrice-Nauwelaerts, 1961).

13. Louis-Bertrand Geiger, *La participation dans la philosophie de saint Thomas d'Aquin*, 2d ed. (Paris: J. Vrin, 1953). Cf. R. J. Henle, *Saint Thomas and Platonism* (The Hague: Martinus Nijhoff, 1956); and Arthur Little, *The Platonic Heritage of Thomism* (Dublin: Golden Eagle Books, 1949).

Metaphysics of the Moslem Avicenna—the notion of participation had already been transformed in several Neoplatonic ways, which nevertheless still bore the indirect influence of Plotinus and Proclus.

What is most important for the present topic is that the notion of *esse* took possession of center stage. No doubt Thomas enriched his conception of *being* as *esse* through meditation and reflection upon the Biblical text in which God names Himself: "I am Who Am."[14] But it must also be said that the notion of *esse* seems to have been enriched especially by the Pseudo-Dionysian meditations upon unity, goodness, and beauty.[15] What is of the greatest import is that in the mind of St. Thomas this enriched notion of *esse* was to come into association with the Aristotelian doctrine of *act* (*energeia, actus*).[16] What seems to have recommended this joining of the notion of *esse* with the act-potency relation is that only through the latter relation can the simultaneous unity and compositeness of limited beings be realized: "In every composite there must be act and potency. For several things cannot become absolutely one unless among them something is act and something potency."[17] The meeting of the notion of *esse* with the doctrine of act-potency left both *esse* and *act* transformed and transvalued in what is now widely considered to be St. Thomas's existential metaphysics. At its core is the doctrine of the *primacy of existential act*.[18]

For some students of St. Thomas, history was the way into the concrete. This was true of Etienne Gilson. In the same year in which his

14. See J. Owens, *Aquinas on Being and Thing* (Niagara: Niagara University Press, 1981), 17–18.

15. For the influence of Avicenna, see Georges C. Anawati, "Saint Thomas d'Aquin et la Métaphysique d'Avicenne," in *St. Thomas Aquinas 1274–1974: Commemorative Studies*, vol. 1, 449–65. And in the same volume, for the more general background, see Louis Gardet, "Saint Thomas et ses Prédécesseurs Arabes," 419–48.

16. Clarke, "The Limitation of Act by Potency," concludes that, in Thomas's early period up to the *Summa Contra Gentiles* (1261–1264), "the limitation principle is never found expressed in terms of act and potency but exclusively in its traditional Neoplatonic form [that being is limited by essence or form] or a close paraphrase" (190, n. 48).

17. SCG I, chap. 18: "Nam in omni composito oportet esse actu et potentiam. Non enim plura possunt simpliciter unum fieri nisi aliquid sit ibi actus, et aliud potentia." See also the entire question on the simplicity of God: ST I, q. 3. Cf. Clarke, "The Limitation of Act by Potency," 191, n. 48.

18. The recognition, articulation, and advocacy of the primacy of existential act in St. Thomas is too widespread to document. Among its most impressive proponents are Jacques Maritain, *Existence and the Existent* (New York: Pantheon, 1948); Joseph De Finance, *Être et agir dans la philosophie de Saint Thomas*, 3d ed. (Rome: Presses de l'Université Gregorienne, 1965); and Joseph Owens, *An Interpretation of Existence*, 2d ed. (Houston: Center for Thomistic Studies, 1985).

study of St. Thomas, *Le Thomisme*, first appeared (1919), Gilson called for a "living neo-scholasticism" which would demand of reason—as St. Thomas had done centuries before—*all* that it could tell us of all that is.[19] This too was a call for a philosophy of concrete reality, to be sure; but it was not yet an explicit recognition of the primacy of existential act. That did not come for another two decades. Through his later work, Gilson's name came to be linked with Thomistic existentialism.[20] And indeed, the recognition of the primacy of *esse* as act can be seen in retrospect to be the culmination of Gilson's early and constant emphasis upon the concrete order of realities that presented themselves directly to our senses. In philosophical theology, Gilson emphasized the question of the existence of God, and made use of the real distinction of essence and existence in order to distinguish God from creatures. Both his direct realism and his theological bent are already present in the work of the 1920s. The work of the next decade, however, shows a growing awareness of the paramountcy of existential act within the general problematic of a Christian philosophy of being. But existence is still considered largely within the discussion of the existence and nature of God.

There is not as yet the explicit extension of the existential principle (*esse*) to the whole range of metaphysical problems. The growing emphasis upon existential act broke through explicitly only in the revision of the fourth edition of *Le Thomisme* in 1942. The primacy of existential act was to receive an even more elaborate statement in consideration of the broad sweep of the history of philosophy in *L'être et l'essence*,[21] with its strong emphasis upon judgment, and in *Being and Some Philosophers*.[22] As Gilson became more and more aware of the omnipresent primacy of *esse* in St. Thomas, and more and more convinced of the importance of existential act in his own philosophy, he developed the existentialism of act against the background of its purported absence among thinkers in whom he might have expected to have found it present. And he characterized their philosophies as philosophies of essence, or "essentialisms." Whatever the utility of

19. In a review of *Le retour à la scolastique* by Gonzague Truc, *Revue Philosophique de la France et de l'Etranger* 88 (1919): 322–24.

20. See, for example, John T. Noonan, Jr., "The Existentialism of Etienne Gilson," *The New Scholasticism* 24 (1950): 417–38, esp. 421–22; and J. Collins, "History in the Defence of Metaphysics," *The Review of Metaphysics* 2, n. 8 (1948): 105–25.

21. Etienne Gilson, *L'être et l'essence* (Paris: J. Vrin, both the first edition [1948] which stirred such controversy; and the 2d rev. ed., 1962).

22. Etienne Gilson, *Being and Some Philosophers* (Toronto: Pontifical Institute of Mediaeval Studies, 1949; 2d rev. ed., 1952).

such a broad category, it had the effect of focusing in concrete, quasi-historical terms the question of the relation of essence to *esse*.[23]

Impetus and confirmation of the primacy of *esse* in St. Thomas was advanced also by the lively discussion that arose in the later forties and early fifties out of the textual study of St. Thomas's autograph manuscript of the third article of the fifth question of his commentary on the *De Trinitate* of Boethius. The resulting controversy, while it left some unconvinced,[24] helped to bring matters to a head.[25] The carefully nuanced position arrived at by St. Thomas, after several formulations that left him unsatisfied, makes it clear that Thomas himself had come to recognize the paramount and primordial role to be played in metaphysics by the judgment (in distinction from the simple apprehension and abstraction of essences or natures). The judgment is paramount, according to St. Thomas, precisely because in it alone can the metaphysical significance of the concrete reality of being be affirmed. Paradoxically, however, that affirmation of being *as being* can come about only by an initial judgment that is negative in form, which he called the judgment of separation (*separatio*). This *separatio* pointed to the unique character of the notion of *being* that underlies the science of metaphysics.

The *being* considered by metaphysics, Thomas tells us in this autograph text, is not arrived at by an immediate grasp of a content in simple apprehension, the first operation of the mind. Instead, it is arrived at in its concrete reality only through the second operation of the mind, the judgment. But the judgment is to be seen, not as a simple combination or copulation of concepts, subject and predicate. Rather, in fashioning that combination, the judgment turns the mind back to some context of *being*, and ultimately to the context of real, actual, existential *being*. In addition to its copulative function which

23. See my *What Has Clio to Do with Athena? Etienne Gilson: Historian and Philosopher* (Toronto: Pontifical Institute of Mediaeval Studies, 1987), 9, 17–24.

24. E.g., Edward Simmons, "In Defence of Total Abstraction," *The New Scholasticism* 29 (1955): 427–40.

25. See *In Librum Boethii De trinitate quaestiones quinta et sexta*, ed. Paul Wyser (Fribourg/Louvain: Nauwelaerts, 1948); and also *Expositio super librum Boethii De Trinitate*, ed. Bruno Decker, 2d ed. (Leiden: Brill, 1959); in addition, *The Division and Methods of the Sciences: Questions V and VI of his Commentary on the De Trinitate of Boethius*, trans. Armand Maurer, 3d rev. ed. (Toronto: Pontifical Institute of Mediaeval Studies, 1963), esp. xxii–xxx. Maurer remarks: "Only in the final redaction does he [Thomas] bring out the crucial importance of judgment and the act of existing (*esse*) grasped in that act" (xxvi). See the study (of St. Thomas's redactions in the autograph manuscript) by Louis-Bertrand Geiger, "Abstraction et séparation d'après S. Thomas *In de Trinitate* q. 5, a. 3," *Revue des sciences philosophiques et théologiques* 31 (1947): 3–40, esp. 24–28.

unites concepts, then, the verbal force of the judgment unites the mind with reality—or, in the case of a false judgment, fails to do so.

This means, however, that the significance of the *being* (*ens*) that "first falls into the mind"[26] is not exhausted by the simple grasp that forms ordinary universal concepts, such as "animal" or "plant," or even "reality." Rather, this initial *being* holds within itself and offers to the mind the promise of a further operation, by which the knower returns to that *being* from which the mind has first taken its content. The turn to the concrete on the part of these recent Thomistic scholars has had as its effect to disclose something that was there all along in St. Thomas's thought and works: the modern *turn* to the concrete has led us to see the *return* to the concrete that animates the very thought of St. Thomas himself.

If the foregoing is true, then a proper and more or less adequate notion of *being* cannot be formed by simple abstraction; it cannot be captured by simple apprehension. What is required, St. Thomas tells us, is judgment.[27] This holds for the ordinary exercise of the mind, and what is required for the metaphysical notion is the unique judgment of separation which recognizes that, whether there are actually existent immaterial beings or not—and, philosophically speaking, only further argument can tell us that—still we are entitled to affirm that *being itself* need not be restricted to material existence.

Metaphysics is the methodical study of the very character of *being itself*, and the *separatio* that stands at the threshold of metaphysics holds several implications for that study. Among them is the recognition that *being* is not merely an object standing over against the mind that recognizes it. Rather, the universality of *being* is such that it enfolds the mind itself into its absolutely ample lap. Its horizon is without limit, even though the *beings* that first fall within the compass of the mind are themselves, one and all, limited beings. *Being* can be appreciated even prior to metaphysics as indefinite yet positive, comprehensive yet concrete. *Being* names whatever *is* in any way, and all that *is* in any way. We have seen that the term *being* (*ens*) is given by virtue of and drawn from *actual being* (*ens actu*), and properly derived from

26. Thus, e.g., *De veritate*, q. 21, a. 4, ad. 4: "illud quod primo cadit in apprehensione intellectus est ens," to which Thomas immediately adds: "Thus the intellect necessarily attributes being to everything it apprehands" (Leonine, p. 603). See also *In De Trinitate*, q. 1, a. 3, obj. 3: "Ens est illud quod primo cadit in conceptione humana, ut Avicenna dicit" (Decker, p. 69); and *In I Metaph.*, lect. 2, n. 46: "primo in intellectu cadit ens" (Marietti, p. 13); and yet again, *De veritate*, q. 1, a. 1, c.: "illud autem quod primo intellectus concipit quasi notissimum et in quod conceptiones omnes resolvit est ens . . ." (Leonine, p. 5).

27. Cf. my article, "Enriching the Copula," *The Review of Metaphysics* 27 (1974): 492–512.

the *act of being* (*actus essendi*). To express this, Thomas uses the Latin *esse*, the verbal infinitive meaning "to be." Often enough, the term *esse* is used as a substantive synonymous with *ens*, but texts abound in which he uses it to indicate with all its verbal force the root of *ens*, and to mean the actuality (*actus essendi*) by which (*quo*) a being *is* and is *a being*.

Now, while Thomas insists upon *esse* as the root of all that is—this is the intimacy and depth of *ens* by virtue of *esse*—he equally insists that *ens* by virtue of *esse* is the absolutely comprehensive horizon of all that is—for the mind attributes *being* to everything that falls within its compass. And so we might say that *esse* is, in a sense, intensively comprehensive. It might be said to be a concrete universal, not in Hegel's sense, but in the sense in which the community of being is universal. *Esse* is both the root and the branch of St. Thomas's thought because in *esse* we find the root and branch of all reality, its breadth and its depth, its intension and its extension. If only the root is considered, we lose the openness and universality that is the condition of intelligibility and we lose the relatedness and reality of the shared community of all things which is the condition of their being. On the other hand, if we consider only the universality, if we consider only the comprehensive character of *being*, if we take *being* only as horizon, then we have the branch without the root. The doctrine of *esse* as root and branch requires us to surmount the well-established distribution of meaning into universal and particular. It forces us to face the paradox of *being*, and to find in *ens qua esse* the unity that makes of the universe a community of beings, and the richness that makes of it a work of generosity.

I have traced out in a very incomplete way certain stages in the modern recovery of the concrete in the thought of St. Thomas Aquinas. My account has culminated in the widely held view of his metaphysics as a metaphysics of being rooted in and inspired throughout by the primacy of *esse* as existential act. It may seem that such an interpretation is more single-minded than that of the master himself, a trifle forced. And it must be said that sometimes where we might like to have him stress *esse* in his writings it is not mentioned. It is tempting to think that Thomas had not quite thought through the role of *esse* in all of its implications and in all of its possible applications. It may be thought, too, that the uniqueness of his understanding of *esse* led him to tone down its primacy in order to conform to the terminology and the conceptual horizon of the schools. There may be some truth in this latter point. But the texts on *esse* are so prevalent throughout his works from the earliest to the latest that such a view must be qualified. And the qualification, I suggest, is the following. Thomas lived in a disputatious milieu in which argument was met by counter-argument. Is it possible, then, that Thomas employed a principle of economy? I mean that he answered an objection and developed a solution with just those principles that are sufficient to answer that objection or complete that solution. If form and matter, or substance and accident, suffice in answering an objection or clarifying a confusion or establishing a point, then he finds them sufficient. He does not feel the need to go beyond the horizon of the question itself unless forced to challenge a hidden assumption or a misunderstanding. He feels no need to trot out his own deep view in its entirety on every occasion. That does not make a teacher; it produces a bore. Thomas was not a Polonius of one wise word, not even the most important word, not even *esse*.

The primacy of *esse* as existential act is the root of the real distinction which has become an emblem of Thomistic metaphysics; or, to use the language of St. Thomas himself, the real composition of created being. I will close, then, with a brief look at several ways in which the composite character of created beings is expressed in Thomas from the point of view of the primacy of *esse* as existential act.

Thomas received from Avicenna the language of the *accidentality* of *esse* to essence in limited beings.[28] In Thomas the doctrine is meant to express the contingent and composite character of finite beings; no creature exists by right of its own nature or essence. Its existence (*esse*) comes to it, so to speak, "from without," that is, from God as creative cause.[29] Without doubt, the meaning that Thomas attaches to the accidentality of *esse* in finite being sustains the primacy of *esse* as existential act.[30]

28. See *Quodlibet* 2, q. 2, a. 1, ad 2: "esse est accidens, non quasi per accidens se habens, sed quasi actualitas cuiuslibet substantiae; unde ipse Deus, qui est sua actualitas, est suum esse" (Marietti, p. 24).

29. G. Anawati, "St. Thomas d'Aquin et la Métaphysique d'Avicenne," writes: "St. Thomas admits that essence is distinct from existence in all being other than God, and this is one of the central positions of his metaphysics. He will even say *esse est adveniens extra* (De ente 4); but that does not mean here that existence adds itself to the essence from outside, as would an accident [that is one of Thomas's criticisms of Avicenna on this point], but that it comes to it from an efficient cause that is transcendent to the essence, hence exterior to it, and this is God" (465).

30. Ibid. "Starting from the essence Avicenna forcefully considers the *esse* which affects it as an accident. St. Thomas, on the other hand, starts from the existing being and makes of *esse* what is the most intimate and deepest in the being; the relation of *esse* to the essence is not the relation of two entities of the same order, of an accident

Suppose, however, that we reverse the language? Suppose that—once, just for fun, serious fun—I was to give to these reflections on the primacy of *esse* the title: "The accidentality of essence." Suppose then that we say that limited essence is accidental to *esse*. Does this alter anything? Does it throw a different light upon the relation of essence and *esse*? The reversal has this advantage: it discounts in the most radical way the potentiality of the essence. I say "discounts," not "denies." The reversal is not meant to reject the language of substance with its affinity for the order of essence. Admittedly, the language of substance, subject, and supposit has its utility; but the reversal displaces any pretended primacy or autonomy that limited essence might claim in the metaphysical order. For this reversed way of speaking says: What is at issue is not *esse*, but essence.[31] Of course, this assumes that we have proven the existence of God as *Ipsum esse subsistens*, that we have shown that God's nature or essence is identically his existence, and have set forth his creative action *ex nihilo*. There is *ipsum esse* in the creature, then, because there is *Esse Ipse*. From the perspective of the primacy of *esse* as existential act, then, what is at issue is essence; I mean essence that is other than *esse*, limited essence, the essences of creatures. If I were to rescue the metaphor in the title of this essay, I should say that the actuality of the root of *esse* makes the very branches (the form, nature, and essence) of the tree of being themselves possible. From this reversal, the question is not: Why anything at all? Why not rather nothing? The question is: Why any *thing* at all? Why not simply *esse*?

Viewed from the point of essence, the *esse* of created being is accidental. A number of terms in the Thomistic lexicon can be misunderstood to reflect a starting-point in essence which is only subsequently overcome by a shift to *esse*. Thus, the concrete essence of a creature is sometimes designated as "*that which* is" (*id quod* as distinct from *esse* as *quo*). Gerald Phelan has expressed the essence in modal fashion, so that the essence is taken as the way, manner, or mode according to which the being exists.[32] This is a reversal in favor of the primacy of

---

to a substance, even from a logical point of view; but the relation of act to potency. The two points of view are entirely different. Between the Avicennian extrinsicalism of the act of being, says M. Gilson, and the Thomistic intrinsicalism of the act of being, no reconciliation is possible. We pass from the one to the other not by way of evolution but by way of revolution."

31. Gilson remarks in "Compagnons de route," in *Etienne Gilson: philosophe de la chrétienté*, ed. Jacques Maritain (Paris: Editions du Cerf, 1949), 191–92, that "one does not explain *esse*, it is what explains everything else." The language is reminiscent of St. Thomas's own use of *praeter esse*, "everything else besides *esse*," SCG II, chap. 52.

32. Gerald B. Phelan, "The Being of Creatures," *Proceedings of the American Catholic Philosophical Association* 31 (1957): 118–25.

esse as act. The reversal does not contradict the act-potency relation; indeed, it stresses the total orientation of form in the widest sense (essence taken metaphysically) to *esse* as act. This brings out the super-formality of *esse*, which is more formal than form.[33]

Finite *being* is also spoken of as that which "has being" (*habens esse*).[34] Now what is the character of this "having"? It is translated as "the possession of the act of existence"; and this is unexceptional. Except that this is no ordinary possession by which essence is said to possess existence. The Latin *habens* and its associated forms provide fruitful semantic soil for metaphysical reflection.[35] The anthropologists nowadays are proud of their *homo habilis*, by which they mean "the man with aptitude." And so we might say that essence has existence insofar as it is apt for *esse*. This has the advantage that it downplays the element of possession which—especially in the modern sense of property—implies a possessor prior to possession; it stresses instead a radical aptness, in the sense in which a pianist "has" a talent—not so much that he or she *owns* something called a talent as that there is that which can be actualized.

In this sense, essence is the most radical *habitus* or disposition, just as in Phelan's terminology essence is the most radical *modus* or modality. God's creative causality, then, is the bestowal of *esse* by, in, and through which He confers upon the being He creates the aptitude to receive.[36] That very aptitude for *esse* is essence. In the communication (*influxus entis*) by the creative power (*Deus creans*), out of which arises the received aptitude, the essence's potency, the created being comes to be; but that communication is from *Esse* (*Ipsum esse subsistens*) and through *esse* (the received *ipsum esse* that is the creature's existence). It can be said then, that *ipsum esse* in the creature comes from "without," if by that we mean "not from the creature but from the creative causality of God." In the language of participation, the creature participates in the *being* communicated by God through the *very being* (*ipsum esse*) that the creature receives in and through that participation. If we discard any spatial connotations, we may call this "extrinsic" participation. Looked at from the point of view of creation, it is God's action as creative cause. But within the creature, all that is in the creature is received through the *esse* that God alone communicates.

33. ST I, q. 8, a. 1, c.: *esse* "is formal with respect to all that is in a thing."
34. *In XII Metaph.*, lect. 1, n. 2419 (Marietti, p. 567).
35. Terms cluster around the basic verb, *habeo*, such as *habilitas* (aptitude, ability), *habitudo* (condition), *habitus* (condition, state, deportment, disposition, character). Of course, as with all metaphysical terms, these must be given a radical and analogous meaning.
36. See Owens, *An Interpretation of Existence*, chap. 5: "Bestowal of Existence."

In St. Thomas's words: "Every created substance attains likeness to God through the very act of existing (*ipsum esse*). . . . Therefore, existence itself (*ipsum esse*) has this status with respect to all created substances: it is their act."[37] We might call this the first and primary causal participation.

But from the point of view of the primacy of *esse* as existential act, we can speak also of a second "intrinsic" participation. It is the participation by which everything else in the creature (*praeter esse*) participates in God's Being in and through participating in the act of existing (*esse, actus essendi*) that is proper to the creature. If the first "extrinsic" participation is causality, the second "intrinsic" participation might be called "constitution."[38] It is the constitution of the finite being.

Habens, then, can be taken as a capacity that, by drawing upon *esse*, can become an ability. The point is important, if only because the negative language of essence as "limitation" (which is valid enough in recognizing the finitude of creatures and attends to the difference between God and creatures)[39] needs to be supplemented in such a way that the positive nobility of the creature—a nobility that derives from *esse* itself[40]—can be accounted for. The stress on the dignity of the creature is one of the most important emphases in St. Thomas's thoughts, and he defends it vigorously. Against Avicenna he defended the efficacy of secondary causes; against Averroes, the integrity of the knower; and against those who held certain views of divine illumination he defended the adequacy of the human knowing-powers.

To close, then. Before God has bestowed *esse*, there is no passive potency; there is no possibility on the part of the creature. Indeed, we can go so far as to say that the creature is relation-to-God (*adesse Deum*). We can truly say that "before" God created the world it was not possible—on the part of the world—for the world to be. Strictly, there was no possibility in the passive sense, because with God all is

37. SCG II, chap. 53 (trans. Anderson, *Introduction to the Metaphysics of St. Thomas Aquinas*, 31).

38. Should the word "intrinsic" seem to accord too much essentiality to the creature, see the remarks of Owens, "Aquinas: Intimacy and Contingency of Existence," 261–62, on the text of St. Thomas (*In I Sent.*, d. 8, exp. 1ae partis textus): "cum nihil sit essentialius rei quam suum esse" (Mandonnet, p. 209).

39. If I have understood the late William Carlo, *The Ultimate Reducibility of Essence to Existence in Existential Metaphysics* (The Hague: Martinus Nijhoff, 1966), this book—so stimulating in many ways—fails to retrieve the positive character of essence, nowhere so clearly as when he says that "essence is the place where existence stops" (103–4). His later efforts (138–39) do not seem sufficient to move from the negative to the positive.

40. SCG I, chap. 28: "Omnis enim nobilitas cuiuscumque rei est sibi secundum esse."

actual. The very possibility on the part of the creature arises only through the gift of *esse*. The nobility of the creature lies in its being the gift of the Creator. Since that gift is a pure gift (*creatio ex nihilo*), it is unconditional in the sense that there are no prior conditions. The very possibility of a response arises only with the gift.

2

Cutting the Gordian Knot of Ontology: Thomas's Solution to the Problem of Universals

JORGE J. E. GRACIA

According to legend, a Phrygian peasant by the name of Gordius was called to the throne in accordance with an oracle of Zeus which prescribed the elevation to that position of the first person to ride up to his temple in a wagon. The king subsequently dedicated his wagon to Zeus, and another oracle prophesied that whoever succeeded in untying the knot of cornel bark made from the traces would be the prince of all Asia. No one had succeeded in untying the knot until Alexander the Great cut it in half with his sword and proceeded to fulfill the prophecy.

The moral of this story has been interpreted in various ways. Some, for example, argue its lesson is that sometimes drastic and violent action is necessary in order to solve certain problems. And, indeed, it is altogether possible that this, or any of the other usual interpretations of the story, is correct. For philosophy, however, the lesson I believe we can learn from this story is that the solution to philosophical problems which seem to defy solution does not always lie within the parameters that have been preestablished for the solution. Indeed, in some cases it is these very parameters which vitiate the issue, precluding the discovery of a way out. In that situation the only way out may be the abandonment of the assumptions inherent in the formulation of the problem.

It is not easy, however, to question the very formulation of a philosophical problem long-debated, going behind the scene as it were, in order to examine and evaluate the assumptions on which it has been based. It takes the kind of intellect and courage that only few philosophers have displayed in the history of philosophy: intellect, because it requires the extraordinary effort of seeing things differently from the way in which they are generally seen; courage, because it implies going against well-accepted opinion at the risk of derision and ridicule.

Nonetheless, and fortunately for us, there have been some figures who have met the challenge. Whether we like it or not, Kant is one of those figures. Indeed, we are still living with the results of the revolutionary way in which he looked at the function of reason in understanding. Wittgenstein is a more recent example of a philosopher who dared look at things differently. My business in this paper, however, is neither with Kant nor Wittgenstein, but with the legacy of Thomas Aquinas. My thesis is that Thomas, like Kant and Wittgenstein, ought to be credited with cutting a philosophical Gordian knot he had inherited: the problem of universals. Specifically, my claim is that Thomas's solution to this problem is the result of looking at the problem in an entirely new way. This caused him to reject an unquestioned assumption that had dominated the formulation and discussion of this problem since its inception in the medieval philosophical tradition.

In order to bring out Thomas's contribution clearly, I divide the discussion into three parts. The first briefly presents the problem of universals; the second discusses the medieval formulation of the problem inherited by Thomas; and the third examines Thomas's position.

1. THE PROBLEM OF UNIVERSALS

The problem of universals is just one of the many issues that can be raised concerning universality. Indeed, the controversy surrounding both the formulation of this problem and its solution may stem in part from confusion concerning the nature of these issues. In order to avoid confusion, then, I would like to begin by presenting what I take to be the problem of universals in terms of four questions:

1. What things are universal?
2. Do universals exist?
3. What is the ontological category to which universals belong?
4. What is the relation of universals to other things?

The first two questions concern the extension of 'universal,' that is, whether the category "universal" extends to anything, and if it does, to which things. These questions may be asked of any predicative category. For example, we may ask what things are cats and whether cats exist. A true answer to the first question is "animals," and a true answer to the second is "yes." In the case of universals, similarly, true answers are sought.

The last two questions involve the determination of the ontological status of universality. This entails locating universality on the ontological map one uses to divide the world. Within an Aristotelian framework, for instance, the map consists of the ten categories and, thus, within that framework one would want to determine into which of those categories universals fit. One may ask, for example, whether universals are substances or accidents and, if they are accidents, one may ask whether they are quantities, qualities, relations, and so on. In answer to these questions one may hold with Plato, for example, that universals are substances. Or, following Hume, one may want to defend the view that universals are nothing but faded images in the mind. In either case, to answer these questions involves both the determination of the ontological category to which universals belong and of the relations of universals to other things. For example, if one were to agree with those authors who hold that universals are mental images, then one must establish as well how those images are related to the minds that have them.

The answer to any one or all of these four questions seems to require a prior understanding of universality. We must know what universality is before we can proceed to ask what things fall into the category, whether the category is instantiated or not, and what the ontological status of universals and their relation to other things is. Owing to a lack of space, however, to undertake an intensional analysis of universality at this point would preempt the possibility of discussing the issue which concerns us most. So, rather than raising the intensional question, I shall adopt an understanding of universality which seems to me to be both correct and concordant with Thomas's own views, although I shall neither try to defend it nor to show that Thomas's position is indeed concordant with it. For our present purposes, then, I shall conceive universality as instantiability. To be universal is to be instantiable. Having adopted this view, it becomes clear that "human being," "white," and "dirt" are examples of universals, while such things as "this human being," "this white," and "that dirt" are not universal. I shall refer to what is not universal, that is, to what is noninstantiable, as individual.[1]

Having presented in general the nature of the problem of universals, I must turn now to the specific medieval formulations of and solutions to it that preceded Thomas. This will make clear his contribution to the historical development of the problem.

1. For a defense of this view of individuality and universality, see my *Individuality: An Essay on the Foundations of Metaphysics* (Albany: State University of New York Press, 1988), chap. 1, 43ff.

2. THE HISTORICAL FORMULATION OF THE PROBLEM IN THE MIDDLE AGES: BOETHIUS AND AVICENNA

Everyone of philosophical importance in the Middle Ages before Thomas's time, and indeed after him as well, discussed at some point or another one or more of the four questions I have identified earlier as comprising the problem of universals. I suspect that even among minor thinkers one could find texts pertinent to this issue if we were so lucky as to have preserved all the writings of medieval theologians. Thus the task of providing the historical background on the problem of universals for Thomas would seem Herculean and hardly possible in a paper of this size.[2] Fortunately, such a history is not necessary here. It suffices that I refer to those figures who played a determining role in the formulation of the problem and presented the most widely discussed solutions to it. There are two figures that I believe are particularly pertinent: Boethius and Avicenna. Boethius is important because he presented the first and most influential formulation of and solution to the problem of universals before 1150, the time at which the translations of ancient and Islamic texts began to enter the Latin West. He set the parameters of the problem and, in spite of the influx of new ideas after 1150, maintained an authoritative position on this issue throughout the period. Avicenna is important because it seems that he provided the immediate point of departure for Thomas. I shall, then, present the historical background to Thomas in terms of Boethius and Avicenna.

Boethius

As is well known, Boethius sets up the problem of universals with three questions that he borrows from Porphyry. We find them in the second edition of his commentary on Porphyry's *Isagoge*: "At present, he [i.e., Porphyry] says, I shall refuse to say concerning genera and species [1] whether they subsist or whether they are found merely as bare mental notions or [2] whether as subsistents they are corporeal or incorporeal, and [3] whether they are separated from sensibles or found in sensibles and in accord with them."[3]

---

2. The only comprehensive attempt at a history of the problem of universals in the Middle Ages is the now dated *Geschichte der Logik im Abendlande* of Carl Prantl, 4 vols. (Leipzig: S. Hirzel, 1855–70; rep. Graz: Akademische druck-U. Verlagsanstalt, 1955).

3. Boethius, *In Isagogen Porphyrii commentorum editio secunda* I, chap. 10, ed. Samuel Brandt, in *Corpus scriptorum ecclesiasticorum latinorum*, vol. 48 (Vienna: Tempsky, 1906; rep. New York: Johnson, 1966), 159: "'Mox,' inquit, 'de generibus ac speciebus illud quidem, siue subsistunt siue in solis nudisque intellectibus posita sunt siue subsistentia corporalia sunt an incorporalia et utrum separata a sensibilibus an in sensibilibus posita

Although Porphyry quite prudently does not attempt to answer these questions, Boethius readily does as follows: "[1] Genera and species subsist in one way [as individual], but are understood in another [as universal]; and [2] they are incorporeal, but [3] they subsist in sensibles joined to sensibles."[4] By "genera" and "species" Boethius means such things as animal and man. By "subsist" one may at first take him to mean "to exist as a substance," that is, in the way a man rather than the color of his skin (an accident) exists. And, indeed, since Boethius is referring to genera and species, it seems entirely appropriate to pose their existence in substantial terms. However, the contrast he makes between "subsist" and "being found merely as bare mental notions" suggests that he may be using a more general understanding of subsistence as simply nonmental existence. This is further confirmed by his answer when he points out that genera and species subsist in sensible things, and joined to them; such a type of existence would not seem to meet the conditions of independence and self-sufficience generally associated with substantial existence. Furthermore, in the explanation he gives of the import of the question, he exchanges "subsist" (*subsistere*) by forms of the verb "to be" (*esse*) as well as by the expression "established in the order of nature" (*in rerum natura constitutum*), all of which indicates that he is not restricting the notion of subsistence to that of substantial existence, as Porphyry may have originally intended.[5]

We may reformulate Porphyry's questions then as follows:

1. Do genera and species exist outside the mind or only in the mind?

2. If they exist outside the mind, are they corporeal or incorporeal?

3. If they exist outside the mind, do they exist separate from sensibles or in them?

---

et circa ea constantia, dicere recusabo.'" For the translation of Boethius's texts I shall be guided by Richard McKeon, although I often depart from his readings. See *Selections from Medieval Philosophers*, vol. 1 (New York: Charles Scribner's Sons, 1929), 91–99.

4. Boethius, *In Isagogen* I, chap. 11, 167: "ipsa enim genera et species subsistunt quidem alio modo, intelliguntur uero alio, et sunt incorporalia, sed sensibilibus iuncta subsistunt in sensibilibus." Prior to reaching this solution he specifies the universal character of genera and species in the mind and their individual character in sensibles; see 166–67.

5. Ibid., 160: "quarum prima [quaestio] est huiusmodi. omne quod intelligit animus aut id quod est in rerum natura constitutum, intellectu concipit et sibimet ratione describit aut id quod non est, uacua sibi imaginatione depingit. ergo intellectus generis et ceterorum cuiusmodi sit quaeritur, utrumne ita intellegamus species et genera ut ea quae sunt et ex quibus uerum capimus intellectum, an nosmet ipsi nos ludimus, cum ea quae non sunt, animi nobis cassa cogitatione formamus. . . ." See Martin M. Tweedale, *Abailard on Universals* (Amsterdam: North-Holland Publishing, 1976), 64.

Boethius's answer to the first question is that genera and species exist both in the mind as universals, and outside the mind as individuals. His answer to the second is that they are incorporeal. And to the third he answers that they exist in sensibles and are joined to them, that is, they are not independent of the world of experience.

There are three important points in Boethius's formulation that should be noted. The first is that, although the fundamental question he seeks to address is the question of the existence of genera and species, he also raises questions, following Porphyry, about their status (corporeality or incorporeality, separate or joined existence) and about their relation to other things, namely, the sensible things in which they are found and to which they are joined. Thus Boethius raises in effect three of the four questions which were identified above as comprising the problem of universals: the extensional question concerning existence and the two ontological questions about status and relations.

The second important point is that Boethius, again following Porphyry, does not question the mental existence of genera and species. Although later thinkers would even question this, one must be sympathetic to Boethius's assumption that if we can raise questions about genera and species it is because they are already in some sense present in the mind.[6] The important issue, then, is not mental existence, but existence outside the mind.

Third, we must note that his solution is to say that genera and species exist not only in the mind but also outside it. Although they do not exist independently of other things, as Plato thought, they do exist in and joined to other things, as Aristotle claimed. Boethius's solution, then, is realistic but not realistic in the Platonic sense, where ideas take on a life of their own, as it were. His view as presented here follows the moderate realism of Aristotle, in which genera and species exist outside the mind, but they are not separate from the world of experience, and are thus individual. Indeed, Boethius explicitly acknowledges that he is following Aristotle, although he admits following Aristotle only because the *Isagoge* is a book about Aristotle's *Categories*.[7]

The kernel of the Boethian solution, then, is that genera and species exist both in the mind and in the world of sensible things. This creates two problems. Both have to do with the relation between what exists in the mind and what exists outside it. One is an epistemic problem.

---

6. Among those who questioned the mental existence of universals is Roscelin of Compiègne (ca. 1050–1120), teacher of Peter Abelard. He is reputed to have held that universals are merely utterances (*flatus vocis*).

7. Boethius, *In Isagogen* I, chap. 11, 167: "idcirco uero studiosius Aristotelis sententiam executi sumus, non quod eam maxime probaremus, sed quod hic liber ad Praedicamenta conscriptus est, quorum Aristoteles est auctor."

If what is outside the mind precedes what is inside it, as Boethius and other thinkers from this period believed, then the question arises as to how mental genera and species are related to and derived from nonmental genera and species.

Boethius is quite aware of this problem and makes some timid suggestions as to how the mind is capable of separating what in reality is united. Just as the mind can consider a line as separate from the object of which, in the world, it is a part, so also it can consider genera and species apart from the sensible things to which they are joined.[8] These remarks were to give rise in the later Middle Ages to elaborate epistemic theories of abstraction, including that of Thomas.

The other problem to which Boethius's solution gives rise is more pertinent for the topic of this paper. He accords a double type of existence to genera and species: in the mind and outside the mind, universal and individual. But this seems to be contradictory, for if it is in the nature of genera and species to exist as individuals outside the mind, how can they also exist as universals in the mind? And if it is in the nature of genera and species to exist as universals in the mind, how can they exist as individuals outside it? Can one and the same thing enjoy two different types of existence?

Clearly this question has to do with unity. It must be remembered that for Boethius, who followed the ancients on this, being and unity are coextensive: Whatever is one is a being and whatever is a being is one.[9] What applies to unity extensionally (being and unity do differ intensionally) also applies to being and vice versa. Indeed, in the same text where Boethius discusses universals he raises the difficulties of something being both one and many (or common) at the same time: "For anything that is common at one time to many cannot be one . . . but if any genus is one in number, it cannot possibly be common to many."[10]

Thus Boethius is aware of the difficulties involved in holding that one and the same thing be both one and many and, consequently, of the corresponding difficulty involved in the same thing having two incompatible types of existence. However, he does not seem to be bothered by the problem, thinking that his answer to Porphyry's ques-

---

8. Ibid., 164.

9. In the very text where he discusses universals, Boethius states the second part of this doctrine. See ibid., chap. 10, 162: "Omni enim quod est, idcirco est, quia unum est."

10. Ibid., 161–62: "omne enim quod commune est uno tempore pluribus, id unum esse non poterit. . . . quodsi unum quiddam numero genus est, commune multorum esse non poterit."

tions and his epistemic explanation of how the mental universal is formed suffice to take care of this issue. He defends his position thus:

For there is nothing to prevent two things which are in the same subject from being different conceptually, like a concave and convex line, which things, although they are defined by diverse definitions and have diverse notions, are nevertheless found in the same subject; for it is the same line which is convex and concave. So too for genera and species, that is, for singularity and universality, there is only one subject but it is universal in one way when it is thought, and singular in another when it is perceived in those things in which it exists.[11]

Subsequent medieval thinkers did not always agree with Boethius. Although some did follow in his footsteps and tried to find ways of maintaining the basic Boethian point of view,[12] there were many others who denied nonmental existence to the universal, restricting it to the mental realm alone. Abelard and other so-called conceptualists and nominalists made up this latter group.

Before I leave Boethius, let me make explicit the assumption contained in his formulation of and solution to the problem of universals that is important for our purposes. It is the assumption that the answer to the problem of universals is either: (a) that universals exist in the mind alone, or (b) that universals exist both in the mind and outside it. When one frames the problem of universals in terms of a question such as Porphyry's, these alternatives seem to be the only ones available. Yet both seem unacceptable. If the universal has only mental existence, the objectivity and scientific validity of our concepts is undermined. And if the universal exists both in the mind and outside it, we fall into the difficulties already mentioned. It is this assumption, contained in the Boethian formulation, that is largely responsible for the failure of the many early medieval attempts to solve the problem of universals. We find a catalogue of these positions in John of Salisbury's *Metalogicon*, where he lists no less than nine

11. Ibid., chap. 11, 166–67: "neque enim interclusum est ut duae res eodem in subiecto sint ratione diuersae, ut linea curua atque caua, quae res cum diuersis definitionibus terminentur diuersusque earum intellectus sit, semper tamen in eodem subiecto reperiuntur; eadem enim linea caua, eadem curua est. ita quoque generibus et speciebus, id est singularitati et uniuersalitati, unum quidem subiectum est, sed alio modo uniuersale est, cum cogitatur, alio singulare, cum sentitur in rebus his in quibus esse suum habet." Note that the terms "singular" and "individual" are used synonymously by Boethius in these passages.

12. Abelard describes a view which resembles the position of Boethius in *Logica nostrorum petitioni sociorum*, ed. B. Geyer, in *Beiträge zur Geschichte der Philosophie des Mittelalters* 21, no. 4 (1933): 518: "Sunt alii in rebus universalitatem assignantes, qui eandem rem universalem et particularem esse astruunt. . . ."

different views concerning universals.[13] Most of these were the result of trying to solve the problem by providing an ontological categorization of universals that would avoid the tension between mental and nonmental existence. Thus we find authors identifying the universal with utterances, word-concepts, acts of understanding, ideas, native forms, sets, states, and so on. None of those answers, however, is successful.

Now let us turn to Avicenna. He represents another historical channel through which the problem of universals reached Thomas.

Avicenna

The connection between Avicenna and Thomas has been well documented already by others. More particularly, the relation of Thomas's view of universals to the position presented in the Latin Avicenna was explored in Joseph Owens's definitive article "Common Nature: A Point of Comparison between Thomistic and Scotistic Metaphysics."[14] I do not intend, therefore, to restate in detail what has already been said by Owens on this matter, but only to summarize briefly the points already noted by him, adding a few precisions that are especially relevant to my argument.

The first point that needs to be stressed is that, like Boethius, the Latin Avicenna begins the discussion of the problem of universals with a formula which, like the questions inherited by Boethius from Porphyry, already tilts the scales toward the kind of ontological commitment that ended up in an impasse. The title of the first chapter of Book 5 of the *Metaphysics* reads as follows: "De rebus communibus: et quomodo est esse eorum."[15] This would easily lead to the kind of alternatives explored by Boethius: Either common things, that is, genera and species, exist in the mind alone or both in the mind and outside of it. Thus Avicenna is working within similar constraints concerning the existence of genera and species. He does, however, make substantial advances in several dimensions of the problem. I shall indicate three in particular.

First, Avicenna introduces a distinction between what accrues to genera and species in themselves and what accrues to them extrinsically and by accident.[16] Second, he asserts that neither universality

13. John of Salisbury, *Metalogicon* II, chap. 17, ed. Clemens C. I. Webb (Oxford: Clarendon, 1929), 91–96.

14. Joseph Owens, "Common Nature: A Point of Comparison Between Thomistic and Scotistic Metaphysics," *Mediaeval Studies* 19 (1957): 1–14.

15. Avicenna, *Metaphysica* 5, 1, in *Opera philosophica* (Venice, 1508; rep. Louvain: Bibliothèque S. J., 1961), fol. 86v1.

16. Avicenna, *Logica* 3, in *Opera philosophica*, fol. 12r1: "Animal autem in se est

(multiplicity) nor singularity (unity), and neither existence in sensibles nor existence in the mind, accrue to genera and species in themselves; they only accrue to them accidentally and extrinsically.[17] Third, he points out that to ask whether genera and species are one or many when considered in themselves is a mistake, for it implies that indeed they are one or the other, while in fact they can be either or both. Such a question is illegitimate and must be rejected.[18] Note, however, that the illegitimacy of this question applies only in the case of unity (that is, singularity) and multiplicity (that is, universality), not existence. The reason will soon become clear.

The significance of these Avicennian moves should not be underestimated, for clearly he is trying to get away from the sort of dilemma faced by Boethius and others. Indeed, he is aware that if, say, "animal" were universal in itself, then there could be no individual animals, and that if "animal" were individual in itself, then it could not be universal.[19] He attempts to escape the dilemma by saying that animal, like other genera and species, is neither one nor the other when considered in itself.[20]

When it comes to existence, Avicenna at first seems to move in the direction he took concerning singularity and universality by indicating that genera and species considered in themselves have neither the sort of existence mental entities have nor the sort of existence extramental entities have.[21] Nevertheless, he does not go far enough in this direc-

---

quoddam intellectum in mente quod sit animal, et secundum hoc quod intelligitur esse animal non est nisi animal tantum."

17. Ibid.: "Si autem praeter hoc intelligitur esse universale aut singulare aut aliquid aliud, iam intelligitur praeter hoc quoddam, scilicet id quod est animal, quod accidit animalitati." And in *Metaphysica,* fol. 86v2: "Sed si proprietas eius est esse unum vel multa, sicut proprietas quae eam sequitur, tunc sine dubio appropriabitur per hoc, sed tamen ipsa non erit ipsum appropriatum ex hoc quod est humanitas; ergo ex hoc quod ipsa est humanitas non est ipsum unum vel multum, sed est aliud quiddam cui illud accidit extrinsecus." And in fol. 86v1, he adds: "Unitas autem est proprietas quae cum adiungitur equinitati fit equinitas propter ipsam proprietatem unum. Similiter etiam equinitas habet praeter hanc multas alias proprietates accidentes sibi."

18. *Metaphysica,* fol. 86v2: "Cum ergo subiectum quaestionis posita fuerit ipsa humanitas secundum quod est humanitas veluti aliquid unum, et interrogaverint nos secundum aliquod contrariorum dicentes, quod aut est unum aut multa, tunc non erit necesse respondere aliquod illorum."

19. *Logica,* fol. 12r1: "Si enim in se esset universale, ita quod animalitas, ex hoc quod est animalitas, est universalis, oporteret nullum animal esse singulare, sed omne animal esset universale. Si autem animal ex hoc quod est animal esset singulare, impossibile esset esse plusquam unum singulare, scilicet ipsum singulare cui debetur animalitas, et esset impossibile aliud singulare esse animal."

20. Ibid.: "In se autem huius nec est universale nec est singulare."

21. *Metaphysica,* fol. 86v1: "Equinitas etenim habet diffinitionem quae non eget universalitate. Sed est cui accidit universalitas, unde ipsa equinitas non est aliquid nisi

tion, accepting that they still have some existence that (1) precedes the being they accidentally have both inside and outside the mind, and (2) is the existence whereby they are what they are (e.g., animal is animal).[22] Indeed, he goes so far as to talk about this existence as "proper" to them.[23] Clearly this is an attempt to bypass the problems involved in saying that universals exist in the mind alone or both in the mind and outside it. But it is a solution that creates a third sort of existence proper to genera and species, similar to the being Scotus was going to confer on natures later on. Indeed, this procedure turns out to be quite unlike the one Avicenna followed concerning the singularity and universality of genera and species, for there he argued that the question whether genera and species are singular or universal must be rejected. But when it comes to existence, although he denies that genera and species considered in themselves have existence in the mind or outside it, he still grants them existence, even if it is existence of a third kind, neither that associated with mental entities nor extramental ones.

Avicenna's solution creates some important problems. In the first place, if genera and species considered in themselves have their own proper existence, in addition to whatever accidental existence they have when they are in the mind or outside it, we must explain how that existence is related to the accidental existence they have in the mind or outside it, and we must make sure that there is no incom-

---

equinitas tantum. Ipsa enim ex se nec est multa nec unum nec est existens in his sensibilibus nec in anima."

22. Ibid., fol. 87r1: "Poterit autem animal per se considerari, quamvis sit cum alio a se; essentia enim eius est cum alio a se, ergo essentia eius est ipsi per se. Ipsum vero esse cum alio a se est quiddam quod accidit ei vel aliquid quod comitatur naturam suam sicut haec animalitas et humanitas; ergo haec consideratio, scilicet ex hoc quod est animal praecedit in esse, et animal quod est individuum propter accidentia sua, et universale quod est in his sensibilibus, et intelligibile sicut simplex praecedit compositum, et sicut pars totum; ex hoc enim esse nec est genus nec species nec individuum nec unum nec multa. Sed ex hoc esse est tantum animal et tantum homo, nec comitatur illud sine dubio esse unum vel multa. . . ."

23. Ibid., fol. 72v1: "Et hoc est quod fortasse appellamus esse proprium; nec intendimus per illud nisi intentionem esse affirmativi, quia verbum ens signat etiam multas intentiones, ex quibus est certitudo qua est unaquaeque res; et est sicut esse proprium rei." The term used in the Latin Avicenna for existence in this passage is *esse* rather than *existere*, which is also used (see n. 21 above). The Latin Avicenna does not seem to distinguish between these. Following this lead, and in order to maintain a certain symmetry in the discussion, I shall not make a distinction between them and will continue to speak about "existence." I shall follow the same procedure in the rest of the paper, although I am aware that in the later Middle Ages important distinctions were made between *esse, existere,* and various types of each. For example, Henry of Ghent referred to the sort of *esse* discussed by Avicenna as *esse essentiae*; see John F. Wippel, *Metaphysical Themes in Thomas Aquinas* (Washington, D.C.: The Catholic University of America Press, 1984), 175–76.

patibility involved. None of this, however, seems easy to do, and in fact it resembles in many ways the quandary in which Boethius and others found themselves before Avicenna.

Secondly, as Owens has pointed out, Avicenna's solution breaks the symmetry between being and unity generally accepted in the Middle Ages. If Avicenna is correct, then genera and species have being in themselves but do not have a corresponding unity. And this means that, contrary to the popular medieval doctrine of the transcendentality of being and unity, being and unity are not coextensional.[24]

In short, Avicenna's solution to the problem of universals makes important advances but still functions within the general assumption, also held by Boethius and most of those who dealt with universals before Thomas, that genera and species must have some kind of existence, and it is only the determination of their kind of existence that is at stake in the problem of universals. But that assumption, of course, leaves open the doors to the controversies concerning universals that characterized the early Middle Ages. It is only Thomas who rejects the assumption in question, framing the problem of universals differently.

3. THOMAS'S BREAKTHROUGH

What Thomas inherited from his historical predecessors was an approach to the problem of universals that assumed that there were only two basic alternatives to the problem. One was to deny that genera and species had any kind of existence outside the mind, with the resulting difficulties for the objectivity of knowledge and the validity of scientific concepts. The other was to accept that genera and species had existence outside the mind, with the resulting difficulties involved in claiming different types of existence for one and the same thing. For Boethius, existence outside the mind was the existence individuals have. This was also true of Avicenna, although he added a peculiar existence which genera and species had on their own. Thomas's solution was simply to ignore this assumption, cutting the Gordian knot of the controversy. Instead of accepting the terms of the question that had been laid out before him, he dismissed the question by indicating that neither existence nor unity (not just unity as Avicenna had believed) essentially apply to such things as man and white; they are only accidental attachments to them. In more contemporary jargon we could say that to speak of the existence or nonexistence of such things

24. Owens, "Common Nature," 4.

as man or white is a category mistake which leads to the kind of impasse that has characterized the history of the problem of universals. It is wrong, therefore, to ask whether man or white considered in themselves exist in the mind or outside of it, for existence does not apply to them as such. What exist in the mind are universal concepts, such as the concept of man or the concept of white. And what exist outside the mind are individual things, such as Peter (this man) or the white color of Peter's skin (this white). But let us look at Thomas's position in more detail in order to see how he avoids the conceptual logjam which preceded him. The key discussion occurs in *De ente et essentia*.

I should begin by noting that Thomas's discussion of the problem of universals is cast in the terminology of "natures" rather than the terminology of "genera" and "species" in vogue before 1150.[25] This has two advantages at the outset. In the first place, it clearly sets the problem in a metaphysical rather than a logical context. Boethius had formulated the problem of universals in his translation and commentary on Porphyry's *Isagoge*, which is an introduction to the *Categories*, the first book of Aristotle's Organon. Indeed, Porphyry's ostensive reason for not pursuing an answer to the three questions he had raised concerning genera and species was that the questions were too deep for beginners (i.e., students of logic).[26] We might surmise that he did not want to deal with them because they pertain to metaphysics rather than logic, properly speaking. Boethius, on the other hand, felt no such scruples and gave an answer to the questions which mixed metaphysics and epistemology in spite of the fact that the questions were cast in logical terms—genera and species—and presented in a logical context. All this served to mix metaphysical, epistemological, and logical issues in the early part of the Middle Ages in a way that was not always helpful. With the change of terminology from genera and species to natures and the exploration of the problem in a fundamentally metaphysical treatise, *De ente et essentia*, Thomas clearly separates the metaphysical aspects of the problem of universals from its epistemic and logical ones. He also deals with its logical and particularly its epistemic dimensions, but he does so in other, more appropriate contexts.[27]

---

25. Even in the texts of Avicenna the term "nature" is not as common as it was to become in the thirteenth century; he prefers to speak of genera and species and to use concrete examples of them such as animal and man. For a discussion of nature in Avicenna and Aquinas, see James A. Weisheipl, "The Concept of Nature: Avicenna and Aquinas," in *Thomistic Papers I*, ed. Victor B. Brezik (Houston: Center for Thomistic Studies, 1984), 65–87.

26. In Boethius, *In Isagoge*, 159.

27. See, e.g., ST I, q. 85, aa. 1–3.

The second advantage is that the terminology of natures extends the problem of universals to cover not only substantial predicates such as animal and man, but also accidental predicates, such as "white" and "three feet wide." The reasons for the use of genera and species to pose the problem of universals can be easily understood. First, philosophically, the problem raised by the existence or nonexistence of the referent of substantial terms is quite obvious. Second, historically, the context where the problem was raised for Porphyry and Boethius was that of the secondary substances which Aristotle had introduced in the *Categories*. But consistency requires that if one raises the question of universals about substantial predicates, one should also raise it about accidental predicates. In the early Middle Ages, following Boethius's lead, most discussions of universals were cast in terms of substantial predicates, resulting in a one-sided and somewhat distorted view of the problem. Moreover, although many thinkers were quite aware of the extension of the questions involved in universals to terms other than substantial ones, none of them developed a common terminology, a way of expressing them, that would incorporate the complete breadth of the issue.

So much for the advantages of the new terminology. But now we may ask: What are these natures about which Thomas speaks if they are not the same as genera and species?

We find the answer to this question in chapters 1 and 2 of *De ente et essentia*. In a paragraph pregnant with meaning in spite of its apparent simplicity, Thomas explains the terminology:

Because the definition telling what a thing is signifies that by which a thing is located in its genus or species, philosophers have substituted the term 'quiddity' for the term 'essence.' The Philosopher frequently calls this 'what something was to be'; that is to say, that which makes a thing to be what it is. It is also called 'form,' because form signifies the determination of each thing, as Avicenna says. Another term used for this is 'nature,' using 'nature' in the first of the four senses enumerated by Boethius. In this sense anything is called a nature which the intellect can grasp in any way; for a thing is intelligible only through its definition and essence. That is why the Philosopher, too, says that every substance is a nature. The term 'nature' in this sense seems to mean the essence of a thing as directed to its specific operation, for no reality lacks its specific operation. The term 'quiddity' is derived from what is signified by the definition while 'essence' is used because through it, and in it, a being exists.[28]

28. Thomas Aquinas, *De ente*, chap. 1: "Et quia illud per quod res constituitur in proprio genere uel specie est hoc quod significatur per diffinitionem indicantem quid est res, inde est quod nomen essentie a philosophis in nomen quiditatis mutatur; et hoc est etiam quod Philosophus frequenter nominat quod quid erat esse, id est hoc per

What is important to note in this paragraph is that the terms "quiddity," "essence," "form," and "nature" are coextensional; that is to say, they denote one and the same thing. But they are not cointensional, for their connotations are different. Just like "the author of the *Categories*" and "the most famous student of Plato," they have the same referent but different meanings. Now this point has an important result, namely, that for the formulation of the problem of universals and its solution any of these terms will do. The reason is simple: the problem of universals concerns existence and ontological status, not meaning. Therefore, the conceptual distinctions connoted by these terms are immaterial to it. Indeed, it is because of this that we find the problem of universals discussed variously in terms of form, quiddity, essence, and nature.

At this point, however, a difficulty arises which is particularly obvious with respect to the term "form." The difficulty arises in the context of the Aristotelian doctrine of hylomorphism. According to this doctrine, substances such as Socrates are composed of both form and matter. This entails that form does not contain matter since it is united to it in order to make up the composite. But if form, as noted earlier, is coextensive with essence, and essence is expressed by the definition, then form must include matter, for the definition of a material composite must make reference to matter.[29]

This difficulty leads Thomas to make a distinction between what he calls "the form of the part" (*forma partis*) and "the form of the whole" (*forma totius*). The form of the part is the form which unites to matter and, therefore, does not include matter. For this reason it is to be considered a kind of incomplete or partial form, as it were. The form of the whole by contrast is the complete form and thus includes matter

---

quod aliquid habet esse quid. Dicitur autem forma, secundum quod per formam significatur certitudo uniuscuiusque rei, ut dicit Auivenna in II Methaphisice sue. Hoc etiam alio nomine natura dicitur, accipiendo naturam secundum primum modum illorum quatuor quod Boetius in libro De duabus naturis assignat: secundum scilicet quod natura dicitur omne illud quod intellectu quoquo modo capi potest, non enim est res intelligibilis nisi per diffinitionem et essentiam suam; et sic etiam Philosophus dicit in V Methaphisice quod omnis substantia est natura. Tamen nomen nature hoc modo sumpte uidetur significare essentiam rei secundum quod habet ordinem ad propriam operationem rei, cum nulla res propria operatione destituatur; quiditatis uero nomen sumitur ex hoc quod per diffinitionem significatur; sed essentia dicitur secundum quod per eam et in ea ens habet esse" (Leonine, pp. 369–70). For the translations of texts from *De ente et essentia* I am following, with occasional modifications, Armand Maurer's translation *On Being and Essence*, 2d rev. ed. (Toronto: Pontifical Institute of Mediaeval Studies, 1968). For the cited text, see 31–32.

29. *De ente*, chap. 2 (Leonine, pp. 370ff.).

in its definition. As Thomas puts it: "in the case of composite substances the term 'essence' signifies the composite of matter and form."[30]

From this we can gather that the problem of universals cannot concern the form of the part, for what is said of a composite does not concern only one of its parts, but the whole being. Thomas illustrates the point with reference to two predicates, "man" and "humanity":

> It is clear, then, that the essence of man is signified by the two terms 'man' and 'humanity,' but in different ways, . . . since the term 'man' expresses it as a whole, because it does not prescind from the designation of matter but contains it implicitly and indistinctly. . . . That is why the term 'man' can be predicated of individuals. But the term 'humanity' signifies the essence of man as a part, because its meaning includes only what belongs to man as man, prescinding from all designation [of matter]. As a result it cannot be predicated of individual men.[31]

For these reasons, then, the problem of universals concerns only the nature or essence understood as the form of the whole, that is, as the complete essence.

But if this is so we may ask, following in the footsteps of those who preceded Thomas: Does the nature exist outside the mind or not? Interestingly enough, Thomas does not begin the discussion of the ontological status of natures with this question, an indication perhaps that we are right in saying that he rejects the traditional formulation of the problem of universals. Rather, he begins by introducing a distinction between two ways in which a nature may be considered, which he borrows from Avicenna. First, a nature may be considered absolutely, that is, according to its proper meaning. Now, since the proper meaning of a nature is given by its definition, only what is included in the definition pertains to the nature when it is considered absolutely. Thus when the nature "man" is considered absolutely, such things as white or black are excluded from it. The nature "man" absolutely

---

30. Ibid.: "nomen essentie in substantiis compositis significat id quod ex materia et forma compositum est" (Leonine, p. 370). The notion of essence raises some other interesting questions as well, some of them in relation to more contemporary issues. See Martin T. Woods, "The Reduction of Essence in the Thought of Thomas Aquinas and Edmund Husserl," *The Thomist* 53 (1989): 443–60, and Francisco Ugarte Corcuera, "Estudio sobre la esencia," *Sapientia* 36 (1987): 171–94 and 255–62.

31. *De ente*, chap. 2: "Sic igitur patet quod essentiam hominis significat hoc nomen homo et hoc nomen humanitas, sed diuersimode, . . . quia hoc nomen homo significat eam ut totum, in quantum scilicet non precidit designationem materie sed implicite continet eam et indistincte . . . ideo predicatur hoc nomen homo de indiuiduis. Sed hoc nomen humanitas significat eam ut partem, quia non continet in significatione sua nisi id quod est hominis in quantum est homo, et precidit omnem designationem; unde de indiuiduis hominis non predicatur" (Leonine, p. 373).

considered includes only animality and rationality and whatever else is implied by these predicates.[32]

The second way in which a nature may be considered is according to the existence it has in this or that. And this time predicates that are not part of its definition, or implied by it, may be predicated of it, but only accidentally, because they are not part of the essence. Thus, while absolutely considered man could not be said to be white or black, the fact that Socrates is white and Socrates is a man, permits us to speak of the essence "man" as being accidentally, in this man, white.[33]

The examples that Thomas provides illustrate quite well the reasons for the introduction of the distinction between the nature absolutely considered and the nature considered according to the existence it has in different things. For if it were in the nature of man as such—the nature absolutely considered—to be white, for example, then no man could be anything other than white. What we call black human beings could not be considered human. And if it were in the nature of human beings to be black, it would be impossible for human beings to be white. Thus it is not in the nature of man to be white or black, even if it is in the nature of man to have some skin color. Yet there are both white and black human beings, and this entails that somehow the nature of man can acquire these colors in certain circumstances. This is what Thomas means by saying that the nature, as it is in this or that, can have attributed to it accidentally what does not belong to it in itself and essentially.

For Thomas the nature considered absolutely is "neutral" with respect to all features *not* included in its definition.[34] Indeed, in the example with which we have been working, it makes sense to say that the nature of man is neutral with respect to white or black since in itself, absolutely considered, it is neither white nor black. But under particular circumstances the nature of man can, in this or that human being, become white or black.

The neutrality of the nature considered absolutely entails, more-

32. Ibid., chap. 3: "Uno modo secundum rationem propriam, et hec est absoluta consideratio ipsius: et hoc modo nichil est uerum de ea nisi quod conuenit sibi secundum quod huiusmodi; unde quicquid aliorum attribuatur sibi, falsa erit attributio. Verbi gratia homini in eo quod homo est conuenit rationale et animal et alia que in diffinitione eius cadunt; album uero aut nigrum, uel quicquid huiusmodi quod non est de ratione humanitatis, non conuenit homini in eo quod homo" (Leonine, p. 374).

33. Ibid.: "Alio modo consideratur secundum esse quod habet in hoc uel in illo: et sic de ipsa aliquid predicatur per accidens ratione eius in quo est, sicut dicitur quod homo est albus quia Sortes est albus, quamuis hoc non conueniat homini in eo quod homo" (Leonine, p. 374).

34. For text, see n. 37 below.

over, that it is a mistake to ask whether it has features that are not included in its definition. To ask whether the nature of man considered absolutely is either white or black is, using language introduced earlier in this section, a category mistake. It is like asking, as Ryle would say, whether the paella tastes blue or red. The paella tastes good or bad, salty or not, spicy or bland, but not blue or red, for blue and red are not predicates that apply to the way paellas taste. Of course, the situation with the nature "man" and the predicates "white" and "black" is not exactly symmetrical with respect to the example of the paella tasting blue or red. According to Thomas, under particular circumstances man can be said to be white and/or black, while paellas can never be said to taste blue or red. But the situation is exactly the same when it comes to essential predicates. My point is that, according to Thomas, there are certain predicates which are only accidentally associated with natures and thus cannot be predicated of them essentially.

But what does all this have to do with the problem of universals? The answer is, a great deal. For what was said concerning white and black applies, *mutatis mutandis,* to existence and nonexistence, unity and multiplicity. It is Thomas's view that the nature considered absolutely is neutral with respect to existence and unity. The nature may exist in diverse ways, but it does so precisely because neither existence nor unity are included in its definition.[35] As Thomas puts it:

This nature [considered as it exists in this or that] has a twofold existence: one in singulars and the other in the mind, and accidents follow upon the nature because of both. In singulars, moreover, the nature has a multiple existence corresponding to the diversity of singulars, but none of these types of existence belongs to the nature from the first point of view, that is to say, when it is considered absolutely. It is false to say that the essence of man as such exists in this singular: if it belonged to man as man to exist in this singular it would never exist outside the singular. On the other hand, if it belonged to man as man not to exist in this singular, human nature would never exist in it. It is true to say, however, that it does not belong to man as man to exist in this or that singular or in the mind. *So it is clear that the nature of man, considered absolutely, abstracts from every type of existence, but in such a way that it prescinds from no one of them.*[36]

35. Joseph Bobic, *Aquinas On Being and Essence: A Translation and Interpretation* (Notre Dame: University of Notre Dame Press, 1965), 129.

36. *De ente,* chap. 3: "Hec autem natura habet duplex esse: unum in singularibus et aliud in anima, et secundum utrumque consequuntur dictam naturam accidentia; in singularibus etiam habet multiplex esse secundum singularium diuersitatem. Et tamen ipsi nature secundum suam primam considerationem, scilicet absolutam, nullum istorum esse debetur. Falsum enim est dicere quod essentia hominis in quantum huiusmodi,

And Thomas adds elsewhere concerning the nature considered in itself: "If someone should ask, then, whether a nature understood in this way [i.e., absolutely] can be called one or many, we should reply that it is neither, because both are outside the concept of humanity, and it can happen to be both."[37]

We should refrain, then, from asking whether the nature considered in itself is one or many, for to answer this question implies saying something about natures that does not apply to them essentially. In this Thomas follows Avicenna, as we saw above. However, the fact that he also extends the nature's neutrality to existence, contrary to what Avicenna held, should lead us to surmise that according to him we should also refrain from asking whether the nature in itself exists or does not. True, Thomas does not actually put it this way, but everything else he says suggests a parallel between existence and unity. Besides, the transcendental symmetry he accepted between being and unity supports the point. If our surmise is correct, we may ask whether this or that individual exists or whether there is one or many individuals of a certain type. We may also ask whether we have a concept of a certain type in our minds or not. But we should not ask whether natures considered absolutely are one or many, exist or do not exist in this or that way. These are improper questions that can be answered only by rejecting the alternatives posed by them and saying, with Thomas, that none apply.

Of course, this answer does not prevent Thomas from holding that the nature as it is in this or that thing can acquire different types of existence as well as diverse types of unity. As noted earlier, the nature may acquire two basic types of existence: in individual things, where it is both individual and multiplied in accordance with their number, and in the mind, where it is again individual as a mental concept present in an individual mind but also related to all individual instances of the nature found outside the mind and thus universal.[38] The universal for Thomas, then, is properly speaking an individual mental entity which enables us to think about each of a multiplicity

---

habeat esse in hoc singulari, quia si esse in hoc singulari conueniret homini in quantum est homo, nunquam esset extra hoc singulare; similiter etiam si conueniret homini in quantum est homo non esse in hoc singulari, nunquam esset in eo: sed uerum est dicere quod homo, non in quantum est homo, habet quod sit in hoc singulari uel in illo aut in anima. Ergo patet quod *natura hominis absolute considerata abstrahit a quolibet esse*, ita tamen quod non fiat precisio alicuius eorum" (Leonine, p. 374; emphasis added).

37. Ibid.: "Vnde si queratur utrum ista natura sic considerata possit dici una uel plures, neutrum concedendum est, quia utrumque est extra intellectum humanitatis, et utrumque potest sibi accidere" (Leonine, p. 374).

38. Ibid. (Leonine, p. 375).

of nonmental entities. The nature, both in the mind and outside it, exists as individual, although with different relational features. Finally, as noted already, the nature in itself is neutral with respect to these types of existence.

It is in this way, then, that Thomas answers the four questions that were understood above to comprise the problem of universals. With respect to the first, which asked what things are universal, Thomas answers that only concepts, such as "the concept of man" and "the concept of white," are universal. However, in addition to concepts there are natures, such as "man" and "white," and individuals, such as "this man" and "this white." With respect to the question concerned with the existence of universals, Thomas responds that universals exist in the mind alone.[39] However, natures exist not only in the mind, but also as individuated in individual things, although natures in themselves are neutral with respect to being. Regarding ontological type, since universals are concepts, we must surmise that they are accidents of the mind in which they are found. We may also conclude that the ontological status of natures, whether considered in themselves or as they are found in individuals, will depend on their definitions: substances will be substances and accidents will be accidents. Finally, the relation of universals and natures to other things will depend on their ontological status. For example, universals, being accidental, will relate to minds as accidents relate to substances. And the same applies to natures considered in themselves or in individuals, depending on the ontological status prescribed by their definitions.

All these points are important for an understanding of Thomas's legacy concerning the problem of universals. However, in all these, one point stands out: Thomas's masterstroke concerning the problem of universals was to reject the formulation and the ontological assumption contained therein that had been handed down to him by his predecessors. That formulation gave him two basic alternatives from which to choose: either universals exist outside the mind or they do not. On the one hand, to say that the universal exists only in the mind is unsatisfactory because it puts into question the objectivity and validity of our concepts, and moreover it fails to explain the existence of instances of universals outside the mind. On the other hand, to say that universals exist both in the mind and outside of it seems to lead to a contradiction insofar as contradictory predicates are said of the same thing. Thomas's solution was to reject the alternatives before him, indeed, to reject the whole question as inappropriate. Instead,

39. How this is so is not easy to determine. See Francis P. Clarke, "St. Thomas on 'Universals'," *The Journal of Philosophy* 59 (1962): 720–25.

he posited natures as ontologically neutral and thus allowed them to acquire seemingly incompatible types of unity and existence, but only accidentally.

His solution was no doubt inspired by Avicenna's view, but Thomas went further on two important counts. First, as Owens has already suggested, Thomas rejected the existence that Avicenna accorded to the nature in itself. Second, and even more important than that, he rejected implicitly the formulation of the problem of universals in terms of the type of existence to be accorded to natures. I believe he rejected that formulation because he saw that, once its terms are set, a certain conceptual machinery is put into motion that is difficult to stop and which leads to the puzzles which are commonplace in discussions of the problem of universals.

Unfortunately, not all those who followed after Thomas understood the advantages of his position, and most reverted to the situation that had preceded him.[40] This is the case with Duns Scotus, for example, whose view was to confer being and unity to the nature considered in itself. Ockham, feeling uncomfortable with Scotus's move, opted for the elimination of natures except as they are found in the mind. Both Scotus and Ockham accepted the terms of the dilemma Thomas had escaped and as a result paid the consequences which had been clear from the earliest discussions of the problem of universals in the Middle Ages.[41]

40. Indeed, some contemporary scholars argue that even Thomas himself accords some kind of being to the nature considered in itself. See, for example, Ralph W. Clark, "Saint Thomas Aquinas' Theory of Universals," *The Monist* 58 (1974): 163–72. And others hold that "it is nonbeing." See B. Ryosuke Inagaki, "Thomas Aquinas and the Problem of Universals: A Re-Examination," in *Studies in Philosophy and the History of Philosophy*, ed. John K. Ryan, vol. 4 (Washington, D.C.: The Catholic University of America Press, 1969), 188.

41. Among prominent contemporary authors who follow the lead of Scotus and Ockham perhaps the most obvious is W. V. Quine. See "On What There Is," in *From a Logical Point of View* (Cambridge: Harvard University Press, 1961).

3   **Aquinas on Goodness and**
Moral Goodness

DAVID M. GALLAGHER

INTRODUCTION

To speak of the good and human action is to speak of moral goodness, that peculiar sort of goodness which comes to be in the choices and actions of free agents. Normally we approach this topic only to ask why one sort of action is morally good and another morally bad or evil. In fact, this often is held out as the primary task of ethics: to discover or devise some rule or rules, some set of principles by which actions might be judged as morally good or bad. We may, however, raise a yet more fundamental question: What precisely is the nature of moral goodness? Once raised, this question immediately generates a flurry of related ones. Is moral goodness located primarily in moral agents themselves, or is it in their actions, or is it perhaps in the things effected by those actions? Is moral goodness the only sort of goodness, the only thing "really" good, in comparison with which all other goods lose their claim to that title? If there are many sorts of goods, how is moral goodness related to nonmoral goodness? We might put this question in the following manner; How is moral goodness related to ontological goodness, or again, how is goodness in the realm of freedom related to goodness in the realm of nature?

Thomas Aquinas, like anyone who ventures into the arena of moral discourse, had to face these questions. Unlike most, however, he brought into that arena a rare combination, a union of breadth in philosophical reflection, of consistency of thought, and of a profound sense of the interrelatedness of philosophical questions. Above all, he brought to these questions the full weight of his metaphysics, for here, as on almost every page of his corpus, Aquinas drives relentlessly to the being of things. And this drive takes on special importance in the question of moral goodness, since, for Thomas, the good is above all a metaphysical notion.

This paper will attempt to describe Thomas's understanding of moral goodness: what it is, where it is located, and how it is related to other kinds of goodness. It will consist of two parts, the first dealing with Thomas's understanding of the good in general, that is, good as a metaphysical notion, and the second treating specifically the notion of moral goodness. Having reached a precise understanding of moral goodness, we shall be in a position to understand why it is that moral goodness has so central a place in the perfection of a human being.

I. THE NOTION OF GOOD IN GENERAL

When we try to understand the good, or grasp the meaning of the term "goodness," we face a seemingly impenetrable swirl of different instances and kinds of goodness. These instances are so many and so various as to discourage, indeed almost defy, any attempt to unify them. Each kind of thing has its peculiar sort of goodness, distinct from that of other things. The goodness of a good book is not that of a good meal; neither is identical with or even similar to the goodness of a good man. Moreover, any single thing can be at once good in several ways. The cherry tree is good for the beauty of its blossoms, its yield of fruit, its shade, the wood it supplies. We encounter things at once good and bad: the barking dog is good for the master of the house, bad for the burglar. Such flux hardly promises the discovery of any distinctive quality or set of characteristics to which the term refers of the sort we might easily produce for words like "dog" or "book" or "sweet." The meaning of "good," it seems, is either impenetrable or simply shatters into unrelated fragments.[1]

Nevertheless, Aquinas discerns a unity within the many uses of the term. In the opening lines of the *Nicomachean Ethics,* while asserting that all human activity is directed to some good, Aristotle had remarked that "the good has been well defined as that at which all things aim."[2] Thomas, who almost never speaks of the good without citing this passage, takes it as a definition; what is distinctive about the good, what constitutes a good as good, is the simple fact that it is something aimed at, something desired. The things we call good are many, but all share in this: in some way they are the object of desire; they are

1. Georg Henrik von Wright, *The Varieties of Goodness* (New York: Routledge & Kegan Paul, 1963), has attempted to classify the various kinds of goodness. He distinguishes instrumental goodness, medical goodness, the good of a being, beneficial goodness, utilitarian goodness, hedonic goodness, and moral goodness (see chap. 1, esp. 6–18). Unlike Aquinas, however, von Wright does not think that the various instances of goodness can be unified by analogy.
2. *Nicomachean Ethics* 1.1.1094a1–3 (hereafter NE); *Rhetoric* 1.6.1362a23.

desirable. It is precisely this understanding which Aquinas expresses in his oft-repeated phrase: the *ratio boni*—the intelligible content of the term—consists in something being desirable (*appetibile*).[3]

To define the good as simply the desirable would seem not merely to uncover an underlying unity, but beyond that, to point to a certain univocity in its meaning. The notion of the "desirable" seems to provide an intelligible core equally present in each and every instance of the good. This however is not the case. The term "desirable," depending as it does upon the notion of desire for its own intelligibility, will have just as many senses as there are different sorts of desire. And here it is crucial to recognize that, for Thomas, tendency or striving of any sort, from the most basic tendency of bodies to move toward the earth to the most deliberate and intense act of willing in spiritual beings, falls into the category of desire.[4] Thus "desire" is no more univocal than "good." We must simply acknowledge that "desire," "the desirable," and especially the "good" are *analogical* terms: the intelligibilities they embrace escape the unrelatedness of equivocity, yet never achieve the identity of univocity.[5]

It is difficult to express just how analogical the good is for Aquinas. The goodness of God in contrast to that of creatures, goodness in the substantial order as opposed to that of the accidental order, goodness as found in each of the ten categories, goodness as found in different essences or natures, the honest good, the pleasant good, and the useful good; these are only some of the analogies to be found.[6] In fact, the only term that would seem to be more analogical than "good" is "being" itself. It is necessary to emphasize this point, since the cost of overlooking it, for the reader of Aquinas, is grave misunderstanding, if not utter incomprehension.

Let us return to Thomas's definition of the good as the "desirable." From Aristotle's words, one might say that the good is not so much the desirable, as merely the *desired*. A good is simply that at which something aims. On such a reading, to call something good is only to say that it actually is desired, such that, if the desire were to cease, the

3. For example, ST I, q. 5, a. 1, c.: "Ratio enim boni in hoc consistit, quod aliquid sit appetibile: unde Philosophus, in I *Ethic.* dicit quod bonum est *quod omnia appetunt*"; also *De malo*, q. 1, a. 1, c.: ". . . bonum proprie est aliquid in quantum est appetibile, nam, secundum Philosophum in I *Ethic.* optime diffinierunt bonum dicentes, quod bonum est quod omnia appetunt; . . ." (Leonine, p. 5).
4. *In I Ethicorum*, lect. 1 (Leonine, p. 5: 165–75); cf. ST I, q. 59, a. 1, c.
5. *In I Ethicorum*, lect. 7 (Leonine, p. 27: 198–213); cf. ST I, q. 5, a. 6, ad 3.
6. For "*bonum*" used analogically of God and creatures, see ST I, q. 6, a. 1, c., and q. 13, aa. 3–6; for "*bonum*" used analogically of substance and accidents and in the ten categories, see *In I Ethicorum*, lect. 6 (Leonine, p. 23: 125–48); for analogy among honest, pleasant, and useful goods, see ST I, q. 5, a. 6, ad 3.

thing would be no longer good. Goodness, on this reading, is simply the fact of being desired. This view, however, is not Aquinas's. His commentary on these first lines of the *Nicomachean Ethics* is illuminating in this regard. There he remarks that good (*bonum*) is among the first and most basic of things; *bonum* is so basic in fact, that the Platonists were able to consider it absolutely first, prior even to being.[7] Now, Thomas continues, things which are most basic cannot be known or described in terms of anything more basic than themselves, but must be known by what is posterior to them, the way, for example, we know causes by their effects. This is the case with the good: it can be known only by its effect, which is the desire it arouses.[8] In other words, we know or recognize the good by means of the desire directed toward it, and for this reason we necessarily refer to desire when we try to define the good. In terms of our knowledge, desire is prior to good. Nevertheless, the goodness which attracts desire is, in being, prior to that desire. Because the honey is sweet I wish to eat it; because the wood is combustible I gather it for my fire. So goodness is known by its relation to desire, but this relation does not make it be what it is. Rather, goodness is located in the thing itself and is prior to desire. For this reason to be good is to be *desirable*, not merely to be desired; a thing may be desirable even when it is not actually being desired. Thus while the intelligibility (*ratio*) of goodness depends upon a relation to desire, goodness itself is found within the very being which is good.

If goodness is located in the thing which is good, how, precisely, are we to characterize the relationship between the thing's goodness and its being? Or, to put the question another way, what is the ontological status of the good? In an early work, the *De veritate*, Thomas approaches this question in the context of the ten categories.[9] As is well known, Aquinas, following Aristotle, maintains that every instance of real being falls into one of ten ultimate genera, either into the category of substance—being which can exist in itself—or into one of the nine categories of accidents such as quantity or quality or relation: kinds of being which do not exist in themselves but only in substances. These ten categories are not species within the larger genus of being; rather,

---

7. *In I Ethicorum*, lect. 1: ". . . bonum numeratur inter prima, adeo quod secundum Platonicos bonum est prius ente . . ." (Leonine, p. 5: 150–51).

8. Ibid. "Prima autem non possunt notificari per aliqua priora, sed notificantur per posteriora, sicut causae per proprios effectus. Cum autem bonum proprie sit motivum appetitus, describitur bonum per motum appetitus, sicut solet manifestari vis motiva per motum" (Leonine, p. 5: 153–58).

9. *De veritate*, q. 21, a. 1 (Leonine, pp. 591–95).

they are what Thomas terms special modes of being, various ways in which existing things (*entia*) can exist.[10]

Aquinas, following once again Aristotle's discussion of the good in the *Nicomachean Ethics*,[11] points out that the good or goodness is not limited to any one category, but rather is to be found in all of them. Usually a particular term is limited in range to a single category. Thus "cat" or "dog" or "oaktree" always refer to substances; "red" and "white," "hot" and "cold," "generous" and "stingy" always refer to qualities; "large" and "small" to quantities; "near" and "far" to place, and so on. Each of these designates one particular mode of being. "Good," on the other hand, is not limited to one of the categories, but can be predicated in any of them. We can speak of good men (substance), good color or good temperature (quality), a good size (quantity), a good place (place), and so on. As Thomas says, the good is divided equally into all the categories.[12]

This observation leads Thomas to maintain that goodness is not a special mode of being; the term "good" does not point to anything that would narrow or determine being (*ens*) to a particular mode; it does not place being into one of the genera.[13] Good is somehow coextensive with being. Still, good is not a synonym for being; we really do mean something different when we say that a thing is and that it is good. In terms of meaning, good adds something to being, but, Thomas argues, it is not possible for good to add anything *real* to being, since if it did, it necessarily would determine being to a particular mode. He concludes, finally, that there is a distinction between good and being, but only a distinction in reason (*rationis tantum*).[14] What good adds to being is a reference to desire or appetite; something desirable is simply a being viewed as the object of desire. If I say that the honey is good because it is sweet, and that the goodness of the honey is its sweetness, I am not pointing to anything other than

---

10. See *De veritate*, q. 1, a. 1, c. (Leonine, pp. 4–6), and q. 21, a. 1, c. (pp. 592–94).

11. NE 1.6.1096a12–1097a14.

12. *De veritate*, q. 21, a. 1, c.: "Secundo autem modo inveniuntur aliqua addere super ens quia ens contrahitur per decem genera, quorum unumquodque addit aliquid super ens, non quidem aliquod accidens vel aliquam differentiam quae sit extra essentiam entis sed determinatum modum essendi qui fundatur in ipsa existentia rei. Sic autem bonum non addit aliquid super ens, cum bonum dividatur aequaliter in decem genera ut ens, ut patet In I Ethicorum" (Leonine, p. 593). Cf. *Sententia Libri Ethicorum*, lect. 6 (Leonine, p. 23: 125–48).

13. *De veritate*, q. 21, a. 1, c.: "Et ideo oportet quod [bonum] vel nihil addat super ens vel addat aliquod quod sit in ratione tantum; si enim adderet aliquod reale oporteret. quod per rationem boni contraheretur ens ad aliquod speciale genus" (Leonine, p. 593).

14. Ibid.: ". . . bonum . . . addat aliquid super ens quod sit rationis tantum."

the sweetness. What I am doing is viewing or taking that sweetness as something which is desired or desirable. Likewise, if I think the wood good because it burns, its goodness is its combustibility; it is the combustibility seen as the object of desire.

Goodness is not, in the good thing, a distinct characteristic or quality over and above the substantial and accidental modes of being. It is always one of those modes taken in reference to desire. It is like the difference between the first President of the United States and the husband of Martha Washington. What I *mean* when I use these two descriptions is not the same (*secundum rationem*), but the thing I am describing is one and the same thing (*secundum rem*).[15]

In a later work, the *Summa theologiae*, Thomas argues once again for the identity of good and being in things. This argument is briefer and, more importantly, takes a different path from that of the *De veritate*. Moreover, it introduces an absolutely central notion, that of a being possessing an appetite or desire for its own perfections. This notion, what we might term "self-appetite," opens up a deeper and richer understanding of the goodness of things. Let us turn briefly to Aquinas's discussion (ST I, q. 5, a. 1).

He begins with his fundamental understanding of the good as that which is desirable. Immediately, however, he introduces the notion of the perfect (*perfectum*), asserting that whatever is desirable is so precisely insofar as it is perfect. The desirable is the perfect.[16] Thomas's reason for saying this is that whenever a being desires something, it always is desiring its own perfection. Perfection in this context, means completion; a thing is perfect to the extent to which it is complete, that is, to the extent to which it does not lack anything. Thus to say that a thing seeks its perfection is to say that it desires either to maintain the degree of completion it now enjoys or to achieve an even greater degree of completion.

Having argued that the good is always the perfect, Thomas must next show how the perfect is always something existing (*ens*) if he wishes to conclude that being and good are the same in things (*secun-*

15. *De veritate*, q. 21, a. 2, c. (Leonine, p. 596). In more contemporary terms, we might say that good and being differ in sense but have the same referent. Eleanore Stump and Norman Kretzmann use precisely this language to describe Thomas's understanding of the relation between the two terms. See "Being and Goodness," in *Divine and Human Action: Essays in the Metaphysics of Theism*, ed. T. Morris (Ithaca: Cornell University Press, 1988), 282, 284.

16. ST I, q. 5, a. 1, c.: "Respondeo dicendum quod bonum et ens sunt idem secundum rem: sed differunt secundum rationem tantum. Quod sic patet. Ratio enim boni in hoc consistit, quod aliquid sit appetibile: unde Philosophus, in *I Ethic.*, dicit quod bonum est *quod omnia appetunt*. Manifestum est autem quod unumquodque est appetibile secundum quod est perfectum: nam omnia appetunt suam perfectionem."

dum rem). Thomas must show that the perfect as such is always what exists. Anything, he says, is perfect insofar as it is in act. This is clear if we consider the notion of completion; so long as a being only *could* be something but *is not*, it contains unfulfilled potential and so is not yet complete. Thus to be complete or perfect, something must possess its perfection *in act*. Perfection always implies actuality. But for anything to be in act it must have the most basic of all acts, the act of being (*actus essendi*). This, Thomas says elsewhere, is the act of acts and the perfection of perfections: without existence nothing is in act at all, and certainly nothing could be perfect or complete.[17] The conclusion, then, is that for anything to be perfect it must have being; that is, the *perfectum* is always *ens*.[18]

Let us summarize the path Aquinas's argument has taken: The good by definition is the desirable; the desirable is the perfect; the perfect is always in act; only what exists is in act. We conclude, then, that whatever is good is something existing. The identity of good and being is to be found in the notion of act. The actual as such, as opposed to the potential, is that which is (and not what merely could be), that is, the actual is the existing. The perfect, on the other hand, is also the actual, for as we have just seen, to be perfect or complete always implies actuality. If we look at the actual as what exists, we see it as being (*ens*); if we look at the actual insofar as it is perfect and thus desirable, we see it as good (*bonum*). *Secundum rem*, in the things themselves, good and being are the same, but what we mean when we say good remains distinct from the meaning of being (*secundum rationem*). Good adds to being a reference to desire.

In order to grasp the full import of this argument, we need to focus our attention on two points: 1) the fact that perfection is always relative to essence or nature, and 2) the claim that any being, in its desiring, seeks its own perfection. With respect to the first point, the relation of perfection to essence, Thomas states several times that a thing is said to be perfect when it lacks nothing "*according to the mode of its perfection.*"[19] Now to say nothing is lacking is simply to point to completion. But to speak of the "mode of perfection" is to point to the fact that what constitutes perfection or completion has a determinate

---

17. *De potentia*, q. 7, a. 2, ad 9 (Marietti, p. 192); ST I, q. 3, a. 4, c.; q. 4, a. 1, ad 3.
18. ST I, q. 5, a. 1, c.: "Intantum est autem perfectum unumquodque, inquantum est actu: unde manifestum est quod intantum est aliquid bonum, inquantum est ens: esse enim est actualitas omnis rei, ut ex superioribus patet. Unde manifestum est quod bonum et ens sunt idem secundum rem: sed bonum dicit rationem appetibilis, quam non dicit ens."
19. ST I, q. 4, a. 1, c.: ". . . perfectum dicitur, cui nihil deest secundum modum suae perfectionis."

content, a content which is proper to the kind of being in question. According to the kind of being it is, each thing has its own proper actualization. Thus, what constitutes completion for an oak tree is very different from the completion of a dog or of a human being. Each of these is a distinct kind of thing; that is to say, each has a distinct nature or essence, and consequently we can speak of their perfection only in relation to their particular natures.[20] Another way of putting this is to say that each thing has its own *due* perfections; certain perfections are "owed" (*debitum*) to it according as it is a certain kind of thing, perfections not owed to another kind of thing. Thomas's usual example is that of sight: sight is a due perfection for an animal, but not for a stone. Without sight a dog is imperfect, while a stone is not.[21] A being's goodness or perfection, then, will consist in the possession of all the perfections due to its nature or essence.

The second key point is that each thing, in desiring, desires its own perfection. Why is this important? Because it means that the desirability by which the thing is a good thing is not primarily said with reference to the desire of some other being. A being can be said to be good solely by reference to its own desire for its own perfection.

Let us look at this point more closely. If the good is characterized as the desirable, there must always be some desire, actual or potential, in reference to which it is desirable. Upon first understanding the good as the desirable, one usually thinks of instances in which things are good by reference to the desire of other beings, especially human beings. In our examples of honey and wood this was the case; both were taken to be good because they were desirable for human beings. In our daily commerce with the world, this is probably the most common way things are taken to be good. This is most evident in the case of artificial things. Being made precisely for human use, their goodness corresponds to some human desire. A good car is a desirable car, but what counts for desirability in a car depends solely upon what human wants the car was designed to satisfy.

In natural beings, on the other hand, goodness or desirability can be said in terms of the thing's own desire. Each thing desires first to exist—Thomas holds that all things resist corruption insofar as they are able—and second, to achieve its full completion. This is most manifest perhaps in the case of living things; they both maintain them-

20. ST I-II, q. 71, a. 1, c.: ". . . in hoc enim consistit uniuscuiusque rei bonitas, quod convenienter se habeat secundum modum suae naturae." Cf. ST I, q. 5, a. 5, c.
21. ST I, q. 48, a. 5, ad 1: ". . . quia malum privatio est boni, et non negatio pura, . . . non omnis defectus boni est malum, sed defectus boni quod natum est et debet haberi. Defectus enim visionis non est malum in lapide, sed in animali: quia contra rationem lapidis est, quod visum habeat"; also a. 3, c.

selves in existence (nutrition), and in addition always struggle towards their fulfillment (growth and reproduction). Thus for any being, he says, both existence and the possession of its due perfections are objects of desire. Being the sort of thing it is, each thing has a natural desire or inclination for its own perfection.[22] This sort of "self-desire" in natural things explains why it is that we can speak of such things as good not merely insofar as they provide some benefit for human life, but simply as they are in themselves.[23]

Here we have the basis for Thomas's well-known view that being and good are convertible. If all beings desire their own existence, then existence will always be a good, and each thing, insofar as it exists, will be a good thing. Proceeding in the other direction, whatever is good must exist, for, as we have seen, all perfection implies the act of being. Hence wherever we find one we necessarily will find the other, that is, they are convertible.[24]

Thomas's thesis that good and being are convertible may seem to imply that evil is not really possible. If evil is opposed to good and all that is is good, there seems no room for evil. Thomas might reply that, true enough, there is no room for evil, but then evil does not take up any room. Evil, he says, is a privation, the lack of a perfection which a being should enjoy. The simplest case is something like blindness which is not itself anything, but only the absence of a due perfection, namely, sight. All that exists is good insofar as it exists and possesses perfections due to it; nevertheless, a being may lack certain perfections and so, in some respects, be evil.[25] Nothing, however, can be wholly evil, since privation always exists in a subject and that subject, as an existing thing, is good.[26]

22. *De veritate*, q. 21, a. 2, c.: "Omnia autem quae iam esse habent illud esse suum naturaliter amant et ipsum tota virtue conservant; . . ." (Leonine, p. 596). SCG I, chap. 37: ". . . unumquodque suam perfectionem appetit sicut proprium bonum"

23. Thomas's view that all beings are good insofar as they desire their own existence and perfection is thoroughly treated by Larry Donohoo, "The Nature of Desire: St. Thomas Aquinas's Primary Account of Desire" (S.T.L. diss., Dominican House of Studies, Washington, D.C., 1988), 45–61.

24. For texts in which Thomas argues for the convertability of *ens* and *bonum* in terms of a being desiring its own existence, see *De veritate*, q. 21, a. 2 (Leonine, p. 596); ST I, q. 5, a. 3. For a distinct argument, see *De veritate*, q. 1, a. 1, c. (Leonine, pp. 4–5). See also Jan Aertsen, "The Convertability of Being and Good in St. Thomas Aquinas," *The New Scholasticism* 59 (1985): 449–70.

25. ST I, q. 48, aa. 2–4; *De malo*, q. 1, aa. 1–2 (Leonine, pp. 3–13); SCG III, chaps. 7–9. While Thomas denies that evil has existence or being according to the mode of being which is divided among the ten categories, he does allow that it has the sort of being found in the truth of propositions. Thus, for example, blindness has being insofar as it is true to say that blindness occurs in animals. For this, see ST I, q. 48, a. 2, ad 2; *De malo*, q. 1, a. 1, ad 20 (Leonine, pp. 8–9).

26. ST I, q. 48, aa. 3–4; *De malo*, q. 1, a. 1, c. (Leonine, pp. 5–6).

Here we encounter a distinction which will figure largely in our discussion of why moral goodness is so central to human perfection. To say something exists simply (*simpliciter*) does not imply that that thing is good simply. Something is said to be *simpliciter*, Thomas says, as soon as it exists. For it to exist it must have substantial being (*esse*), by which a being exists actually and not merely potentially. If we say that John exists or simply is, we are referring to his substantial being. If we say, in addition, that John is white or tall or intelligent, we cannot say simply that he is, but must qualify the "is": we say he is white or is tall or something else. In other words, when we say that something is simply or in an unqualified manner (*simpliciter*) we are referring to its substantial being. If we wish to refer to the substance in terms of other, superadded determinations—its accidents—we speak of it existing, but only *secundum quid*, in a certain respect. Thus in terms of being, something is *simpliciter* through its substantial being, and is *secundum quid* through its additional accidental determinations.[27]

With the good, just the opposite occurs. A thing is not said to be good merely because it has the perfection of substantial existence. If we say a horse is a good horse, we mean much more than that it simply exists. Goodness is said with reference to perfection and perfection always implies completion, and so a thing is said to be good simply when it is simply complete, that is to say, when it has its full completion. Completion of this sort goes beyond simple substantial existence; it requires the superadded perfections proper to the sort of being in question. Thus a diseased horse would not be simply good. We could say that it is good insofar as it is an existing horse, but clearly it is necessary to add that qualification. This view implies that a being is good simply, only if it enjoys certain perfections beyond that of simply existing as a substance; a thing will be good *simpliciter*, through perfections in the accidental order.[28]

---

27. ST I, q. 5, a. 1, ad 1: "Ad primum ergo dicendum quod, licet bonum et ens sint idem secundum rem, quia tamen differunt secundum rationem, non eodem modo dicitur aliquid *ens simpliciter*, et *bonum simpliciter*. Nam cum ens dicat aliquid proprie esse in actu; actus autem proprie ordinem habeat ad potentiam; secundum hoc simpliciter aliquid dicitur ens, secundum quod primo discernitur ab eo quod est in potentia tantum. Hoc autem est esse substantiale rei uniuscuiusque; unde per suum esse substantiale dicitur unumquodque ens simpliciter. Per actus autem superadditos, dicitur aliquid esse *secundum quid*, sicut esse album significat esse secundum quid: non enim esse album aufert esse in potentia simpliciter, cum adveniat rei iam praeexistenti in actu."

28. Ibid.: "Sed bonum dicit rationem perfecti, quod est appetibile: et per consequens dicit rationem ultimi. Unde id quod est ultimo perfectum, dicitur bonum simpliciter. Quod autem non habet ultimam perfectionem quam debet habere, quamvis habeat aliquam perfectionem inquantum est actu, non tamen dicitur perfectum simpliciter, nec bonum simpliciter, sed secundum quid"; cf. *De veritate*, q. 21, a. 5, c. (Leonine, pp. 605–6).

Among the perfections which go beyond the simple existence, the activities or operations of a being constitute its ultimate perfection. The thing's existence and the qualities and characteristics due it according to its nature or essence are all ordered to its proper activities or operations. This is seen most easily in the case of living things. The perfection of such beings lies in their activities. Ultimately, then, a thing will find its perfection and its goodness in its operations.[29]

II. MORAL GOODNESS

To describe Thomas's understanding of moral goodness, we must first clarify what he means by the term "moral" itself. In the first question of the *Prima secundae*, at the very beginning of his discussion of the moral life, he explicitly equates moral acts with what he calls "human acts" (*actus humanus*).[30] Human acts, he says, are those acts over which a person has dominion or control, those acts which, when one does them, one could do differently or even not at all. Thomas distinguishes these acts from those things which a person does but does not control. While in a state of drunkenness or rage, while sleep-walking, or even while distracted, people carry out many actions over which they have no control. Aquinas calls these "acts of man" (*actus hominis*): they are things a person does, but not in a properly human way.[31] There is a very real difference between blinking (usually an act of man) and winking (always a human act).

Human acts, insofar as they are acts over which an agent has control, are said to be *voluntary* acts. These are actions in which agents move themselves to act on the basis of some deliberation. That is to say, voluntary action is action done thinkingly. To speak of action done thinkingly, however, is not to confuse thought and action. Thinking alone neither is nor produces action; it is quite a different thing to think about eating dinner and actually to eat it. In order to eat dinner, if it is to be a human act, I must *choose* to eat. While never without thinking, human action is always more than thinking, and this something more, the source of the actual motion, is *will*. Human actions,

---

29. SCG III, chap. 20: ". . . bonitas autem rei non solum in esse suo consistit, sed in omnibus aliis quae ad suam perfectionem requiruntur, ut ostensum est: manifestum est quod res ordinantur in Deum sicut in finem non solum secundum esse substantiale, sed etiam secundum ea quae ei accidunt pertinentia ad perfectionem: et etiam secundum propriam operationem, quae etiam pertinent ad perfectionem rei." Cf. ST I, q. 6, a. 1, c.
30. ST I-II, q. 1, a. 3, c.: ". . . nam idem sunt actus morales et actus humani"; also q. 18, a. 5, c.; q. 21, a. 2, ad 3.
31. ST I-II, q. 1, a. 1, c.

for Aquinas, are actions done thinkingly and willfully or, as he himself
expresses it, actions which proceed from a deliberate will (*a voluntate
deliberata*).[32] Moral action, action within the control of an agent, voluntary action, willed action, human action: these terms all have the
same extension.

Let us focus particularly on one of these terms, that of *willed acts*.
Moral action is action which proceeds from the will; to the extent that
an action is willed, to that extent it is moral. Behind this claim, however, lies the whole of Thomas's psychology, especially his theory of
faculties or powers, for he understands the will precisely as a power
of the soul.

As is well known, for Aquinas all the activities of any living being—
including any human being—must ultimately arise from its soul,
which is the form and active principle of the body. These activities,
however, do not proceed from the essence of the soul directly, but
rather through the mediation of certain powers or faculties which the
soul possesses and by which it acts. Thus when a person sees, he does
so through his power of sight, he remembers through his power of
memory, he understands through his power of intellect; he walks,
runs, or otherwise moves his body by means of his motive power.[33]

Yet it would be clearly insufficient to describe the activity of human
agents solely in terms of these kinds of powers. When we refer to
activities such as seeing, remembering, or walking simply in themselves, it is enough to explain them simply in terms of their respective
powers or faculties: the powers of sight, and memory, and the motive
power. But if we consider them insofar as they are carried out voluntarily—if we take them as *human* acts—then these powers are not
alone sufficient. None of these powers can account for the fact that
the activity which arises from them has arisen *voluntarily*. Common
experience testifies that the exercise of many powers lies within a
person's control. Thus I see or leave off seeing when I want to;
whether I walk or not depends upon my choice.[34] Of course, not all
activities are voluntary; in fact the very same activity may in one instance be voluntary and in another not: I must strain to remember a

32. ST I-II, q. 1, a. 3, c.: ". . . actus dicuntur humani, inquantum procedunt a
voluntate deliberata."
33. For Thomas's doctrine of the soul and its powers, see ST I, qq. 76–78. For a
general description see Etienne Gilson, *The Christian Philosophy of St. Thomas Aquinas*,
trans. L. K. Shook (New York: Random House, 1956), 187–222. For some of the historical precedents of his theory see Pius Künzle, *Das Verhältnis der Seele zu ihren Potenzen.
Problemgeschichtliche Untersuchungen von Augustin bis und mit Thomas von Aquin* (Freiburg:
Universitätsverlag Schweiz, 1956).
34. ST I-II, q. 9, a. 1, c.: ". . . voluntas movet alias potentias animae ad suos actos:
utimur enim alii potentiis cum volumus"; cf. q. 16, a. 1, c.

name or face, yet a smell or song may suddenly stir up a childhood memory.

The point here is that when an activity is done voluntarily, there must be some power beyond the powers which cause the activity as such, a power by which that activity receives its voluntary character. This power is the will. The will, says Aquinas, can move the other powers to their acts, and when it does so, it renders those acts voluntary. In fact, we can define the will precisely as that faculty by which acts are voluntary acts, or, in equivalent terms, that faculty by which actions are within the control of an agent.[35] This distinction between the act of will which moves other powers and the acts of the other powers which are moved is precisely the distinction between the interior act and the exterior act, a distinction which figures prominently in Aquinas's moral doctrine.[36]

Will is not, however, pure spontaneity, a sort of wild card by which a person randomly determines himself to actions. Voluntary action is always deliberate or thinking sort of action; when thinking ceases to be operative, as in a state of rage, there can be no voluntary action. Similarly there is no voluntary act when a person acts from ignorance, because in such a case one does not thinkingly or deliberately direct one's action to effect what in fact the action causes to happen.[37] In other words, voluntary action must be willed action, but it must also be deliberate action, action carried out on the basis of thinking and judgment. In short, will is a *rational appetite* and its inclinations and motions must be governed by reason.

In sum, moral actions are acts of the will itself or acts carried out because they have been commanded by the will. Consequently, to discover the precise character of moral goodness, we must look to the will and its acts. Aquinas holds that it is in the will's relationship to reason that moral goodness arises. In this relationship there is a *debitum*, a particular kind of relationship which by nature ought to obtain, but which can and often is broken. When the will follows reason properly, that is, is properly ordered to reason, moral goodness is

---

35. For example, ST I-II, q. 21, a. 2, c.: "Tunc autem actus imputatur agenti, quando est in potestate ipsius, ita quod habeat dominium sui actus. Hoc autem est in omnibus actibus voluntariis: quia per voluntatem homo dominium sui actus habet, . . ." For a characterization of the will in terms of control (*dominium*), see *De veritate*, q. 22, a. 4 (Leonine, pp. 619–21).

36. For the distinction between interior and exterior act, see ST I-II, q. 18, a. 6, c. For the role of this distinction in Thomas's moral theory, see David Gallagher, "Aquinas on Moral Action: Interior and Exterior Act," *Proceedings of the American Catholic Philosophical Association* 64 (1990): 118–29.

37. For Thomas's discussion of the factors which render acts involuntary, see ST I-II, q. 6, aa. 4–8.

present; if for some reason that ordination, a due perfection for the will's acts, is lacking, the resultant privation will be moral evil. If, then, moral evil is a deficiency, we might obtain the clearest view of moral goodness by studying moral evil and discovering the precise nature of the privation which constitutes it. Indeed, Thomas's fullest treatments of the proper relationship of will to reason are actually found in his discussions of sin, in particular, moral or voluntary sins.[38]

Thomas uses three terms to designate evil: *malum* (evil), *peccatum* (fault or sin), and *culpa* (moral sin or moral fault). *Malum* or evil has the broadest extension; *peccatum* or fault is a category within *malum*, and *culpa* or blame an even narrower category, a subset as it were of *peccatum*. Evil (*malum*), can be applied, as we have seen, to any privation of a due good. For each kind of thing, certain goods or perfections are proper and are said to be due or owed to it. There may be something lacking in the thing itself, or there may be a lack in the thing's activity or operations; deficiencies or privations of both sorts are evils. Fault, in contrast to evil, applies only to the deficiencies or privations found in *activities* or *operations*; any activity, natural or technical or moral, which is not what it ought to be according to its kind is a fault (*peccatum*). Thus, if we took a shortsighted person, both his eyes and his acts of seeing would be evil, but only the acts of seeing would be faults (*peccata*). So too, both a musician's lack of proper conditioning and the consequent mistakes he makes while playing are evils, but only the mistakes in playing would be faults (*peccata*). Voluntary acts which are defective or suffer some privation constitute a special class of faults, the evil of which receives the title "*culpa*" or "*malum culpae*" or blame. I shall refer to this class of evils as "moral fault." *Culpa* or moral fault is precisely moral evil.[39]

Since moral fault is a specification of fault in general (*peccatum*), it follows that the structure of the specific evil found in voluntary acts is a particularization of what occurs more generally in faults. How

---

38. ST I-II, q. 71, and *De malo,* q. 2.

39. *De malo,* q. 2, a. 2, c.: "Set considerandum est quod hec tria, malum, peccatum et culpa, se habent ad invicem ut communius et minus commune. Nam malum communius est: in quocumque enim, sive in subiecto sive in actu, privatio forme aut ordinis aut mensure debite mali rationem habet. Set peccatum dicitur aliquis actus debito ordine aut forma sive mensura carens. Unde potest dici quod tibia curva sit mala tibia, non tamen potest dici quod sit peccatum, nisi forte eo modo loquendi quo peccatum dicitur effectus peccati; set ipsa claudicatio peccatum dicitur: quilibet enim actus inordinatus potest dici peccatum vel nature vel artis vel moris. Set rationem culpe non habet peccatum nisi ex eo quod est voluntarium: nulli enim imputatur ad culpam aliquis inordinatus actus, nisi ex eo quod est in eius potestate. Et sic patet quod peccatum est in plus quam culpa, licet secundum communem usum loquendi apud theologos pro eodem sumantur peccatum et culpa" (Leonine, p. 33); cf. ST I-II, q. 21, a. 1, c.; ST I, q. 48, a. 5, c.

should we describe what occurs in a fault? According to Thomas, an act of any sort is evil, that is, a fault, when in some manner it fails to achieve its end. The shortsighted person does not see clearly; the musician does not play the song correctly; in both cases the act does not fully achieve that to which it was ordained.[40] Not only does the act fail to achieve its goal, but, Thomas adds, the cause of the failure is that the act strayed from the *rule or measure* (*regula vel mensura*) that should have governed it. The activity has its own rule or measure, a way it ought to have been carried out; the failure to achieve the end is a consequence of the failure to observe the proper rule or measure. There is a proper way to play a piece and the musician's fault consists precisely in his failure to observe it (e.g., playing a wrong note); so too the eye has a natural way of focusing, and a failure to conform to it constitutes a defect in the act of seeing.[41]

Here we touch upon a central element of Thomas's understanding of fault. Activities, both of nature and of art—and, as we shall see, voluntary actions—have rules by which they are measured. In this context, rule should not be understood only as something which is written or spoken, such as a law or a set of instructions, nor is it even necessarily something grasped intellectually. In the case of natural things, for example, Thomas says that the rule which governs activity is merely the natural inclination from which the activity arises and by which it is guided. For example, in the instinctual behavior of animals the instinct itself would be the rule and measure of the activities.[42] In the case of rational beings the rule takes the form of law. The important element, however, is not the form which the rule or measure takes but the fact that there is a proper or due way in which activities should be carried out, such that for any act to be carried out as it should, it must conform to its rule. The perfection of an activity depends upon its conformity to its rule.

Aquinas maintains that the activities of all beings other than God

40. Thomas explicitly takes this doctrine over from Aristotle (see following note). In *Physics* 2, Aristotle offers as an argument for his teleological view of nature the fact that mistakes (*hamartiai*) occur in both art and nature. Such mistakes, he maintains, are possible only if the acts are directed to some end (199a33–b5). For Thomas's commentary on this passage, see *In II Physicorum*, lect. 14, n. 263 (Marietti, pp. 129–30).

41. *De malo*, q. 2, a. 1, c.: ". . . peccatum enim, ut Philosophus dicit in II Phisicorum, contingit et in his que sunt secundum naturam et in his que secundum artem, quando non consequitur finem natura vel ars propter quem operatur. Quod autem finem non consequatur operans per artem vel per naturam, contingit ex hoc quod declinatur a mensura vel regula debite operationis; que quidem in naturalibus est ipsa nature inclinatio consequens aliquam formam, in artificialibus vero est ipsa regula artis. Sic igitur in peccato duo possunt attendi, scilicet recessus a regula vel mensura et recessus a fine" (Leonine, p. 29).

42. ST I-II, q. 21, a. 1, c.

have a rule which they themselves do not establish, but to which their actions must conform if they are to achieve their end. God is himself the rule and measure of his acts and he alone has no measure outside himself. For this reason, Thomas states, God cannot sin. Thomas illustrates this point with a simple example, that of a carpenter cutting wood. If the carpenter's hand were the rule and measure of his cutting, then it would be impossible for the carpenter to make a mistake or fault; wherever he cut would be exactly where he ought to have cut.[43]

Thus fault (*peccatum*), in the wide sense which pertains to activities of all kinds, contains two essential elements: (1) there is an act which is directed to an end and fails to achieve that end; and (2) that act does not conform to its rule or measure. These elements, of course, are related. An act does not arrive at its goal *because* it did not follow its rule. According to Aquinas, this second element, that of transgressing the rule, pertains more to the intelligibility (*ratio*) of fault than failure to achieve a goal.[44] Here again his examples are illuminating. If someone were to swallow a stone and were unable to digest it, the natural powers of digestion would have acted without achieving their end; nevertheless, there would be nothing lacking in their activity. The stone is simply undigestible. Similarly, if a doctor prescribed the correct medicine for an illness, but the patient neglected to act in such a way that the medicine could take effect, there would be no fault on the part of doctor, despite the fact that the end was not achieved. Nothing is lacking in either the stomach's or the doctor's activity, and so there is no fault. In fact, Thomas says, if the doctor were to prescribe incorrectly and the patient still managed to regain his health, the doctor's act would remain faulty because he had not followed the rule applicable to the case.[45]

Let us now turn our attention to moral fault (*culpa*), the kind of fault found in voluntary action, or, more accurately, the kind of fault found in the acts of the will. Here too there is a rule or measure of action, with the possibility of conformity or lack of conformity, but in the case of the will's acts there is not a single rule, but several. Let us turn to Thomas's characterization of moral fault wherein he describes these rules.

A human act is evil [*malum*] from the fact that it lacks its due commensuration. Commensuration for any particular thing, however, arises from a comparison to some rule; if it should depart from that rule it will be incommensurate.

43. ST I, q. 63, a. 1, c.; *De malo*, q. 1, a. 3, ad 9 (Leonine, p. 17).
44. *De malo*, q. 2, a. 1, c.: ". . . magis est de ratione peccati preterire regulam actionis quam etiam deficere ab actionis fine" (Leonine, p. 29).
45. Ibid.

Now the rule of the human will is twofold: one proximate and homogeneous, viz., reason itself, and another which is the first rule, viz., the eternal law which is, so to speak, God's reason [*quasi ratio Dei*].[46]

As in the activities of art or nature, so too in human acts there is a rule or measure. The measure in this case is, first of all, reason itself. The will's act is evil or morally faulty when it does not conform to what reason judges should be done; it is good or right (*rectum*) when it does so conform.[47] How does Thomas understand that reason itself is a rule for actions? To see this we need to consider Thomas's understanding of nonrational beings and the rules governing their activities. All such beings, he maintains, living and nonliving, have their actions determined for them *by nature*: stones fall to the earth, plants grow toward the sun, animals act by instinct. The rule of their activity is implanted, so to speak, within them. Human beings, in contrast, go beyond such pre-ordained modes of activity, and instead they act according to their own deliberation. Reason, in its practical or deliberative function, assumes the directive role which, in nonrational beings, is played by natural inclination or instinct. In any given circumstances, rational agents themselves must determine what the proper course of action is. That is to say, the rule which governs their actions in concrete situations comes only from reason.[48]

Perhaps the clearest case of moral fault, in which the will does not follow reason, is what Aristotle called moral weakness or *akrasia*. It often happens that a person, in the grip of passion, does what he knows to be wrong, at times after having decided earlier not to do it. Here a person does what, from the point of view of reason, is a bad thing to do. A similar situation arises in the case of a person who acts out of willful ignorance. Ignorance prevents such an agent from making a proper judgment concerning what should be done, and as a result the action is not in accord with the rule of reason.[49]

46. ST I-II, q. 71, a. 6, c.: "Habet autem actus humanus quod sit malus, ex eo quod caret debita commensuratione. Omnis autem commensuratio cuiuscumque rei attenditur per comparationem ad aliquam regulam, a qua si divertat, incommensurata erit. Regula autem voluntatis humanae est duplex: una propinqua et homogenea, scilicet ipsa humana ratio; alia vero est prima regula, scilicet lex aeterna, quae est quasi ratio Dei." Cf. SCG III, chap. 6: "Privatio autem ordinis aut commensurationis debitae in actione est malum actionis." When Thomas says that the rule of reason is *homogenous* with the will he has in mind the Aristotelian principle that a measure must be homogenous or somehow of the same kind as that which it measures (*Metaphysics* 10.1053a24). For this, see ST I-II, q. 19, a. 4, ad 2.

47. ST I-II, q. 21, a. 1, c.

48. For a clear exposition of this point, see SCG II, chap. 47, *Amplius*, and chap. 48, *Praeterea*.

49. For Thomas's treatment of moral weakness, see ST I-II, q. 77; for acts done in ignorance, q. 76.

We must note that in neither case does the agent act without any sort of reason whatsoever, the way a person would while drunk or in a state of rage. Since moral evil presupposes voluntary action, there must be operative a rational judgment about what is to be done. This judgment governs the will's act which gives rise to the action. Nevertheless, in the instances described the judgment is not a true judgment; the reason involved is not right reason (*recta ratio*); it has not directed the action to the proper end.[50]

These examples imply that reason is not a rule unto itself. The very possibility of willing bad action points to a further rule, one by which reason in its practical functioning is itself measured. This rule, Thomas maintains, is law. Rule and measure, for rational beings, takes on the specific form of law, universal precepts directive of action which are grasped by reason.[51] This is what Thomas, in the text quoted above, referred to as the "first" rule. Eternal law, the order put into created things by God, provides the ultimate rule and measure of action, the rule and measure to which reason itself must conform. Not only eternal law (the first law) but also all the intermediate levels of law, human law, natural law, and divine law, provide a rule for reason. Hence Thomas refers at times to moral evil as the will's lack of conformity to law, especially to eternal law.

Thus reason provides the rule of action, only if it is in conformity with its own rule. It is a ruled rule. If one reads Thomas closely, one finds that Thomas almost always speaks of the will's proper order, not simply to reason, but to the *order* of reason or to the *rule* of reason. These expressions are his way of noting that there is an order to which practical reason must conform.[52]

If we say that the will, in moral fault, follows an erroneous judgment of reason, it might seem that moral evil should be located primarily in reason itself and only derivatively in the will. Thomas rejects this view, however, because he believes that, in the final analysis, such errors stem from the will. According to his doctrine of choice, the rational judgment which actually directs the will in an act of choice,

---

50. We may say that the will in such cases inclines to the apparent good but not the true good. For this, see ST I-II, q. 18, a. 4, ad 1: ". . . bonum ad quod aliquis respiciens operatur, non semper est verum bonum; sed quandoque verum bonum, et quandoque apparens." See also Thomas's description of false prudence (ST II-II, q. 47, a. 13).

51. ST I-II, q. 90, a. 1, c.: "Respondeo dicendum quod lex quaedam regula est et mensura actuum, secundum quam inducitur aliquis ad agendum, vel ab agendo retrahitur: . . ."

52. E.g., ST I-II, q. 71, a. 2, ad 4: "Lex autem aeterna comparatur ad *ordinem* rationis humanae sict ars ad artificiatum. Unde euisdem rationis est quod vitium et peccatum sit contra *ordinem* rationis humanae, et quod sit contra legem aeternam" (emphasis added). Cf. q. 19, aa. 3–4; q. 21, a. 1, c.

the *iudicium electionis,* is a free judgment, that is, could be other than it is. This freedom, he says, stems from the will, and thus the fact that the judgment is erroneous and does not embody what is truly good should be attributed to that power. Consequently, he holds that the seat and ultimately the source of moral evil is in the will itself.[53]

It follows from this discussion that moral evil is the will's lack of ordination to the rule of reason in its acts. Moral goodness, in contrast, is precisely the will's ordination to that rule.[54] A person will be morally good to the extent to which his voluntary actions are in conformity with the rule which governs them. We should note, however, that the will's act has a goodness other than its moral goodness. Simply as an act, it is a kind of being, and as such is good, so that even a morally bad act is good to this extent. It is not the act as act which is bad, but the act as deficient in its ordination to the rule of reason. Without the proper ordination, the will's act suffers a privation, it falls short of the *plenitudo essendi,* the fullness of being, which is due to it by nature.[55]

The understanding of moral goodness we have just developed locates it quite clearly in acts of the will, in acts such as choice, intention, or consent. Does not such a characterization, however, overly restrict its range or extension? Are we not overlooking other very real and important instances of moral goodness? There is, in the first place, the goodness a person enjoys by possessing moral virtues; we call those who possess moral virtue morally good, yet virtues for Thomas are

53. In ST I-II, Thomas distinguishes three kinds of sins, those arising from ignorance (*ex ignorantia,* q. 76), those caused by weakness of will (*ex passione,* q. 77), and those caused simply by a bad will (*ex certa malitia,* q. 78). In each case there is the ignorance of choice, although the ignorance differs for the different kinds of sin. These differences are spelled out in ST I-II, q. 78, a. 1, ad 1: "Ad primum ergo dicendum quod ignorantia quandoque quidem excludit scientiam qua aliquis simpliciter scit hoc esse malum quod agitur: et tunc dicitur ex ignorantia peccare. Quandoque autem excludit scientiam qua homo scit hoc nunc esse malum: sicut cum ex passione peccatur. Quandoque autem excludit scientiam qua aliquis scit hoc malum non sustinendum esse propter consecutionem illius boni, scit tamen simpliciter hoc esse malum: et sic dicitur ignorare qui ex certa malitia peccat." Ignorance of each type is caused by the will, except in the case of invincible ignorance; in that case, however, there is not considered to be any sin at all on the part of the will (see q. 76, aa. 1–4). For his doctrine of the *iudicium electionis* and its freedom, see *De veritate,* q. 17, a. 1, ad 4; q. 22, a. 15, c.; q. 24, aa. 4–6.

54. ST I-II, q. 21, a. 1, c.: ". . . omnis actus voluntarius est malus per hoc quod recedit ab ordine rationis et legis aeternae: et omnis actus bonus concordat rationi et legi aeternae."

55. ST I-II, q. 18, a. 1, c.: "Sed quia de ratione boni est ipsa plenitudo essendi, si quidem alicui aliquid defuerit de debita essendi plenitudine, non dicetur simpliciter bonum, sed secundum quid, inquantum est ens: . . . Sic igitur dicendum est quod omnis actio, inquantum habet aliquid de esse, intantum habet de bonitate: inquantum vero deficit ei aliquid de plenitudine essendi quae debetur actioni humanae, intantum deficit a bonitate, et sic dicitur mala: . . ."; cf. *De malo,* q. 2, a. 3, ad 2 (Leonine, p. 37).

not themselves acts but only dispositions to a kind of action, that is, they are habits. In the second place, it seems proper to say that moral goodness and moral evil are found not only in the will's acts, but also in the actions an agent performs in the world. If we assert that a particular murder was a moral evil, we refer not simply to the choice but also to the performance of the murder and even to the death of the person killed. So it seems that we need a broader understanding of moral goodness, one that will embrace all that is commonly considered to fall under the term.

It is indeed the case that we call things other than acts of the will morally good. When we do so, however, we are speaking analogously. "Moral goodness," like the general term "good," is analogous. When used differently, the term has different senses; yet as is characteristic of analogy, there is one sense to which all the rest are related and from which they take their meaning. In the case of moral goodness, this primary instance is the goodness of the will's acts which arises from their conformity to the rule of reason. In all its other senses, the term gains meaning by reference to this central case.

Thus the moral virtues are so called precisely because of their ordination to choice. A moral virtue, Thomas frequently repeats, is a *habitus electivus,* a habit whose proper act is an act of choice. In fact, at one point he describes the acts of the virtues as simply the good use of free will (*liberum arbitrium*).[56] Similarly, he maintains that the virtues of courage and temperance, taken in themselves, can be the proper disposition of the sense-appetites in which they inhere; but, if through a lack of prudence they do not issue in acts which accord with the rule of reason, they cannot be called moral virtues. In this case they are good, but they are not *morally* good because they are not a cause or principle of morally good acts of the will.[57]

Similarly, Thomas quite clearly holds that the actual performance of what has been chosen—he calls this the exterior act—is morally good or bad only insofar as it is commanded by the will.[58] Insofar as it is carried out willfully, its goodness or badness is the goodness or badness of the interior act of the will; from the moral point of view, in fact, the two acts are really one.[59] It is proper then to speak of outward actions as morally good or bad, but only by reference to the goodness or badness of the will's act from which they stem.

---

56. ST I-II, q. 55, a. 1, ad 2: "Nihil est enim aliud actus virtutis quam bonus usus liberi arbitrii."

57. ST I-II, q. 55, a. 3, ad 2; q. 56, a. 4, c.; cf. q. 71, a. 3, c.; for the doctrine that there is no moral virtue without prudence, q. 58, a. 4, c.

58. ST I-II, q. 20, a. 2, ad 3; *De malo,* q. 2, a. 2, c., ad 5, ad 6 (Leonine, pp. 33–34).

59. ST I-II, q. 20, a. 3, c.

We have in the case of moral goodness a situation parallel to Aristotle's famous example of health. Health is said primarily of an animal and secondarily both of food which conserves the animal's health and of urine which is a sign of health. Neither the food nor the urine is healthy the way the animal is healthy, yet both are properly called healthy by reference to the animal.[60] So too, neither moral virtue nor the performance of an action is morally good the way the will's act is. Moral virtue is morally good insofar as it is a disposition to a morally good act; the exterior act is morally good insofar as it is the effect of a morally good will; neither is morally good in just the same way as the acts of the will. Thus we can say that moral goodness, in its principal sense, is the goodness of acts of the will.

Let us now address our final question: why is it in terms of moral goodness that a person is called good simply (*simpliciter*)? When we say "John is good," why do we mean that he is good morally, such that when we refer to other sorts of goodness we have to qualify our statement, saying, "John is a good doctor, a good athlete, a good pianist"?

To answer this question we must return to a point we saw earlier in our discussion of goodness in general. Good, unlike being, is said simply of something which possesses its ultimate perfection. The ultimate perfection of any being lies in its *operations*; accordingly, it is in terms of its proper operations that it possesses or lacks that which makes it good simply. When the proper operations are what by nature they ought to be, the being which carries them out is good; if, on the other hand, the operations fall short of their natural fullness, the being is not good.

This dependency of goodness on operation holds true for human beings just as it does for all other beings. A person will be good or bad simply according to the goodness or badness of his proper operations, and the proper operations of human beings are always human acts. Again, as we saw earlier, human acts are precisely those acts which one does in a properly human fashion (*ex voluntate deliberata*). The goodness of these acts depends upon the goodness of the will which is their source. Hence the operations of human beings are good operations *simpliciter* when they are done in a morally good way.

Such a view does not imply that moral goodness is the only goodness a man can have. Each person possesses a wide range of goods: physical health or physical beauty, talents and abilities, knowledge, technical or artistic skills; these are all good things and a person is better for having them. Better healthy than sick, better beautiful than ugly, bet-

---

60. *In IV Metaph.*, lect. 1, nn. 536–37 (Marietti, pp. 151–52).

ter wise than ignorant. These goods, however, seen in relation to the operations or actions a person carries out, are only potential; in themselves they are not activities or operations. To possess wisdom or knowledge is not actually to consider it, to possess a musician's skill is not to play a piece, to be healthy is not to engage in vigorous activity. It is true, in each case, that a person possessing knowledge or skills or health can do what someone who lacks them cannot. Nevertheless, the possession of such qualities and the exercise of the corresponding actions remain distinct.[61]

For such qualities to actually issue in operations, activities such as thinking, playing music, or hiking, an act of the will is required. In other words, such good qualities or possessions (*res habitae*)[62] are only potencies or capacities to activities and are actualized by the will. A person may refuse to use some capacity; he might use it for the wrong reason or at the wrong time or in the wrong circumstances; he might even willfully make mistakes as he performs some particular activity. Thus, whether or not all the good qualities other than goodness of the will in fact give rise to activities which are perfections of the person as such, that is to say, whether they give rise to some good human action, depends ultimately on how that action is willed.

The result of this line of reasoning is to say that the goodness of all operations or activity depends upon the goodness of the will. The goodness of human operations, in other words, depends upon moral goodness. And since, as we have said, a being is said to be good simply by reference to its operations, we can say that a man is good simply because of his moral goodness. Aquinas says that all other goods are only potencies to good operation and for this reason a person who possesses them is said to be good only in a qualified way: a good physicist, a good pianist, a good athlete.[63] "Good and evil," he states, "are said simply according to act, but only qualifiedly according to potency."[64]

---

61. *De malo*, q. 1, a. 5, c.: ". . . bonum enim et malum dicitur simpliciter quidem secundum actum, secundum vero quid secundum potentiam; posse enim esse bonum vel malum, non simpliciter set secundum quid bonum vel malum est. Actus autem est duplex, scilicet primus, qui est habitus vel forma, et secundus, qui est operatio, sicut scientia et considerare. Actu autem primo inherente adhuc est potentia ad actum secundum, sicut sciens nondum actu considerat set considerare potest. Simpliciter ergo bonum vel malum attenditur secundum actum secundum, qui est operatio; secundum vero actum primum attenditur bonum vel malum, quodammodo secundum quid" (Leonine, pp. 23–24).

62. ST I, q. 48, a. 6, c.

63. *De malo*, q. 1, a. 5, c.: "Manifestum est autem quod in habentibus voluntatem per actum voluntatis quelibet potentia et habitus in bonum actum reducitur: quia voluntas habet pro obiecto universale bonum, sub quo continentur omnia particularia bona

CONCLUSION

Let us conclude with some remarks about the relation of moral goodness to ontological goodness. "Ontological goodness" is not a phrase Aquinas himself uses; nevertheless, he does distinguish between the goodness accruing to a thing insofar as it enjoys existence as a substance, and the further goodness it acquires through additional determinations in the accidental order. Now if we understand by ontological goodness that which arises from a being's simply existing, that is, its substantial being, then the ontological good is clearly distinct from the moral good. Moral goodness arises in acts of the will which are, in metaphysical terms, accidents of an already existing substance. Even within the will's act, moreover, we can distinguish between the act's simple exercise—willing as such—and its ordination to the rule of reason. Here again, the goodness of the act insofar as it has existence is not identical with the further goodness of its ordination to reason. So there is, then, a real sense in which we can contrast moral and ontological goodness.

Nevertheless, if by ontological goodness we mean simply the goodness that is found in being as such, and if, in addition, we recognize that being includes both substantial and accidental being, then moral goodness, far from being opposed to ontological goodness, is actually a specification of it. That by which a person is called morally good, the ordination of the will to reason, is a portion of that person's being, a portion due to him by nature. Morally good action is the fulfillment of being, the *plenitudo essendi,* demanded by the very nature of a human being as rational and as free.

Moral goodness, for Aquinas, is never separate from nature; it is, rather, a natural fulfillment or perfection. Nevertheless, in the actualizing of natural perfections there lies a fundamental difference between moral agents and other beings, a difference which underlies the propensity to see a radical separation between nature and freedom. All beings have a natural goodness; most beings achieve that

---

propter que operantur potentie et habitus quecumque. Semper autem potentia que tendit ad finem principalem, movet per suum imperium potentiam que tendit ad finem secundarium, sicut gubernatoria ars imperat navifactive, et militaris equestri. Non enim ex hoc ipso quod aliquis habet habitum gramatice bene loquitur: potest enim habens habitum non uti habitu aut contra habitum agere, sicut cum gramaticus scienter soloecismum facit; sed tunc recte operatur secundum artem, quando vult. Et ideo homo quid habet bonam voluntatem dicitur simpliciter bonus homo, quasi per actum bone voluntatis omnibus que habet bene utatur, ex hoc vero quod habet habitum gramatice, non dicitur bonus homo, set bonus gramaticus; et similiter est de malo" (Leonine, p. 24). Cf. ST I, q. 48, a. 6, c.

64. See n. 61.

goodness by nature. But it is the singular privilege of free beings to attain to their natural perfection, not by nature, but by choice. In this, rational and free beings find themselves infinitely distanced from the remainder of nature. Yet, for all that, rational beings remain part of nature. In fact, it is precisely in this realm, in the realm of freedom, that nature reaches its fulfillment.

4   Aquinas on Moral Responsibility in the Pursuit of Knowledge

GREGORY MARTIN REICHBERG

The past few years have witnessed a renewed interest in Aquinas's moral teaching. Much of the attention has focused on his theory of practical rationality, with numerous studies treating the various ways in which practical reason functions to guide human action. The inverse approach however, which asks whether the life of theoretical reason is itself conditioned by practical reason and choice, is surprisingly rare. From this perspective one asks not how reason operates within moral action but rather how the use of reason itself can be taken as a matter for moral judgment. Does the concrete orientation of our cognitive activity have any moral significance? Do there exist good dispositions toward the pursuit of knowledge that can be cultivated or vitiated by the knowing subject? Can knowledge be sought in a morally bad manner? If so, what would constitute a morally good approach to the acquisition of knowledge?

With the exception of a few articles, little attention has been devoted to understanding Aquinas's theory of the moral employment of theoretical reason.[1] Despite this neglect, it can be demonstrated that Aquinas does indeed formulate a carefully constructed teaching on how moral responsibility applies to the pursuit of knowledge. As one of a few major thinkers in the tradition to give sustained treatment to this question, he can serve as an engaging and illuminating interlocutor for current discussions on epistemic virtue and responsibility. In

---

1. Articles on this topic include: John Hugo, "Intelligence and Character: A Thomistic View," *The New Scholasticism* 11 (1937): 58–68; Martin Grabmann, "Scientific Cognition of Truth: Its Characteristic Genius in the Doctrine of St. Thomas Aquinas," *The New Scholasticism* 13 (1939): 1–30; Thomas M. MacLellan, "The Moral Virtues and the Speculative Life," *Laval Théologique et Philosophique* 12 (1956): 175–232; Mary William, "The Relationships of the Intellectual Virtue of Science and Moral Virtue," *The New Scholasticism* 36 (1962): 475–505.

this essay I shall endeavor to present a sketch of Thomas's approach to the ethics of theoretical knowing, while seeking to manifest its relevance for contemporary debate on this theme.

I. KNOWLEDGE WITHOUT A KNOWER: AVERROISM AND ITS CONTEMPORARY COUNTERPART

A normative inquiry concerning the moral employment of reason is by no means a novelty within the western philosophical tradition. Plato's discussion of philosophical character in the *Republic*, Aristotle's elaboration of the "intellectual virtues" in the *Nicomachean Ethics*, Hume's chapter in the *Treatise* on "curiosity, or the love of truth," and Kant's elucidation of the morally good *Denkungsart* (mode of thought) are but a few of the many examples that might be gleaned from the history of philosophy. Schiller gives succinct expression to this type of inquiry when, having asked whether it is "enough to say that all enlightenment of the understanding is worthy of respect only inasmuch as it reacts upon character," he replies in the negative, insisting that "to a certain extent it also proceeds from character. . . ."[2]

In contrast, a typical modern approach to the use of reason is exemplified by the ideal of the computer, which appears "to think" precisely without being a living, personal subject. To speak here of moral responsibility would clearly be nonsensical, since only a "self " can be a moral agent. "One speaks of a 'reliable' computer, not a 'responsible' one. A person can be judged responsible or irresponsible only if he/ she is clearly regarded as an agent. . . ."[3]

It would be worthwhile investigating the historical causes which have contributed to the rise of an a-personal, morally neutral conception of reason in modern times. Some philosophical historians claim that this constitutes one of the essential cleavage points distinguishing modernity from the ancient and medieval worlds. For instance, Hans Blumenberg describes the modern conception of scientific rationality as founded upon the "integration, through 'method,' of a potentially infinite sequence of inquiring subjects active in temporally extended functional complexes—subjects whose individual lives and needs (in regard to truth) can neither be the point of nor the standard against which to measure the totality of knowledge to be realized. To both the ancient world and the Middle Ages, a knowledge that neither

---

2. Freidrich Schiller, *On the Aesthetic Education of Man,* ed. E. M. Wilkinson and L. A. Willoughby (Oxford: Oxford University Press, 1967), Eighth Letter, 53.
3. Lorraine Code, *Epistemic Responsibility* (Hanover, N.H.: University Press of New England, 1987), 51.

related to nor could be made to relate to the capacity of the individual and his existential fulfillment was still an altogether remote idea."[4]

Recent developments in epistemology and ethics, and more particularly in the area now referred to as "responsibilist epistemology," have attempted to renew links with this older tradition of philosophical inquiry by elaborating theories of epistemic virtue and responsibility. Such theories have arisen in large part as a response to models of rationality which detach the products of knowledge from the concrete epistemic agents who are the source of that knowledge.[5]

One might cite Karl Popper as a clear representative of such a model of rationality. In his formulation of an "Epistemology Without a Knowing Subject," Popper postulates a sharp separation between cognitive activity on the one hand, and the question of truth and falsity on the other. Following Bolzano and Frege, he holds that truth is not the act of a mind but is exclusively the property of propositions. Hence, epistemology is no longer concerned with the study of the knower as such, but rather with the end-products of knowledge: problems, theories, arguments, and in general any statement or combination of statements that can possess truth value. "Knowledge in this objective sense," he writes, "is totally independent of anybody's claim to know; it is also independent of anybody's belief, or disposition to assent; or to assert, or to act. Knowledge in the objective sense is *knowledge without a knower*: it is *knowledge without a knowing subject*."[6]

The rationale for eliminating concrete epistemic *agents* from the field of epistemological inquiry is that such a move can protect scientific knowledge from the errors of psychologism, in order to bolster the value of objectivity. It is fascinating to observe that Aquinas confronted an analogous philosophical project during his own intellectual career, in regard to the Averroistic teaching on the possible intellect, which stirred so much controversy at the University of Paris during the decade that runs from 1260 to 1270.

According to Thomas, the fundamental claim of the Averroists was that individual human beings are not the agents of their own intellectual activity. The agency responsible for truthful acts of intellectual cognition does not belong to individual humans but rather to a separate substance. The Averroistic conception of the separate possible

4. Hans Blumenberg, *The Legitimacy of the Modern Age*, trans. Robert W. Wallace (Cambridge: MIT Press, 1985), 317–18.

5. For example, see Code, *Epistemic Responsibility*, 8. For an even more recent treatment of this theme, see James A. Montmarquet, *Epistemic Virtue and Doxastic Responsibility* (Lanham, Md.: Rowman and Littlefield, 1993).

6. Karl R. Popper, *Objective Knowledge, An Evolutionary Approach* (Oxford: Clarendon Press, 1979), 109.

64   GREGORY MARTIN REICHBERG

intellect, Popper's theory of epistemology without a knower, and Blumenberg's "potentially infinite series of inquiring subjects" which characterizes modern scientific rationality, are alike in that the individual
epistemic agent ceases to be the locus of objective knowledge.

Again, like Popper, it was precisely a desire to avoid any taint of
subjectivism that motivated the Averroists. Since humans are all capable of knowing the same uniform reality, for example, we can all
cognize the same tree in front of us, this must be possible, they concluded, because we all participate in the same intellectual act. Humans
perceive a uniform reality by virtue of a unique receptive intellect
which is shared by them all. Thomas summarizes this position in his
De unitate intellectus: "Therefore it is impossible that the things understood should be two in number in me and in you. There is, therefore,
only one thing [understood] and the intellect is only one in number
for all."[7] The same point is made even more succinctly in the early
work *De ente et essentia* where Thomas writes that "the Commentator
. . . wanted to conclude that the intellect is one in all men from the
universality of the apprehended form."[8]

Now the Angelic Doctor does not take this problem lightly, for he
too is firmly committed to the objectivity and intersubjectivity of
knowledge. "It must therefore be simply admitted," he writes, "that
what is understood of one thing, for example, a stone, is one only, not
merely for all men but also for all beings that understand."[9] However,
Thomas is just as firmly committed to the position that the intellectual
act is exercised in a fully individual manner by singular agents. The
phrase "hic homo singularis intelligit," is restated throughout the *De
unitate intellectus* as a kind of leitmotif.

This leads Thomas to embrace a seeming paradox. The faculty of
knowing is particularized in each individual human being. This includes both the agent and possible intellects, which together concur
to produce the concrete act of intellection in human knowers. As fully
singularized operations, acts of intellection are as exclusively unique
as the individual agents who accomplish those operations. But at the

7. *De unitate*, chap. 5: "Ergo impossibile est quod sint duo intellecta in numero in
me et in te; est ergo unum tantum, et unus intellectus numero tantum in omnibus"
(Leonine, p. 311: 128–31). All translations of this work are taken, with some alterations,
from *On the Unity of the Intellect against the Averroists*, trans. Beatrice H. Zedler (Milwaukee: Marquette University Press, 1968).
8. *De ente*, chap. 3: "Et ideo patet defectus Commentatoris in III De anima qui uoluit
ex universalitate forme intellecte unitatem intellectus in omnibus hominibus concludere . . ." (Leonine, p. 375: 107–10).
9. *De unitate*, chap. 5: ". . . est ergo simpliciter concedendum quod intellectum unius
rei, puta lapidis, est unum tantum non solum in omnibus hominibus, sed etiam in
omnibus intelligentibus" (Leonine, p. 312: 159–63).

same time, the act of intellectual knowing is other-directed. The formal object which specifies this act is not the soul itself or the knowing faculty, but the manifold field of being, *ens universale*.

We thus encounter the paradox of an intellectual activity which is fully individualized in each person, but which at the same time is formally specified by a knowledge of the universal. On Thomas's view, any adequate explanation of intellectual cognition will need to account for these two poles present in human knowledge: singularity of the act and universality of the object. This point is stated clearly in the final chapter of the *De unitate intellectus*:

> It is therefore one thing which is understood both by me and by you. But it is understood by me in one way and by you in another, that is, by another intelligible species. And my [act of] understanding is one thing, and yours, another; and my intellect is one thing, and yours another. . . . Whence also my intellect, when it understands itself to understand, understands a certain singular act; but when it understands "to understand" absolutely, it understands something universal.[10]

Although Thomas does not further elaborate on the distinction between these two senses in which the intellect can be said "to understand," the meaning is fairly clear. "To understand absolutely" (*intelligere simpliciter*) is to engage in an act of direct cognition, whereby the intellect is referentially conformed to its objects. Such directly intended objects of intellection are "something universal," because entities are always posited before the human intellect in a state of abstraction and universality that comes to them through their existence in concepts. It is precisely the conceptual nature of human knowledge which accounts for the fact that objects of cognition are not private data in solitary selves, but fully public data for intersubjective discourse.

In a second sense, to say that the intellect "understands itself to understand" (*intelligit se intelligere*) is to consider the act of knowing in relation to the agent whose faculty is concretely engaged in that act. As the actuation of a determinate power of a fully individualized soul, the cognitive act will be as particular as the substance whence it derives. Speaking of the knowledge communicated from teacher to pupil, Thomas notes that although "it is the same in relation to the thing known" it is nevertheless "individuated in me and in him."[11]

---

10. *De unitate*, chap. 5: "Est ergo unum quod intelligitur et a me et a te, sed alio intelligitur a me et alio a te, id est alia specie intelligibili; et aliud est intelligere meum, et aliud tuum; et alius est intellectus meus, et alius tuus. . . . Vnde et intellectus meus quando intelligit se intelligere, intelligit quendam singularem actum; quando autem intelligit intelligere simpliciter, intelligit aliquid uniuersale" (Leonine, p. 312: 226–38).

11. *De unitate*, chap. 5: "Ex hoc autem apparet quomodo sit eadem scientia in dis-

The act of a knowing power is, ontologically, an accident inhering in the soul through the mediation of its powers and habitus.

Thomas takes this point a step further, and suggests that the metaphysical principle *actus sunt solum singularium* is reduplicated on the level of the intellectual agent's inward awareness of the completed cognitive act: "whence also, my intellect, when it understands itself to understand, understands a certain singular act." As Thomas explains elsewhere, it is the privilege of the intellect to be present to itself in its operations.[12] For at the same time that I know some universal aspect of being, object of direct intention, I am also obscurely aware of that act of knowing as mine, as belonging to me personally.

II. THE ETHICAL DIMENSION OF AQUINAS'S THEORY OF TRUTH

It is precisely the relation between these two poles—an extramental thing grasped in an abstract and universal mode on the one hand, and the singular act of knowing qua mine, on the other—that Thomas posits at the core of his definition of truth, as outlined in *Summa theologiae* I, q. 16. There he holds that truth is properly speaking the *perfection* of an intellect when it knows its own conformity to a thing

---

cipulo et doctore. Est enim eadem quantum ad rem scitam, non tamen quantum ad species intelligibiles quibus uterque intelligit; quantum enim ad hoc, indiuiduatur scientia in me et in illo" (Leonine, p. 312: 243–48).

12. In ST I, q. 87, a. 1, c., Thomas posits two modes of self-awareness, which are distinguished as "particulariter" and "in universali." The former mode arises from the obscurely felt presence of the self (*mens*) to itself throughout all its individual acts of cognition. In contrast, the latter mode is a conceptually articulated inquiry into the nature of knowledge as a determinate act of the rational soul. In the first instance, self-awareness is concomitant to an act of direct cognition, but not its direct object, whereas in the second instance, the mind reflects back upon itself as the explicit and direct object of inquiry. It is the former and not the latter mode of self-reflection that accompanies every act of judgment.

The distinction elaborated here parallels Dilthey's contrast between two modes of self-awareness: reflexion (*Innewerden*) and reflection (*Besinnung*). *Reflexion* is immediate and nonrepresentational. It expresses "an immediate pre-reflective mode of self-givenness in which the dichotomies of form and content, subject and object characteristic of reflective consciousness do not yet exist" (*Introduction to the Human Sciences*, in *Selected Works*, ed. Rudolf A. Makkreel and Frithjof Rodi, vol. 1 [Princeton: Princeton University Press, 1989], 247, n. 4). In contrast, *reflection* is discursive and representational, it is an "objective placing-before-oneself " (*Vor-sich-stellen*), a "re-presenting in perception of what is contained in reflexive awareness" (254). Dilthey adds that "the reflexive awareness of the act does not undermine the objectivity and immediate certainty of the object; at any given moment they coexist within the same complex configuration of consciousness, as constituents of the same whole" (258). For a discussion of Dilthey's concept of "Innewerden," see the editors' introduction, 24–30.

in the act of judgment.[13] Truth in the fullest sense involves more than a correspondence to reality. This we find already in the senses and when the intellect apprehends a thing's quiddity in a concept. It requires, in addition, a reflective awareness of that conformity, when a knower affirms in the judgment that his or her own cognitive act is indeed conformed to outward reality. In its fullest and most proper sense, "truth" does not simply signify "being true," but rather "knowing the true" (*verum ut cognitum*). This, Thomas concludes, "is the perfection of the intellect."[14]

The epistemological and metaphysical reasons behind Thomas's famous definition of truth as the adequation or conformity of intellect and thing in the mental act of judgment are well known and have been the object of careful and ample study.[15] In my estimation, however, this definition includes an implicit ethical dimension frequently overlooked by Thomistic commentators. Thomas himself refers to this dimension in article 4, which asks whether "bonum secundum rationem sit prius quam verum":

The will and the intellect mutually include one another: for the intellect understands the will, and the will wills the intellect to understand. So then, among things directed to the object of the will, are comprised those that belong to the intellect; and conversely. Whence in the order of things desirable, good stands as the universal, and the true as the particular; whereas in the order of intelligible things the converse is the case. From the fact, then, that the true is a kind of good, it follows that the good is prior in the order of things desirable; but not that it is prior absolutely.[16]

The heart of this passage lies in recognizing the true as a kind of good, "verum est quoddam bonum."[17] Since the true has previously

13. ST I, q. 16, a. 2, c.: ". . . per conformitatem intellectus et rei veritas definitur. Unde conformitatem istam cognoscere, est cognoscere veritatem."

14. Ibid.: "Veritas quidem igitur potest esse in sensu, vel in intellectu cognoscente quod quid est, ut in quadam re vera: non autem ut cognitum in cognoscente, quod importat nomen veri; perfectio enim intellectus est verum ut cognitum."

15. For instance, see the recent treatment of this theme by John F. Wippel, "Truth in Thomas Aquinas," *The Review of Metaphysics* 43 (1990): 295–326; 543–76.

16. ST I, q. 16, a. 4, ad 1: "Ad primum ergo dicendum quod voluntas et intellectus mutuo se includunt: nam intellectus intelligit voluntatem, et voluntas vult intellectum intelligere. Sic ergo inter illa quae ordinantur ad obiectum voluntatis, continentur etiam ea quae sunt intellectus; et e converso. Unde in ordine appetibilium, bonum se habet ut universale, et verum ut particulare: in ordine autem intelligibilium est e converso. Ex hoc ergo quod verum est quoddam bonum, sequitur quod bonum sit prius in ordine appetibilium: non autem quod sit prius simpliciter." Translations of the ST are from the 1947 Benziger edition, with occasional alterations.

17. Thomas's most detailed discussion of the principle "verum est quoddam bonum," is *In VI Metaph.*, lect. 4, nn. 1230–1240 (Marietti, pp. 310–11).

been defined as the perfection of an intellect when it conforms itself to a thing, we can conclude that the good in question is that of an individual epistemic agent, functioning well in the order of knowing. Goodness, as Thomas repeats on many occasions, always qualifies an entity according to the mode of its concrete individuality.[18] Accordingly, to attain truth in the judgment is to achieve an end-state of cognitive completion (*terminus cognitionis*), which is perfective of the individual agent.[19] The Latin word "terminus" is employed here as an equivalent to the Greek "telos," and signifies the full actualization of an immanent process, which is attained within the intellect itself. The referential focus of the act, that *to which* the intellect is conformed, might very well bear on the most universal objects of intersubjective discourse, for instance, the axioms of Euclidean geometry. Nevertheless, the act of being conformed to that object is itself strictly singular, and proper to a particular epistemic agent, who develops in some determinate and concrete way by virtue of that cognitive activity.

In the passage just cited, Thomas further specifies the nature of truth as a kind of good. First of all, qua good, truth is something desirable; it becomes an end eliciting appetitive pursuit. In the second place, the good in question does not exhaust the full potentiality for teleological achievement proper to a human agent, since it represents the perfecting of one faculty among several (i.e., the intellect). Considered in relation to the overall good of the agent, truth is a particular, limited good. Finally, as a partial good of a rational agent, truth falls under the scope of the faculty of will, *voluntas*, which is formally specified by the universal, all-encompassing good of that agent (*bonum perfectum*).[20] In this way, truthful knowing can become the object of voluntary desire. Hence "the will wills the intellect to understand," although Thomas does not specify here whether such an act of will is free or necessitated.

In this initial analysis, Thomas has remained on the level of a metaphysical explanation of the relation holding between the true and the good. However, the opening line from the *ad primum* quoted above does give a hint that this relation is reduplicated, so to speak, on the level of the epistemic agent's self-awareness in the act of knowing truth: "the will and the intellect," he writes, "mutually include one another." The mutual imbrication of these two faculties extends into

18. See, e.g., ST I, q. 5, a. 3, ad 4.

19. ST I, q. 16, a. 1, c.: ". . .terminus cognitionis, quod est verum, est in ipso intellectu."

20. On the nature of truth as a particular good, see ST I, q. 82, a. 4, c., and ad 1; cf. ST I-II, q. 9, a. 1, ad 3: "ipsum verum, quod est perfectio intellectus, continetur sub universali bono ut quoddam bonum particulare."

their acts, for "the acts of the will and of reason are brought to bear on one another, insofar as reason reasons about willing, and the will wills to reason."[21]

Accordingly, a truthful speculative judgment will entail an implicit self-awareness of the agent's cognitive act (knowing *my* conformity to the object), allied with a *desire* for perfective achievement by engaging in that act. In other words, the self-reflection concomitant to the act of judgment, which Thomas emphasizes in his definition of truth, includes an awareness of oneself as an *appetitive* cognitive agent. In knowing truth, the self becomes aware of itself as both knowing being and desiring being, or more precisely as desiring to know being. Thomas makes this point when he writes that "the intellect first (*per prius*) apprehends being itself; secondly, it apprehends that it under-stands being, and thirdly it apprehends that it desires being."[22]

The distinction drawn between these three acts does not denote a temporal order of priority and posteriority, but rather an ontological order of inclusiveness and dependency. A reflection on the self's con-formity to being (truth) presupposes that the self has first directly grasped something about being itself. To invert this order would invite an infinite regress.[23] Correspondingly, to desire the mind's conformity to being as a good to be actively pursued through voluntary desire, presupposes that I have first known something about being and per-ceived the act of knowing being to be of value.

In the earlier *Summa contra gentiles*, Thomas presents a clear descrip-tion of how intellect and will interact within this process of desiring truth: ". . . the will moves the intellect *quasi per accidens* in so far as the act of understanding is itself apprehended as good, and so is desired by the will, with the result that the intellect actually understands."[24] The suggestion here is that the act of understanding (even about the-oretical matters) requires a motion of the will in order to become actual, that is, to become a concretely instantiated activity.

On the basis of these considerations we can trace out four acts which

21. ST I-II, q. 17, a. 1, c.: ". . . actus voluntatis et rationis supra se invincem possunt ferri, prout scilicet ratio ratiocinatur de volendo, et voluntas vult ratiocinari. . . ."
22. ST I, q. 16, a. 4, ad 2: "Intellectus autem per prius apprehendit ipsum ens; et secundario apprehendit se intelligere ens; et tertio apprehendit se appetere ens."
23. This point is clearly drawn in SCG III, chap. 26 (2nd *praeterea*): "Si enim intel-lectus intelligit se intelligere, prius oportet poni quod intelligat rem aliquam, et con-sequenter quod intelligat se intelligere: nam ipsum intelligere quod intellectus intelligit, alicuius obiecti est; unde oportet quod vel procedatur in infinitum, vel, si est devenire ad primum intellectum, hoc non erit ipsum intelligere, sed aliqua res intelligibilis."
24. Ibid.: ". . . voluntas autem movet intellectum quasi per accidens, inquantum scilicet intelligere ipsum apprehenditur ut bonum, et sic desideratur a voluntate, ex quo sequitur quod intellectus actu intelligit."

flow from the grasp of truth in the intellectual act of judgment. By emphasizing the interconnection of these acts, Thomas can indicate how human agents come to appropriate their own cognitive teleology: (1) understanding being as an object of direct intention; (2) apprehending my conformity to being, first phase of reflection; (3) apprehending my own act of understanding being as good for myself, second phase of reflection; (4) desiring this conformity to being as good for myself, intervention of volition into the cognitive order of truth-seeking.

Our reading of question 16 on truth has enabled us to comprehend how Thomas approaches epistemology from within the perspective of the moral agent. From the outset, truth is described as a *value*, attracting the moral agent through the faculty of will, which is the guardian, so to speak, of the total perfection which such an agent is capable of attaining by the use of his or her many faculties. Accordingly, the achievement of moral integrity in each person will require that the intellect's activity be pursued in a manner consistent with, and contributory to, the good of the whole of which it is a part. "For properly speaking, it is not the intellect or the senses that know, but the man who knows through each."[25]

It is precisely this perspective on truth as a good which cannot arise from within the Averroistic position, nor from within the modern view which posits truth as an exclusive property of propositions. For if truth resides in a separate intellect or is a property of self-less statements, what could possibly ground objectivity as a value? Values are always related to concrete agents who pursue ends. To value is to manifest attachment and concern, to regard something as worthy of pursuit. Whether truth is valued, the manner in which it is valued, and why it is valued, are all questions about the concrete stance of the knower in his or her relation to possible objects of inquiry.

Thomas himself refers to this link between truth and value in his commentary on Aristotle's *De interpretatione*: "Truth, as the Philosopher says in *Nicomachean Ethics* 6, is the good of the intellect. Hence, anything that is said to be true is such by reference to intellect."[26]

---

25. *De veritate*, q. 2, a. 6, ad 3: ". . . non enim proprie loquendo, sensus aut intellectus cognoscunt sed homo per utrumque, ut patet in I De anima" (Leonine, pp. 66–67: 131–33). See also ST I, q. 76, a. 1, c., where Thomas argues against the Platonists that the intellect is a *part* and not the whole of man: "Relinquitur ergo quod intellectus quo Socrates intelligit, est aliqua pars Socratis . . ."

26. *In I Periherm.*, 3: "Verum enim, ut Philosophus dicit in VI Ethicorum, est bonum intellectus, unde, de quocunque dicatur uerum, oportet quod sit per respectum ad intellectum. [Comparantur autem ad intellectum uoces quidem sicut signa, res autem sicut ea quorum intellectus sunt similitudines]" (Leonine, pp. 15–16: 107–13). The Leonine editor brackets this sentence to designate a marginal addition by Thomas.

Immediately thereafter, he affirms his adherence to the theory of indirect signification of words, the view that words signify mental concepts and through mental concepts, things. He thereby rejects in advance the theory of direct signification, the view that a thing is directly signified by the word with which a certain meaning is connected, defended by Scotus and Ockham, and which has evolved in our own time into the view that self-less propositions are the locus of truth.[27]

For Thomas, propositions are only true in a secondary sense, insofar as they signify the truth which is in the act of the intellect affirming or denying.[28] The adage "truth is the good of the intellect," expresses how truthful knowing can and should become an object of care and attachment for the epistemic agent, precisely because the agent's whole self is intimately engaged in the act which terminates in conformity with reality. In its formal signification, truth is a perfective state of a personal intellect. Conversely, falsity is a state of deprivation for the intellect, and hence is described by Thomas as its evil, *malum intellectus*.[29] This intrinsic link of truth with the achievement of the self, absent in Averroistic monopsychism, is also missing in contemporary philosophies inspired by the so-called semantic turn.

III. VOLUNTARY CHOICE IN SPECULATIVE KNOWING: *SUMMA THEOLOGIAE* I-II, Q. 17, A. 6

Significantly the most detailed exposition of Thomas's views on the morality of thinking is contained within the *Secunda pars* of the *Summa theologiae*, largely written during his second Parisian regency (1269–72) at the time of his debate with the Latin Averroists. In the prologue to question 6 of the *Prima secundae*, Thomas sets out his intention to study the range of human acts in the light of their voluntariness. Those acts are voluntary which have their interior source in the will's exercise of an efficient and final causality. By emphasizing these two orders of causality Thomas can show that humans have the initiative for their acts in the light of freely chosen ends. Personal responsibility

27. For a discussion of direct and indirect signification in the later Scholastics, see Philotheus Boehner, "Historical Notes on the Concept of Truth in Scholasticism," in *Collected Articles on Ockham*, ed. Eligius M. Buytaert (St. Bonaventure, N.Y.: The Franciscan Institute, 1958), 175–99.

28. ST I, q. 16, a. 8, ad 3: "... propositio ... dicitur habere veritatem quodam speciali modo, inquantum significat veritatem intellectus." Also, *In I Periherm.*, 7: "Dicitur autem in enunciatione esse uerum vel falsum, sicut in signo intellectus ueri uel falsi: set sicut in subiecto est uerum uel falsum in mente ..." (Leonine, p. 36: 41–43).

29. ST I-II, q. 57, a. 2, ad 3: "Bonum autem intellectus est verum, malum autem eius est falsum."

for the concrete direction of voluntary acts becomes so crucial, because each act contributes to the shaping of the agent's character and his ordination to the end.

As part of this overall project, Thomas addresses the issue of voluntariness in the act of knowing. The issue is treated explicitly in I-II, q. 17, a. 6, although it is already addressed in earlier questions, especially part I, q. 82, a. 4, on "whether the will moves the intellect." This theme is also treated in the *De virtutibus in communi*, thought to have been disputed during the same period, which contains an important article on "whether there is virtue in the speculative intellect" (a. 7).

It is likely that the voluntariness of knowing became urgent to address within an intellectual milieu imbued with Averroism, for only agents endowed with individual minds can be held morally accountable for the employment of their cognitive faculties. Moral responsibility in knowing would evaporate if humans were passive recipients of a cognitive agency possessed exclusively by a separate intellect. Correspondingly, in the *Secunda pars* of the *Summa theologiae* Thomas will show that because cognitive activity truly belongs to a voluntary agent, each person is responsible for that activity and its effects upon his character.

His approach in q. 17, a. 6 is to inquire, as a propaedeutic to the study of virtue and vice in the employment of our epistemic acts, whether the act of reason can be exercised freely. The immediate context for this inquiry is the study of acts commanded by the will (*quasi a voluntate imperati*), where the question arises whether the act of reason can be commanded. Thomas describes command (*imperium*) as "an act of reason, presupposing an act of the will, in virtue of which reason, by its command, moves [a faculty] to the exercise of its act."[30] The *imperium* is therefore the result of a combined act of will and intellect, culminating in a practical judgment in which the agent freely decides that a certain act is to be accomplished. It involves the concrete process of free choice (*electio*) as applied to the operation of one of the powers of the soul.

To command, therefore, is to direct the accomplishment of a contingent human action, on the basis of a freely determined choice. Can the act of reason be prescribed in this manner? To answer this question affirmatively would result in placing the act of reason, even speculative reason, under the sway of practical wisdom and the relevant

---

30. ST I-II, q. 17, a. 1, c.: "Unde relinquitur quod imperare sit actus rationis, praesupposito actu voluntatis, in cuius virtute ratio movet per imperium ad exercitium actus."

moral virtues. For the virtue of prudence consists especially in recti-fying the act of command, so that the commanded act conforms to the authentic moral good of the agent.[31]

In the sed contra to q. 17, a. 6, Thomas responds affirmatively that "that which we do of our free will, can be done by our command. But the acts of reason are accomplished through free will. . . . Therefore the acts of reason can be commanded."[32] Immediately thereinafter, he begins his treatment by reminding the reader of the intellect's ability to reflect back upon itself, a reflection which follows upon the speculative act of judgment and which terminates in a practical judg-ment backed up by volitional force: "Since reason reflects back upon itself, just as it orders the acts of other powers, so it can order its own act. Consequently its act can be commanded."[33]

This perspective closely parallels the series of reflective acts which we outlined above in relation to the grasp of truth in the judgment. In the act of knowing a given object the cognitive agent can reflect upon that act and perceive it as something good for the self. As a consequence, that act itself can come to be desired by the will of the agent. In turn, as the primary efficient source of motion in the human agent, the faculty of will initiates the concrete process of movement towards the accomplishment of the desired cognitive act.

Thus, when Thomas writes that "reason can order its own act," he is implying that there are two distinct series of cognitive acts operative in this context: (1) theoretical cognitive acts that directly bear on some aspect of being and (2) a series of cognitive acts that begins with a reflection upon the first act, issuing into a practical judgment backed up by volitional force. The first series terminates in a speculative judg-ment, whereas the second terminates in a free practical judgment commanding the accomplishment of that speculative judgment.

For example, in the present instance I am constructing arguments about the ethics of knowing. My judgments here are speculative in nature. However, I am aware that I am at present engaged in this cognitive activity. The fact that I am now at work on this argument is

31. This is a conclusion that Thomas reaches in ST II-II, q. 47, a. 2, ad 2, where he asserts that the exercise of speculative reason does in fact fall within the scope of prudence: "Quamvis dici possit quod ipse actus speculativae rationis, secundum quod est voluntarius, cadit sub electione et consilio quantum ad suum exercitium, et per consequens cadit sub ordinatione prudentiae."

32. ST I, q. 17, a. 6: "Sed contra, id quod libero arbitrio agimus, nostro imperio agi potest. Sed actus rationis exercentur per liberum arbitrium. . . . Ergo actus rationis possunt esse imperati."

33. ST I, q. 17, a. 6, c.: "Respondeo dicendum quod, quia ratio supra seipsam reflectitur, sicut ordinat de actibus aliarum potentiarum, ita etiam potest ordinare de actu suo."

the result of a practical judgment which I made this afternoon as I set out to work, and continue to make as long as I am working, stating to myself that the construction of this rational demonstration is something that I want to be doing now. This practical judgment is indeed backed up by volitional force, otherwise I might now be relaxing at the pool.

Hence, what was implicit in question 16 on truth here becomes explicit, namely, Thomas shows how inasmuch as the act of reason can be accomplished by voluntary choice, it becomes a matter for morality and thus falls under the scope of ethics.

A host of objections immediately come to mind as soon as one utters the thesis that persons are morally responsible for their mental activity. We often assume that intelligence is an ability that persons possess in unequal measure. For this reason it may appear that a good use of one's mental abilities depends more on innate disposition than on conscious choice. Furthermore, if we affirm that ethical commitments have a direct bearing on our acquisition of knowledge, would this entail the thesis that right thinking is to be equated with moral goodness, and erroneous thinking with moral vice? Is it enough to have good character to think well? Is a grasp of the rule of *modus ponens* somehow dependent on purity of heart? If "to err is human," as common wisdom would have it, then an identification of error with vice would amount to a most unsympathetic judgment to be leveled on the human race.

Thus, at first glance Aquinas's theory of human acts looks rather simplistic and overly rigorous. He appears to be making the traditional Christian claim that human beings are responsible for their actions and extending this even further to cover our activity of thinking. And indeed, he is making such a claim. However, a reading of his writings reveals a very sophisticated version of this strongly responsibilist view of human action. For despite his emphatic affirmation in q. 17, a. 6 that the act of speculative reason can be commanded by a voluntary practical judgment, Thomas immediately adds an important rider. The will's motion does not apply to all aspects of the intellect's activity, but only to one facet of an act characterized by a certain internal complexity.

It is at this juncture that Thomas enunciates a crucial distinction between two different components of a unique act of reason: the *exercise* of the act and the *specification* of the act.[34] Thomas refers to them

34. Thomas employs the specification/exercise terminology in ST I-II, q. 9, a. 1; q. 10, a. 2; and in *De malo*, q. 6 (Leonine, pp. 145–53, esp. 148–50). In other contexts

as "modes" of the same act, suggesting that the distinction consists neither in a purely ideal consideration of reason imposing a logical distinction on a uniform reality, nor in a separation of two unconnected and self-contained parts of the same act. The two modes are really distinct causal aspects of an identical act. Each mode has its own requirements, but the two nevertheless concur in the completion of the same act. Exercise refers to whether or not there is an intellectual act at all, like the on-off switch on a movie projector, whereas specification refers to the object of the act, like the images projected on a screen once the movie projector has been turned on.

What Thomas refers to as the "exercitium actus" is easily correlated with our everyday experience. Just as I can open or close my eyes at will, or walk to the corner store at will, in like manner I can apply myself to the activity of speculative thinking at will. Parents who exhort their children "to sit down and do your homework" are directing not only bodily movements, but especially a mental act, requiring attentiveness and effort. Likewise the need for voluntary effort in knowing is evidenced by the praise or blame accorded to the efforts one invests in this regard: "he is gifted but undisciplined"; "while not the brightest student, she does her work more diligently than the others." Thomas himself makes clear reference to this volitional side of knowing in the previous question (16) concerning "application" (*usus*): "Even speculative reason is applied by the will to the work of understanding or judging. Consequently, speculative reason itself is said 'to be used,' insofar as it is moved by the will, in the same way as the other executive powers."[35]

The application of the intellect to the work of speculative thinking is clearly the kind of activity that leaves room for a choice among several contingent alternatives. The most obvious option is between acting or not acting—thinking about speculative matters or not thinking about speculative matters. I can reflect on the ethics of knowing today, or I can abstain from reflecting on that subject today. Each alternative is within the scope of my voluntary control. Each side presents positive and negative aspects, such that my will is necessitated by neither of the two alternatives.

Moreover, in addition to choosing between an act and its contradictory, it is also possible to make a choice between two positive acts. All

---

Thomas refers to the "specificatio" simply as the ordering of an act "ad obiectum," as in ST I-II, q. 17, a. 6, and II-II, q. 47, a. 2, ad 2.

35. ST I-II, q. 16, a. 1, ad 3: "Ad tertium dicendum quod etiam ipsa ratio speculativa applicatur ad opus intelligendi vel iudicandi, a voluntate. Et ideo intellectus speculativus uti dicitur tanquam a voluntate motus, sicut aliae executivae potentiae."

sorts of alternatives are possible here. One can choose between engaging in: different speculative endeavors (e.g., mathematics or philosophy); speculative or practical cognition (e.g., working on proofs for the existence of God or balancing a checkbook); a cognitive activity or a noncognitive activity (e.g., working on derivation proofs or eating supper).

Either set of alternatives in the act of knowing (to act or not, to act in this way or in that way) fulfills the basic characteristics for an object of free choice. In each case there are at least two options, of a contingent nature, which can be effectuated by an agent with the requisite capacity for the sake of an end. This is the act of reason considered in the mode of its exercise, which "can always be commanded."[36]

In contrast, the *specification* of reason, whereby the mind assents to its apprehended objects, is characterized largely by an absence of alternatives from which to form the basis of a free choice. The issue at this stage of the inquiry is no longer to discern whether the intellect has the power to consider some object or not. We have already determined that the epistemic agent does retain that power. The question to be raised here presupposes that a choice has already been made to consider some object, and consequently that the agent is actually engaged in a determinate act of understanding, for instance, the agent has decided to occupy himself with arithmetic calculations and is presently doing so. Does the epistemic agent retain free choice in relation to the precise manner in which he understands the things that are known? For instance, let us suppose that I am presently considering certain basic properties of numbers. Do I *choose* that $2 + 2 = 4$? Is the act of comprehending and asserting that this is the case an outcome of a free choice? In other words, is mental assent or judgment a kind of choice?

Because all judgments require the formation of propositions, in which a subject and predicate are united by a copula, it is always possible to consider the contradictory proposition. For instance, to assert the truth of the proposition "Every man is a rational animal" presupposes that I have entertained (at least implicitly) the contradictory proposition "Not every man is a rational animal" and denied its truth. For this reason, it may appear that every judgment involves a choice between at least two alternatives: the affirmation and the denial of the same propositional content. But is it actually the case that I am free to choose between the affirmation of a proposition and its denial?

36. ST I-II, q. 17, a. 6, c.: "Sed attendendum est quod actus rationis potest considerari dupliciter. Uno modo, quantum ad exercitium actus. Et sic actus rationis semper imperari potest: sicut cum indicitur alicui quod attendat, et ratione utatur."

Thomas's answer to this question is clear. Assent to *necessary* propositions is not open to choice.[37] The contradictory of a necessary proposition is always excluded precisely because it is impossible and hence is necessarily false. As an impossibility, it is not something an agent could possibly choose, since choice bears only on what is possible. Although the mind can entertain the opposite of a necessary proposition, it can never choose to assent to it. Hence, once the necessity of the said proposition is understood, in turn the mind grasps the impossibility of its opposite, and assent follows "naturally" without choice.[38]

Thomas's discussion in *Summa theologiae* I-II, q. 17, a. 6, on the commanded act of reason, can be summarized as follows. He enunciates unambiguously that the act of reason can always be *exercised* voluntarily, through free choice. The epistemic agent is moved by his or her own will, as from a personal, interior source, to consider some object or other. No internal or external compulsion can constrain an agent to engage in any such act of intellectual consideration. This is true regardless of the necessary or contingent character of the object specifying the act of consideration: ". . . no matter what the object might be, it is in a man's power not to think of it, and consequently not to will it actually."[39]

37. ST I-II, q. 17, a. 6, c.: "Si igitur fuerint talia apprehensa, quibus naturaliter intellectus assentiat, sicut prima principia, assensus talium vel dissensus non est in potestate nostra, sed in ordine naturae: et ideo, proprie loquendo, nec imperio subiacet."

In the case of contingent objects or even necessary objects whose necessity is not perceived by the intellect, Thomas affirms that a motion of the will does indeed intervene to determine assent. In such instances the intelligibility of the object is insufficient to elicit assent and a voluntary choice is required in order that a mental judgment might follow. Key examples of such willed acts of assent are: faith, prudential judgment, or any theoretical judgment lacking evidential warrant, e.g., opinion: "Sunt autem quaedam apprehensa, quae non adeo convincunt intellectum, quin possit assentire vel dissentire, vel saltem assensum vel dissensum suspendere, propter aliquam causam: et in talibus assensus ipse vel dissensus in potestate nostra est, et sub imperio cadit" (ST I-II, q. 17, a. 6, c.). Cf. ST I, q. 82, a. 2; II-II, q. 1, a. 4; *De veritate*, q. 14, a. 1 (Leonine, pp. 436–37); and *De virt. in comm.*, q. un., a. 7 (Marietti, pp. 723–25).

The Thomistic doctrine concerning the voluntariness of assent is best understood as a continuum, with the nonvoluntary judgments about necessary matters at one extreme and the voluntary judgments about purely nonevidential matters at the other. In between the two extremes many different degrees of voluntariness are possible, and it is here that we encounter most of the ordinary judgments made in human life.

38. In ST I, q. 62, a. 8, ad 2, Thomas explains that the assent to a necessary proposition excludes its opposite (contradictory) and therefore occurs naturally: "Virtutes rationales se habent ad opposita in illis ad quae non ordinantur naturaliter: sed quantum ad illa ad quae naturaliter ordinantur, non se habent ad opposita. Intellectus enim non potest non assentire principiis naturaliter notis. . . ."

39. ST I-II, q. 10, a. 2, c.: ". . . potest enim aliquis de quocumque obiecto non cogitare, et per consequens neque actu velle illud." Cf. I-II, q. 6, a. 3, ad 3.

Thomas holds just as emphatically that the *assent* of the intellect to necessary objects in the act of judgment is strictly independent of the voluntary choices of the epistemic agent. In the order of specification, the intellect receives the intelligible imprint of outward reality by virtue of the inner light of the agent intellect. The mental act of speculative judgment does not immediately pertain to the agency of voluntariness and choice, but rather to the receptive agency of the intellect. Although the act of speculative judgment is commanded by the will in the line of its exercise, it is nevertheless elicited directly by the intellect in the line of its specification.

CONCLUSION: VIRTUE IN SPECULATIVE KNOWING

The distinction between exercise and specification enables Thomas to explain in what manner speculative truth does and does not pertain to the domain of morality. Anything done willingly enters the realm of morality. An act can be qualified as morally good or bad to the degree that it is voluntary. The intellectual act will be moral to the precise degree that it is freely chosen.

Clearly, from what we have said above, the *specification* of knowledge lies outside the scope of morality. When the intellect functions well in the speculative order, assent is necessitated by the object, and is not freely chosen. True, we can speak of goodness and badness in relation to the intellect's specification (as when we speak of a good mathematician or a good biologist), but this is not a moral denomination.[40] In this instance, goodness signifies an excellence of the mind, a readiness for pronouncing true judgments concerning a specific range of objects, which depends upon the acquisition of stable dispositions in the knower. These are the intellectual virtues, which have their seat in the possible intellect, actively disposing it to skillfully pronounce its act of judgment.[41]

As qualities which internally shape the possible intellect in conjunction with the senses and the imagination, the virtues of the speculative

40. *De virt. in comm.*, q. un., a. 7, ad 2: "Ille autem qui habet bonitatem secundum aliquam potentiam, non praesupposita bona voluntate, dicitur bonus secundum quod habet bonum visum et auditum, aut est bene videns et audiens. Et sic patet, quod ex eo quod homo habet scientiam, non dicitur bonus simpliciter, sed bonus secundum intellectum, vel bene intelligens; et similiter est de arte, et de aliis huiusmodi habitibus" (Marietti, p. 725).

41. ST I-II, q. 50, a. 4, c.; It is significant that Thomas begins his treatment of the intellectual virtues by noting that the Averroistic conception of a unique possible intellect would preclude any such consideration: "Unde si intellectus possibilis sit unus numero omnium hominum, habitus scientiarum, secundum quos homines diversificantur, non poterunt esse in intellectu possibili sicut in subiecto . . .".

intellect enable the knower to enter into personal relation with objective, universal, and necessary truth. Thomas is quick to point out that these virtues function without a direct rapport to the will, which is the source of morality in human acts:

> For someone is said to have understanding or science when his intellect has been perfected to know the truth, which is the good of the intellect. Although this truth can be something willed, as when a man wills to know the truth, nevertheless it is not in this respect that the aforesaid habitus [the intellectual virtues] are brought to perfection. For it does not follow from the fact that a man has science that he efficaciously wills the consideration of truth, but only that he is capable of doing so. Hence the consideration itself of truth is not science insofar as it is an object of volition, but according as it tends directly to its object.[42]

On this basis, should we conclude that the intellectual virtues function in a manner which is morally neutral? In other words, when Thomas states that these virtues have no internal relation to the will, does he thus intend to remove them from the whole order of morality? To answer this question, we must recall his teaching that acts of judgment are specified only when exercised. To consider some object in act, the epistemic agent must direct his attention to it. Attention can be directed or diverted at will. But the grasp of truth in the judgment is not an act of will but rather the outcome of intellectual skill. Nonetheless, the *desire* to know something and thus to direct attention to it, is constituted by an act of will. Hence, although intellectual virtue does indeed supply a *capacity* for knowing, this capacity only becomes *actual* in the individual knower when animated by the efficacy of voluntary desire.

As we have already seen, the *exercise* of the act of reason is the result of a free choice. In consequence, despite the fact that intellectual virtues do not function as qualities *for* the direction of good choice (*habitus electivus*), it nevertheless remains true that they are always exercised *by* choice. The *will* to apply one's understanding to the act of knowing truth is accordingly never morally neutral. The actual *desire* for knowledge is always either virtuous or vicious, depending on the will of the agent. This act always engages the epistemic agent qua

42. *De virt. in comm.*, q. un., a. 7, c.: "Dicitur enim aliquis intelligens vel sciens secundum quod eius intellectus perfectus est ad cognoscendum verum; quod quidem est bonum intellectus. Et licet istud verum possit esse volitum, prout homo vult intelligere verum; non tamen quantum ad hoc perficiuntur habitus praedicti. Non enim ex hoc quod homo habet scientiam, efficitur volens considerare verum, sed solummodo potens; unde et ipsa veri consideratio non est scientia in quantum est volita, sed secundum quod directe tendit in obiectum" (Marietti, p. 724). Trans. John Patrick Reid, *St. Thomas Aquinas on the Virtues* (Providence: Providence College Press, 1951), 48. Cf. ST I-II, q. 56, a. 3.

moral agent, for it is by the faculty of will that the agent moves himself to engage in deliberate acts of speculative understanding:

From the fact that someone possesses a habitus of speculative science, it does not follow that he is inclined to make use of it, but only that he is made able to consider the truth in those matters about which he had scientific knowledge: [however] that he make use of the acquired science, is due to a motion of the will. Consequently a virtue which perfects the will, as charity or justice, confers the right [moral] use of these speculative habitus.[43]

The aim of this argumentation is to explain how moral considerations enter into the concrete process of knowing. The possession of an intellectual virtue does not shape the moral quality of the intellectual act, it shapes the ability of the agent to perform a truthful judgment. This does not imply that any particular *act* of speculative judgment can be ethically neutral, precisely because the act itself only occurs when an agent so desires, and desire is an act of will which is always morally qualifiable. Thomas therefore concludes that the moral quality of that will-act depends, like all will-acts, on its object and its circumstances. On the part of the agent, the capacity to choose well in this area, as in all areas of moral action, hinges on the possession of the appropriate *moral* virtues.

In the passage just cited, Thomas has applied the conclusion reached in *Summa theologiae* I-II, q. 17, a. 6 on *voluntariness* in knowing, to his subsequent discussion on *virtuous knowing* in q. 57, a. 1. The structures of the arguments in the two articles are exactly parallel. Whereas in q. 17, a. 6, Thomas sought to determine in what measure speculative reason is moved by the will, in q. 57, a. 1, he examines the same faculty in order to determine whether it may be the seat (*subjectum*) of virtue and hence subject to morality. The connection between the two articles is clear, since the ability to move a power freely is the basis for the ability to act morally.

In conclusion, we may say that the intellectual virtues are morally neutral insofar as they can *potentially* serve either a good or a bad end.[44] This distinguishes them from the moral virtues which can never be used for a bad end. This does not mean, however, that the intel-

---

43. ST I-II, q. 57, a. 1, c.: "Ex hoc enim quod aliquis habet habitum scientiae speculativae, non inclinatur ad utendum, sed fit potens speculari verum in his quorum habet scientiam: sed quod utatur scientia habita, hoc est movente voluntate. Et ideo virtus quae perficit voluntatem, ut caritas vel iustia, facit etiam bene uti huiusmodi speculativis habitibus."

44. *De virt. in comm.*, q. un., a. 7, ad 5: "Non enim ex eo quod homo habet scientiam, efficitur bene volens considerare, sed solummodo bene potens; et ideo mala voluntas non opponitur scientiae vel arti, sicut prudentiae, vel fidei, aut temperantiae" (Marietti, p. 725).

lectual virtues can *actually* be employed in an ethically neutral manner. Such neutrality results from a formal mode of consideration, which abstracts from their necessary involvement in the moral life of particular individuals. Taken in their true existential context, the intellectual virtues are exercised within acts of knowing, which as willed acts, are personal acts of the knower. As personal acts they are necessarily moral acts, and as moral acts they are either good or bad. Consequently, the actual *exercise* of the intellectual virtues is *never* morally neutral. Every act of knowing contributes to or detracts from a person's ultimate perfection. And so it is no surprise that Aquinas should introduce a *moral* virtue, *studiositas*, whose function is to incline the knower towards a good ethical use of the speculative intellect and its habitus.[45] Knowing is perfective only when it is guided by this virtue of the will, which rectifies "the appetite and the engagement of the self [*studium*] in acquiring knowledge."[46]

A treatment of the various ways in which reason can be utilized by moral agents thus represents an important theme running throughout the *Summa theologiae*. In the *Secunda pars* especially, Thomas manifests an acute awareness of the role of intellectual activity for the devel-

45. The role of *studiositas*, which regulates the exercise of all the intellectual virtues, is overlooked by Alex C. Michalos in his study, "The Morality of Cognitive Decision Making," in *Action Theory*, ed. M. Brand and D. Walton (Dordrecht: D. Reidel, 1976), 325–40. Michalos maintains that for Aquinas "morality can play a role in decision making only insofar as beliefs are related to overt actions, i.e., only in the realm of what he calls 'prudence.' In that realm there *is* moral virtue in intellectual virtue, but it is only possible because the decisions made are not merely cognitive" (336). It is true that among the intellectual virtues prudence alone involves a determination of the will within the order of specification and in this sense it bears a special relationship to moral virtue. Nevertheless, it is false to conclude that for prudence alone there is "moral virtue in intellectual virtue," since according to Thomas the intellectual virtues are employed virtuously only under the direction of the relevant moral virtues, especially *studiositas*.

46. ". . . studiositas non est directe circa ipsam cognitionem, sed circa appetitum et studium cognitionis acquirendae" (ST II-II, q. 167, a. 1, c.). The mention of a special virtue called "studiositas," which one might translate as "virtue of mental attention," is unique to the *Summa theologiae* within the Thomistic corpus. It is not enumerated among the traditional lists of virtues that Thomas had at his disposal (Aristotle, Cicero, Gregory, Augustine, etc.). He cites no authority to justify the introduction of this new virtue, but merely presents a quote from Proverbs (27:11) which exhorts: "Stude sapientiae, fili mi" (q. 166, a. 1, sed contra). A special moral virtue devoted to the appetite for knowledge does not appear to have figured into his initial plan for the *Summa*, since when the need for such a virtue is mentioned in I-II, q. 57, a. 1, c. (see n. 43), he simply states that "a virtue which perfects the will, such as justice or charity, makes us have good use of the speculative habitus." No mention is made of *studiositas*, the virtue to which he later assigns this role. However, another plausible explanation for his omitting mention of *studiositas* at this juncture in the *Summa* might very well be the novelty of the new virtue. Instead of presenting it here, which would require a more lengthy explanation, Thomas chose to speak in general terms, preferring to introduce the new material later on at the appropriate place in the *Secunda secundae*.

opment of moral character. His concern throughout is to show how theoretical truth, in itself objective, can in fact constitute the agent's subjective good.[47] Simply as an object of the intellect, truth is indeed transsubjective, entirely detached from the will and the passions. But as an object of the will, the act of knowing truth can become the focus for an intense desire for personal achievement. Knowing the objective truth can thus become an end perfective of my singular intellect and the source of a desire which is profoundly "my own."

47. This is nicely summarized in ST I, q. 82, a. 4, ad 1, where Thomas notes that the intellect may be considered from two points of view: "uno modo, secundum quod intellectus est apprehensivus entis et veri universalis; alio modo, secundum quod est quaedam res, et particularis potentia habens determinatum actum."

5 Aquinas's Critique of Averroes' Doctrine of the Unity of the Intellect

EDWARD P. MAHONEY

No doubt St. Thomas Aquinas's best-known attack on Averroes' doctrine of the unity of the intellect is that found in his 1270 *Tractatus de unitate intellectus contra averroistas*. What appears to be less appreciated is that he had already set forth most if not all of the arguments that it contains in earlier works.[1] The aim of this paper will therefore be to review briefly some of Thomas's works that antedate or were written at about the same time as the *De unitate intellectus*. This will enable us to see more clearly what was new in that much-studied treatise.[2] Because of set limits, not all of Thomas's arguments against

---

1. In his comprehensive study, *Friar Thomas d'Aquino: His Life, Thought and Work* (New York: Doubleday, 1974), James A. Weisheipl refers to the *De unitate intellectus* as "a tightly argued refutation of Siger's arguments concerning the nature of the human intellect" (277).He does not indicate that many of its arguments are found in earlier works nor does he specify what is new in it. There are *Corrigenda et addenda* (465–87) in the reprint edition of Weisheipl's book (Washington, D.C.: The Catholic University of America Press, 1983) that I shall cite where appropriate. It is important to note that Marie-Dominique Chenu had already wisely and correctly emphasized the importance of reading the *De unitate intellectus* against the background of Thomas's other works on the topic, the writings of his adversaries (most notably Siger of Brabant), and Stephen Tempier's impending Condemnation of 1270. See his *Toward Understanding Saint Thomas*, trans. and ed. A.-M. Landry and D. Hughes (Chicago: Henry Regnery, 1964), 338.

2. For helpful studies, see Bruno Nardi's introduction to *Tommaso d'Aquino: Trattato sull'unità dell'intelletto contro gli averroisti* (Florence: Sansoni, 1947), 7–89, esp. 60–67 and 74–78; Gérard Verbeke, "L'unité de l'homme: saint Thomas contre Averroès," *Revue philosophique de Louvain* 58 (1960): 220–49; Pasquale Mazzarella, "La critica di San Tommaso all' 'Averroismo gnoseologico'," *Rivista di filosofia neo-scolastica* 66 (1974): 246–83. Both Nardi and Mazzarella pay special attention to the historical development in Thomas's writings. Verbeke's approach is for the most part systematic, but he does note some changes. His study has been reprinted in his *D'Aristote à Thomas d'Aquin. Antécédents de la pensée moderne. Recueil d'articles*, Ancient and Medieval Philosophy: De Wulf-Mansion Centre, Series 1, vol. 8 (Leuven: University Press, 1990), 539–68. More limited in scope is Maurice Nédoncelle, "Remarques sur la réfutation des averroistes par saint Thomas," *Rivista di filosofia neo-scolastica* 66 (1974): 284–92. See also Howard P. Kainz, "The Multiplicity and Individuality of Intellects: A Re-examination of St. Thomas' Reaction to Averroes," *Divus Thomas* (Piacenza) 74 (1971): 155–79, who appears to find

Averroes can be examined here; nor can those that are examined be studied in the detail that they deserve. Special attention will be given to those arguments and analyses in his other writings that reappear in the *De unitate intellectus*. Of particular interest will be his first presentation of arguments against Averroes in his early work on the *Sentences*. This study will close with a listing of some late medieval and Renaissance philosophers who interested themselves in Thomas's arguments, especially as those arguments are presented in the *De unitate intellectus*.

The *Scripta* on the *Sentences*, which are not a strict commentary, appear to have been written during the period 1252–56. In this early work, Thomas takes up the question whether the intellective soul or intellect is one in all humans.[3] Among the initial arguments recounted for the unity of the intellect are several involving fundamental epistemological and metaphysical issues regarding the problem of individuation and problems regarding universal cognition and intelligible species.

The arguments include that a form is only multiplied through matter, whereas the intellect knows all things and is not a *forma materialis*; that if the intellect were individuated by the body, then intelligible species in the intellect would also be individuated and not be actually intelligible, that is, universal; and that insofar as the rational soul is an immaterial substance, subsistent in itself, there can be no diversity in its essence, that is, it cannot be multiplied. Thomas's replies are that the intellect or intellective soul (*anima intellectiva*) is called a material form in that it does give existence as a substantial form and is multiplied with the division of matter but it is also called immaterial with regard to its immaterial operations, such as thinking, which flow from its immaterial powers; that the intelligible species does indeed

---

attractive the thesis of the unity of the intellect, which he relates both to views of Teilhard and to the doctrine of the mystical body of Christ (178–79). I find Kainz's viewpoint implausible.

3. *In II Sent.*, d. 17, q. 2, a. 1 (Mandonnet, pp. 411–30). Thomas also presents Averroes' theory on the unity of the intellect as one of four positions on the nature of the human soul at death in d. 19, q. 1, a. 1 (Mandonnet, pp. 479–84). Thomas's historians seem to have neglected this text. On the dating, see Weisheipl, *Friar Thomas d'Aquino*, 358–59 and 478. The importance of this early work for establishing the development of Thomas's critique was recognized by Carmelo Ottaviano (*Tommaso d'Aquino: Saggio contro la dottrina averroistica dell'unità dell'intelletto* [Lanciano: Carabba, 1930], 60, 68–70) and Bruno Nardi (*Trattato*, 56–59). But they had in fact been anticipated by J. Vinati in his "In opusculum Divi Thomae Aquinatis *De unitate intellectus contra Averroistas*," *Divus Thomas* (Piacenza) 6 (1885): 447–49.

have individual existence in the individual intellect and yet it is the "likeness" (*similitudo*) of the specific nature found in many individuals; and that the soul, unlike the separate substances, is multiplied numerically according to the matter of which it is the perfection or actuality.

Although Thomas takes up the unity of the agent intellect (*intellectus agens*), he notes that some *catholici doctores* identify God as the agent intellect. It is noteworthy that he does not criticize their position. His target is rather the unity of the possible intellect. Thomas lists both Themistius and Theophrastus, on the one hand, and also Averroes, on the other, among those who hold that the possible intellect (*intellectus possibilis*), which is in potency to receiving all intelligible forms, is one for all humans. Since no Latin translation of Themistius's paraphrases on the *De anima* was available at this time, Thomas depends here on Averroes for knowledge of the late ancient commentator's thought. Thomas thus ascribes to Themistius and Theophrastus the view that since both the possible and the agent intellect are one and eternal, so too are the intelligible species. In contrast, Thomas sees Averroes as holding that the agent intellect and the possible intellect are eternal and one for all humans, but the intelligible species (*species intelligibiles*) are not eternal. On the contrary, the intelligible species are understood only when they are abstracted from the phantasms in presently existing human beings.

Thomas now presents the basic analysis of Averroes that he will consistently maintain in his subsequent writings. According to his reading of Averroes—and his claim that Averroes maintained "intelligible species" is surely doubtful—the latter holds that intelligible species have a twofold subject (*duplex subiectum*). The one is the phantasms, in which they have material existence (*esse materiale*) and according to which the species are not eternal, and the other is the possible intellect, in which they have immaterial existence (*esse immateriale*) and according to which they are not generable and corruptible. But Thomas dismisses this explanation on the grounds that the numerically same intelligible species can no more be present in the imagination of an individual human and also in the possible intellect than the numerically same "visible species" (*species visibilis*), that is, the species of color, can be in a wall and in the eye. Indeed he insists that the intelligible species in the possible intellect really has only one subject; the species in the imagination is numerically different. Thomas even suggests that it might be said that the species in the possible intellect are eternal and are not in fact abstracted from phantasms, an outcome contrary to the mind and words of Aristotle (*contra inten-tionem et verba Philosophi*).[4]

Aquinas now relates how Averroes attempts to show that it is not a consequence of his position that there is one existence and operation for all humans. Because of the different phantasms in different humans, the possible intellect is supposedly joined to each individual man by a distinct "union" (*conjunctio*). Accordingly, while one man knows, another will not be knowing, since the intelligible species in the possible intellect will be united to the former but not to the latter. But Thomas judges Averroes' line of reasoning in his attempt to escape to be frivolous (*frivola*). First of all, he again denies that the intelligible species—the form of the possible intellect—is numerically the same as the species in the phantasm. Secondly, he argues that such a "union" of the intellect with the species in the possible intellect does not provide an individual human with the first perfection and substantial existence (*esse substantiale*) that would put him or her into the specific class of being human. And finally, he remarks somewhat sharply that the theory really involves that the separate intellect would know or understand (*intelligat*) what the individual human is imagining, but *this* individual man, namely Socrates, would not in fact understand (*hic homo, scilicet Socrates, non intelligat*). Thomas adds that it would not be difficult to add many other absurdities.

The analysis and critique of Averroes that Thomas has presented in his *Sentences* commentary is basically that which he repeats, though with some nuances and noticeable additions, in his later writings. This

4. St. Thomas himself adopted the doctrine of the *species intelligibilis* and also used it to explicate Averroes' cognitive psychology as found in the "long" commentary on the *De anima*. In doing so, he introduced a foreign element into the latter's thought. For relevant discussion, see Édouard-Henri Wéber, *La controverse de 1270 à L'Université de Paris et son retentissement sur la pensée de S. Thomas d'Aquin*, Bibliothèque thomiste, vol. 40 (Paris: J. Vrin, 1970), 221–30 and 237–38; and Bernardo Carlos Bazan, "La dialogue philosophique entre Siger de Brabant et Thomas d'Aquin," *Revue philosophique de Louvain* 72 (1974): 98–125, who is highly critical of Wéber's book. Bazan also discussed this question of intelligible species in his "Averroes y Sigerio de Brabante: La nocion de 'intellectum speculativum'," in *Actas del V Congreso Internacional de Filosofía Medieval*, vol. 1 (Madrid: Nacional, 1979), 541–49, and "*Intellectum Speculativum*: Averroes, Thomas Aquinas, and Siger of Brabant on the Intelligible Object," *Journal of the History of Philosophy* 19 (1981): 425–46, esp. 431–33. See also my "Saint Thomas and Siger of Brabant Revisited," *The Review of Metaphysics* 27 (1974): 531–53, and "Sense, Intellect and Imagination in Albert, Thomas, and Siger," in *The Cambridge History of Later Medieval Philosophy*, ed. N. Kretzmann, A. Kenny, and J. Pinborg (Cambridge: Cambridge University Press, 1982), 613–15. But see also n. 60 on Siger. The importance of the doctrine of intelligible species in Thomas's critique of Averroes was recognized by Vinati (*Divus Thomas* [Piacenza] 6 [1885]: 447–49; 8 [1887]: 244–46 and 307–8). John of Jandun too attributes the doctrine of intelligible species to Averroes; see nn. 77 and 81 below.

is evident, for example, in his *Summa contra gentiles,* composed both in Paris and then in Italy between 1259 and 1264.[5] After initially setting forth Averroes' view that the possible intellect is separate from humans (Bk. 2, chap. 59), Thomas marshals various arguments against it. They include that man would *be understood* and *not understand* if the possible intellect were united to man through his phantasms; that that through which a thing operates must really be its form; and that man would not be classified in his species as rational nor would he differ from brutes if the possible intellect were separate from him. Thomas repeats his analysis of Averroes' position as involving one intelligible species that has two subjects, namely, the separate possible intellect and the phantasms in individual men, but he dismisses these ideas as frivolous (*frivola*) and impossible (*impossibilia*). He objects that the result would be that the man who has the phantasms would be understood by the possible intellect and would in fact understand nothing. Another objection is that a child belongs to the human species before it leaves the womb and even begins to have phantasms.[6] When Thomas turns directly to demonstrate that there cannot be one possible intellect for all humans, he again argues that on the assumption of the unity of the intellect and the eternity of the human race, the intelligible species in the possible intellect would be eternal, no new intelligible species would be received, and no new sense knowledge would be needed. He emphatically rejects the notion of a twofold subject of intelligible species as an adequate reply, insists that Averroes' theory involves that there is only one act of understanding (*intelligere*) in all humans, denies that that act could be diversified through the phantasms of individual human beings, and rejects taking the cogitative power as an adequate basis for distinguishing humans from brutes.[7]

5. On the dating of the *Summa contra gentiles,* see Weisheipl, *Friar Thomas d'Aquino,* 359–60 and 478. In the "Introduction historique" to *Saint Thomas d'Aquin: Contra Gentiles. Livre premier* (Paris: P. Lethielleux, 1961), René A. Gauthier discusses in detail the dating and the places of composition (20–59). He rejects Gorce's thesis that the work includes an attack on contemporary followers of Averroes at the University of Paris (70–72). See Matthieu-Maxime Gorce, *L'essor de la pensée au moyen âge: Albert le Grand— Thomas d'Aquin* (Paris: Libraire Letouzey et Ané, 1933).

6. SCG II, chap. 59.

7. SCG II, chap. 73. In this chapter, Thomas appears to add a new argument against Averroes that is based on the notion of an intellectual virtue. If the possible intellect, which is the proper subject (*proprium subiectum*) of an intellectual *habitus* or "science," is one for all humans, then any intellectual virtue, for example, grammar, would be the same in every human being. It would even be possible for any individual human to gain at will a knowledge of all the sciences and to do so without the need of a teacher. St. Thomas disallows the rejoinder that it is not the possible intellect but the cogitative power or "passive intellect" (*intellectus passivus*) that is the subject of the intellectual *habitus* of "science." For a related discussion, see the beginning of SCG II, chap. 60.

Several chapters earlier, Thomas had already rejected Averroes' view that man could have his specific difference from the cogitative power, since man differs from the brutes precisely through intellectual knowing. The human being must have a principle or power which is the source of such intellectual activity, namely, the "possible intellect" (*intellectus possibilis*), and which must be "part" of man and not some separate being. In connection with this argument, Thomas adds a moral consideration that appears not to be found in his earlier work on the *Sentences*. It is that since the will (*voluntas*) is connected to this intellectual power, it too must be part of the individual man. Otherwise the human being would be ruled by the will of a separate substance and not be master of his own acts (*dominus suarum actionum*). The result would be impossible and destroy all moral philosophy and social life (*destructivum totius moralis philosophiae et politicae conversationis*).[8] Thomas returns to this moral consideration when he takes up the theory of a single and separate agent intellect as set forth by Alexander of Aphrodisias and Avicenna. He argues against this position on the grounds that man would then not direct himself (*agens seipsum*) and would thus not be master of his own acts (*dominus suarum operationum*) nor would he merit praise or blame (*nec meretur laudem aut vituperium*). All moral science and political life (*tota scientia moralis et conversatio politica*) would then perish, a result that Thomas judges to be inconvenient (*inconveniens*).[9] Finally, another feature of Aquinas's critique of Averroes not found in his *Sentences* should be identified. It is the notable emphasis on the *text* of Aristotle in order to show that Averroes' doctrine on the soul and intellect is contrary to Aristotle's own. This mode of attack will be developed more fully and play a central role in the *De unitate intellectus*.[10]

Averroes' doctrine on the unity of the intellect is again presented and criticized in the *Prima pars* of Thomas's most celebrated work, the *Summa theologiae*, written in Italy between the Spring of 1266 and the Spring of 1268.[11] He takes up Averroes' theory of the possible intellect

8. SCG II, chap. 60.

9. SCG II, chap. 76. On the significance of Thomas's stress on will and moral responsibility in his critique of Averroes, see the helpful remarks of Verbeke, "L'unité," 225–28.

10. SCG II, chaps. 61, 69, 70, 73, 77, and 78. Nardi presents as "the true novelty" (*la vera novità*) of the *Summa contra gentiles* Aquinas's endeavor to declare Averroes' interpretation of Aristotle to be a sham by appealing to the text of the *De anima* (*Trattato*, 61–62). Nardi notes that this critique will be resumed and enlarged in the *De unitate intellectus*.

11. On the dating of the *Summa theologiae*, see Weisheipl, *Friar Thomas d'Aquino*, 217

and once again objects to what he takes to be Averroes' postulating two subjects of the intelligible species and his claiming that the possible intellect is united to individual humans through intelligible species. This sort of union (*continuatio*), Thomas insists, does not suffice to explain how the action of the intellect would belong to Socrates. Neither Socrates nor his phantasms would understand; rather, they would *be understood* by the separate intellect. As Thomas sees things, Aristotle explained how this man understands (*hic homo intelligit*) by maintaining that the intellective principle is the form of this individual man.[12] Thomas also attacks the mode of union of a single intellect to individual men as one principal agent to many instruments on the grounds that this theory really involves that there is only one knower (*unus intelligens*) and that individuals do not have their own individual activities. Referring to Averroes by name, Thomas denies that the diversity of phantasms in different humans could cause any distinction of intellectual operations.[13]

Another work from this period is the *Quaestio disputata de spiritualibus creaturis*, presumedly composed in Italy during 1267–68.[14] Thomas attacks Averroes' supposed doctrine of the twofold subject of intelligible species and the notion of a union of the possible intellect with an individual man through the intelligible species as insufficient to explain how this individual man would understand (*hic homo singularis intelligat*). The latter can be accounted for only by the possible intellect existing formally in this man (*formaliter inesse huic homini*) as a knowing

---

and 361. Thomas gives another argument against the doctrine of the unity of the intellect in ST I-II, q. 50, a. 4, a text that appears to have been neglected in the scholarly literature. It is that those maintaining the unity of the possible intellect must hold that the *habitus* perfective of cognition, for example, the *habitus* of the various sciences, are not in the intellect as their subject (*subiectum*) but are in the internal senses. Thomas insists that such a view is opposed both to Aristotle and also to the truth of the matter, since habits relate to operations that belong to powers, and thinking is the proper act of the intellect. This argument had been offered in the SCG II, chaps. 60 and 73. See n. 7 above. It does not appear in the *De unitate intellectus* nor does it seem to be found in Thomas's work on the *Sentences*.

12. ST I, q. 76, a. 1. Thomas also writes here of a theory—which is not Averroes' own—that would see a separate intellect united to humans not through intelligible species but simply as their mover (*motor*). It is not evident that this theory, which Thomas views as that of followers of Plato, was put forth by contemporary "Averroists" at the time of the writing of the *Prima pars*. See the judicious remarks of Nardi, who points out that matters change in the *De unitate intellectus*, where followers of Averroes do attempt to use the "mover" theory to save Averroes' thesis on the separate intellect (*Trattato*, 66–67). See n. 51 below.

13. ST I, q. 76, a. 2.

14. On the dating of the *Quaestio disputata de spiritualibus creaturis*, see Weisheipl, 250–51 and 365.

power.[15] Later in the work, Thomas raises a moral and religious consideration already met in the *Summa contra gentiles*. He states that Averroes' doctrine of one possible intellect is contrary to the faith, since it takes away the rewards and punishments of the next life (*praemia et poenae futurae vitae*). He also thinks that it can be shown to be impossible by "the true principles of philosophy" (*vera principia philosophiae*). Even granting that an individual man could know by means of a separate intellect (*intellectus separatus*), Thomas insists that inconveniences (*inconvenientia*) still result. One is that different humans would have the same activity or operation. Another is that the possible intellect would already have received intelligible species abstracted from the phantasms of past human beings and so would not need our phantasms. The replies contain further discussions regarding intelligible species and their individuation and the way in which an immaterial intellective soul can be the form of the human body.[16]

Thomas also appears to have finished his commentary on the *De anima* in Italy before his return to Paris.[17] Of special interest are passages in Book 3, where he presents, though in far less detail, arguments and distinctions met in earlier works. He thus opposes anyone who would separate the intellect from the body as a single separate substance on the grounds that the one expressing this opinion must himself understand it if he is to be given a hearing. But that means

15. *De spiritualibus*, a. 2 (Marietti, p. 375).

16. *De spiritualibus*, a. 9 (Marietti, pp. 402–5).

17. For the sake of convenience, I will first cite the Leonine edition and then *In Aristotelis librum De anima commentarium*, ed. A. M. Pirotta, 4th ed. (Rome: Marietti, 1959). Weisheipl allows that Book 1 could have been a series of lectures presented by Thomas at Rome to young Dominican students (216). He takes Thomas's statement: "Sunt autem plura alia quae contra hanc positionem dici possunt; quae alibi diligentius pertractavimus; sed hic hoc unum sufficiat quod ad hanc positionem sequitur quod *hic homo* non intelligit" (Leonine, Bk. 3, chap. 1, p. 207a; Marietti, Bk. 3, lect. 7, n. 695, p. 167) to refer to the SCG II, chap. 56 and following (482). In a detailed preface in the Leonine edition, René A. Gauthier presents evidence to argue that the work was composed at Santa Sabina in Rome between November 1267 and September 1268 and thus before the *De unitate intellectus* of 1270 (283*–88*), that it was not directed against Siger or "Parisian Averroism," of which Thomas was unaware (285*, 288*, and 293*), and that its tone is serene in contrast to that of the prologue of the *De unitate intellectus* (224*–35*). Gauthier underscores that Thomas cites Averroes by name just once in the commentary and that he presents only a brief resume of the more detailed critique of Averroes' theory that he had given in earlier works, most notably in the *Summa contra gentiles* (227*). Gauthier argues that Thomas's reference to his more diligent treatment "elsewhere" (*alibi*) of the many other things that could be said against the unity of the possible intellect is not a reference to the *De unitate intellectus* but must be a reference to the critique in the *Summa contra gentiles* (284*–85*; see also 227*–28* and 234*). Nardi had already anticipated this explanation and had argued that the commentary is "certainly" prior to the *De unitate intellectus* (*Trattato*, 65, n. 1).See also Gauthier's "Quelques questions à propos du commentaire de St. Thomas sur le 'De anima'," *Angelicum* 51 (1974): 451.

that *this* very man himself understands (*hic homo intelligit*) and that he does so formally (*formaliter*) by means of the possible intellect which cannot then be separated from him in existence.[18] Thomas expresses surprise that some have so easily erred regarding the separation of the intellect when the meaning can be gathered from the text of Aristotle (*ex littera sua*).[19]

Thomas once again attacks the mode of union that he attributed to Averroes in previous works, namely, the twofold subject of the intelligible species.[20] And in the following chapter, he re-emphasizes his own distinction of the intelligible (*intellectum*) and the intelligible species. The latter are not the *obiectum intellectus* or *quod intelligitur* but rather that by which the possible intellect understands (*quo intelligit*). Those who argue for the unity of the intellect on the grounds that the intelligible (*intellectum*) is the same for all fail to comprehend that the intelligible species is not the *intellectum* but rather the "likeness" (*similitudo*) of that intelligible as it exists in the soul. The many intellects have their own "likenesses" of what is the same quiddity in the order of things. Consequently, there will be the same thing understood (*res intellecta*) in all of those numerically distinct intellects.[21]

The *Quaestio disputata de anima* appears to have been authored by Aquinas shortly after his return to Paris in 1269. The unity of the possible intellect is discussed in articles 2 and 3. Thomas underscores that for Aristotle a man knows by means of that intellect. Consequently, it cannot be a separate substance that serves as a principal agent using humans as its instruments. Once again he rejects the thesis of the twofold subject of the intelligible species and compares the union of the intellect to us through phantasms to that of the union of sight to a wall through the colors in it. Man will *be understood, not understand*, just as the wall will *be seen, not see*. Thomas rejects as impossible that the act of knowing or understanding (*intelligere*) of a single possible intellect could be multiplied and so belong to this human being or that human being. In that case, when two humans would know the same thing they would in fact have the numerically same act of understanding (*intelligere*). Accordingly, Thomas argues that the

18. *In De anima*, Bk. 3, chap. 1 (Leonine, pp. 205b–6a, ll. 282–305; Marietti, lect. 7, n. 690, p. 166). On Thomas's use of the *hic homo intelligit* argument both here and in the *De unitate intellectus* to reduce the opponent to a self-contradiction, see Nédoncelle, "Remarques," 284–86, 288, and 290. For evaluations that various historians have made of Thomas's appeal to *hic homo intelligit*, see n. 47 below.

19. *In De anima*, Bk. 3, chap. 1 (Leonine, p. 207b, ll. 372–76; Marietti, lect. 7, n. 699, p. 167).

20. Ibid. (Leonine, p. 206ab, ll. 306–52; Marietti, lect. 7, n. 691–94, pp. 166–67).

21. Ibid., chap. 2 (Leonine, p. 213ab, ll. 264–79; Marietti, lect. 8, n. 718).

possible intellect must then be the power of the individual human soul and be multiplied according to the number of human bodies.[22] Thomas is careful to add that while the many human intellects have their own intelligible species, that which they know by means of those different intelligible species is universal and one for all.[23] It should also be noted that Aquinas again refers to *quidam Catholici* who hold that the agent intellect is God. Against them he argues that there must also be an active principle in us rendering phantasms actually intelligible.[24]

Lastly, we must note the allusions to Averroes' doctrine in Thomas's *Compendium theologiae*, a work whose dating has been disputed. He presents arguments against someone who would say that the intellect is incorruptible but is only one in all humans. To show that this is impossible he pursues the tactic of forcing the opponent to admit something that cannot at all be denied. Supposing that this man understands (*hic homo intelligit*), for example, Socrates or Plato, the opponent could not even deny this unless he in fact understood its very meaning. Accordingly, by denying it is the case he affirms it, since he himself understands. Moreover, he formally (*formaliter*) understands by reason of his form, namely, his intellect, while another man understands by reason of his form, namely, his intellect. But they cannot have the numerically same form. Therefore, there cannot be one intellect.[25]

Thomas refers to "some" (*aliqui*)—presumably he means Averroes—who have attempted to escape the force of this argument by stating that intelligible species exist both in our phantasms and in the

22. *De anima*, aa. 2–3 (Robb, p. 64–88). Weisheipl considers the questions on the *De anima* to have been composed shortly after Thomas's return to Paris and to be directed against "Averroists" in the Arts Faculty (*Friar Thomas d'Aquino*, 250–54). In contrast, Fernand Van Steenberghen, *La philosophie au XIIIe siècle*, Philosophes médiévaux, vol. 9 (Louvain: Publications Universitaires and Paris: Béatrice-Nauwelaerts, 1966), 430, and *Maître Siger de Brabant*, Philosophes médiévaux, vol. 21 (Louvain: Publications Universitaires and Paris: Vander-Oyez, 1977), 49, believes that Thomas's discussion of the unity of the intellect "develops in perfect serenity" (*se deroule en parfaite sérénité*) and concerns Averroes himself and not any Parisian "Averroists." He notes the sharp contrast to the tone of the *De unitate intellectus*. Bernardo Bazán reaches the same judgment, arguing that Thomas shows that he does not know Siger's position as found in the *Quaestiones in tertium De anima*. See the introduction to Bazan's edition of *Siger de Brabant: Quaestiones in tertium De anima, De anima intellectiva, De aeternitate mundi*, Philosophes médiévaux, vol. 13 (Louvain: Publications Universitaires and Paris: Béatrice-Nauwelaerts, 1972), 68*–74*.

23. *De anima*, a. 3, ad 7 (Robb, p. 85).

24. Ibid., a. 5 (Robb, pp. 99–100).

25. *Comp. theol.*, chap. 85 (Leonine, pp. 108b–10b). On the various datings proposed, see the preface of H.-F. Dondaine in the Leonine edition, p. 8, and Weisheipl, *Friar Thomas d'Aquino*, 387–88.

possible intellect in such fashion that the possible intellect is joined and united (*continuatur et unitur*) to us and we can understand through it. Thomas dismisses their response as worthless (*haec responsio omnino nulla est*), since the intelligible species are abstracted from phantasms; they do not exist in the phantasms. We would *be understood* by the single separate intellect; we would *not ourselves understand*. Finally, if the intellect were one in each of us, then we would have numerically the same act of understanding (*intelligere*). But it is impossible that numerically the same activity belong to different agents.[26]

We come finally to St. Thomas's *De unitate intellectus contra Averroistas*, the work that must be of central focus in this paper.[27] In all likelihood it was written early in 1270, that is, before Bishop Stephen Tempier issued his condemnation.[28] There is no evidence whatever that Thomas wrote this work from whole cloth on the occasion of a threat presented by some in the Arts Faculty. It is clear that the arguments that Thomas marshals here against Averroes' theory are for the most part those that he had developed in his earlier writings. Indeed, at the very beginning of the work Thomas himself alludes to the fact that he had already written much against Averroes and the theory of the unity of the possible intellect (*contra quae iam pridem plura conscripsimus*).[29] Nonetheless, there are two things that distinguish this opusculum from Thomas's earlier discussions, namely, the far more detailed analysis of the writings of Aristotle that it contains and also the use of William of Moerbeke's translation of Themistius's paraphrases on Aristotle's *De anima*. Both the text itself of Aristotle and Themistius's interpretation of it are used as weapons to discredit Averroes as a genuine and trustworthy interpreter of Aristotle.[30]

26. *Comp. theol.*, chap. 85 (Leonine, p. 109ab).
27. For the sake of convenience, the Latin text found in the Leonine edition and in Keeler's edition will both be cited. See Leonine, vol. 43, pp. 291–314, and *Sancti Thomae Aquinatis: Tractatus de unitate intellectus contra averroistas*, ed. Leo W. Keeler, Textus et Documenta: Series Philosophica, vol. 12 (Rome: Pontificia Universitas Gregoriana, 1957). Hereafter all references will be to the chapter divisions found in both editions. References to paragraph numbers are only to the Keeler edition.
28. On the dating and historical background of the *De unitate intellectus*, see Van Steenberghen, *Siger de Brabant d'après ses oeuvres inédites*, vol. 2: *Siger dans l'histoire de l'aristotelisme*, Les philosophes belges, vol. 13 (Louvain: Éditions de l'Institut supérieur de philosophie, 1942), 546–50; idem, *Maître Siger*, 57–61; Mahoney, "Sense, Intellect and Imagination," 613–15. On Thomas and the 1270 condemnation, see John F. Wippel, "The Condemnations of 1270 and 1277 at Paris," *The Journal of Medieval and Renaissance Studies* 7 (1977): 179–83. See also Kurt Flasch, *Aufklärung im Mittelalter? Die Verurteilung von 1277* (Mainz: Dieterich, 1989).
29. *De unitate*, chap. 1, par. 1 (Leonine, p. 291a; Keeler, p. 2).
30. For discussion, see Gérard Verbeke, "Thémistius et le 'De unitate intellectus' de saint Thomas," in *Thémistius: Commentaire sur le Traité de l'âme d'Aristote. Traduction de*

At the very beginning of the work, Thomas discerns a widespread error about the intellect that takes its origin from statements of Averroes. The latter strives to assert that the possible intellect (*intellectus possibilis*) is a certain substance that exists separate from a body, is in no way united to it as a form, and is one for all human beings. Aquinas admits that he has already written many things against these statements, but because of the impudence of those who err (*errantium impudentia*) in this way, he proposes to write some things that will confute their error. In all likelihood, Thomas is referring to contemporaries at Paris, Siger of Brabant in particular.[31]

Thomas's initial attack on Averroes' doctrine of the unity of the intellect deserves special note, since it involves what can be called a "moral argument." He indicates that the doctrine of the unity of the intellect contradicts the truth of the Christian faith (*veritas fidei Christianae*). Once diversity of intellects is taken away, all that will remain after death will be one intellect. Consequently, differentiation of rewards and punishment and all retribution (*retributio praemiorum et paenarum*) will be eliminated.[32] Although Thomas does not return again to precisely this consideration from faith, namely, rewards and punishment for an individual immortal human soul, he does later address a somewhat different "moral argument" that we have already met in Thomas's earlier writings. He suggests that if there is only one intellect for all humans, then there will also be only one will (*voluntas*) and all the principles of moral philosophy (*moralis philosophiae principia*) will be destroyed, since personal moral responsibility will have been eliminated.[33] Thomas ends his introductory remarks indicating that he

---

Guillaume de Moerbeke, ed. G. Verbeke, Corpus Latinum Commentariorum in Aristotelem Graecorum, vol. 1 (Louvain: Publications Universitaires, 1957), pp. xxxix–lxii; Edward P. Mahoney, "Themistius and the Agent Intellect in James of Viterbo and Other Thirteenth Century Philosophers (Saint Thomas, Siger of Brabant and Henry Bate)," *Augustiniana* 23 (1973): 434–38; idem, "Saint Thomas and Siger of Brabant Revisited," 535–36; idem, "Sense, Intellect and Imagination," 614. Vinati had already identified in the Greek text and discussed the passages Thomas presents from Themistius; see *Divus Thomas* (Piacenza) 4 (1883): 107–10; 7 (1886): 100. On Thomas's use of Moerbeke's translation of Themistius in his commentary on the *De anima*, see Verbeke, "Thémistius et le commentaire de S. Thomas au De anima d'Aristote," in *Thémistius: Commentaire*, ix–xxxviii, and Gauthier, "Preface," 273*–75*, cited above in n. 17.

31. *De unitate*, chap. 1, par. 1 (Leonine, p. 291a; Keeler, pp. 1–2). Whether Thomas had before him Siger's early *Quaestiones super III de anima* or perhaps *reportationes* of students that provided the content of the teaching not only of Siger but also of other "Averroist" masters has been the subject of scholarly discussion. See Nardi, *Trattato*, 74; Van Steenberghen, *Siger de Brabant d'après ses oeuvres inédites*, 2: 557; idem, *Maître Siger*, 59–61 and 347; Bazan, "Introduction," 72*–74*, esp. n. 36.

32. *De unitate*, par. 2 (Leonine, p. 291ab; Keeler, p. 2).

33. Ibid., par. 81 (Leonine, p. 306b; Keeler, p. 51); and also par. 89 (Leonine, p. 307b; Keeler, p. 57).

intends to show Averroes' position contradicts the principles of philosophy no less than the teachings of the faith. This he will do first of all by showing that that position totally disagrees with Aristotle's mind and words.[34]

The overall structure of the *De unitate intellectus* is a division into five chapters. The plan of the work follows Thomas's reply to the two key errors already mentioned above, namely, that the possible or potential intellect is not the true substantial form of the human body and that it is in fact numerically one for all human beings. Chapters 1–3 are Thomas's critique of the first error, while Chapters 4–5 are his retort to the second error.[35]

In chapter 1, Thomas begins by showing that Aristotle's own definition of the soul at *De anima* 2.1.412b5–6, involves that the soul is the first act of a physical organic body, its substance and essence. He then addresses himself to the dualistic Platonic view that the soul is united to the body more as a mover and a ruler (*motor et rector*) than as a form.[36] He takes Aristotle to have rejected such a conception in his remarks on the sailor-ship analogy at *De anima* 2.2.413a8–9.[37] Thomas then denounces Averroes and his followers for erroneously (*perverse*) interpreting Aristotle's views on how the intellect can be "soul," whether and how it can be "part" of the soul, and how it can be separate from the body.[38]

Thomas underscores that that whereby something primarily operates is the form of that thing insofar as it is operative. When Aristotle spoke of the soul as the act of the physical body, he also meant this to apply to the intellectual part and not just the vegetative and sensitive parts. Thomas concludes that Aristotle's position was that that whereby we think is the form of the physical body.[39] He strengthens his case by adding a string of further relevant quotations from Book 2 of the *De anima*.[40]

34. Ibid., par. 2 (Leonine, p. 291b; Keeler, pp. 2–3).
35. For an outline of the work along with a section-by-section summary, see Ottaviano, *Tommaso d'Aquino: Saggio*, 83–97. Van Steenberghen presents a succinct summary of the work in his *Siger de Brabant d'après ses oeuvres inédites*, 2: 633–36, that reappears almost to the word in his later *Maître Siger*, 347–51. See also his *Thomas Aquinas and Radical Aristotelianism*, trans. S. F. Brown, D. J. O'Meara, J. F. Wippel (Washington, D.C.: The Catholic University of America Press, 1980), 54–59. Beatrice H. Zedler presents an analysis in her translation: *Saint Thomas Aquinas: On the Unity of the Intellect against the Averroists*, Medieval Philosophical Texts in Translation, vol. 19 (Milwaukee: Marquette University Press, 1968), 11–17.
36. *De unitate*, par. 3–4 (Leonine, pp. 291–92; Keeler, pp. 3–4).
37. Ibid., par. 5 (Leonine, p. 292a; Keeler, p. 5).
38. Ibid., par. 7–8 (Leonine, pp. 292b–93a; Keeler, pp. 7–8).
39. Ibid., par. 10–11 (Leonine, p. 293b; Keeler, pp. 8–9).
40. Ibid., par. 13 (Leonine, pp. 293–94; Keeler, pp. 9–10).

Thomas takes Book 3 of the *De anima* to discredit Averroes' perversely misinterpreting Aristotle's statement (*De anima* 2.3.415a11–12)
that the speculative intellect is of a different nature (*altera ratio*). As
Aquinas correctly notes, Aristotle (*De anima* 3.4.429a10–11) clearly
speaks of the part of the soul whereby it knows and understands.[41]
Thomas explains that Aristotle's procedure is to make precise and
determinate here in Book 3 what he had left indeterminate in Book
2.[42] In Aquinas's judgment, Aristotle's own words make manifestly
clear and leave no room for doubt that his view of the possible intellect
was that it belonged to the soul, which is itself the act of the body, but
in such fashion that the intellect has no bodily organ.[43]

In chapter 2, Thomas pursues another line of attack. He attempts
to show that not only the Latins (*Latini*) but also the Greeks (*Graeci*)
and Arabs (*Arabes*) held that for Aristotle the intellect is multiplied
according to the number of human beings. William of Moerbeke's
translation of Themistius's paraphrases on the *De anima* provides
Thomas with a new weapon against Averroes not available to him
previously. Indeed, he now sees Themistius in a different light, since
previously he had to rely on Averroes' presentation of the ancient
commentator's thought. Thomas quotes passages from Moerbeke's
translation that he takes to show that both the possible intellect and
the agent intellect are parts of the human soul for Themistius.[44]
Thomas concludes Chapter 2 with the charge that Averroes was not
so much a Peripatetic as he was a "depraver of Peripatetic philosophy"
(*philosophiae peripateticae depravator*).[45]

In the following chapter, Thomas presents various arguments to
prove against Averroes that the intellect is a potency of the soul, which
is itself the form of the body; nonetheless, this potency is not the act

41. Ibid., par. 14 (Leonine, 293b; Keeler, pp. 10–11).
42. Ibid., par. 15 (Leonine, p. 294b; Keeler, pp. 11–12).
43. Ibid., par. 26 (Leonine, p. 296b; Keeler, p. 19); see also par. 50 (Leonine, p. 301a; Keeler, p. 33).
44. Ibid., chap. 2, par. 51–58 (Leonine, pp. 301a–2b; Keeler, pp. 33–37).
45. Ibid., par. 59 (Leonine, p. 302b; Keeler, p. 38). Gauthier points out that Thomas had already begun to speak in the *Summa contra gentiles* of Averroes as having tried to corrupt (*depravare*) Aristotle's thought ("Préface," 224a*–25a*). He rightly considers as new in the *De unitate intellectus* that Thomas presents Averroes as having perversely expounded not only Aristotle but also the Greek commentators, namely Alexander, Themistius, and Theophrastus (227b*–28a*). Thomas can thus speak of Averroes as the *depravator* and *perversor* of peripatetic philosophy. Nardi had in fact already characterized as "the true novelty" (*la vera novità*) of the *De unitate intellectus* Thomas's extensive quoting of Themistius's paraphrases on the *De anima* to throw in Averroes' face that he had falsified not only Aristotle's thought but also that of Theophrastus and Themistius (*Trattato*, 75). See my study, "Themistius and the Agent Intellect," 425–26 and 434–38. I read Gauthier's study when revising this article for publication.

of any organ.[46] He considers the first argument to be Aristotle's own, namely, that the soul is the first thing whereby we live and think and that it is therefore a certain essence and form (*ratio et species*) of a particular body (*De anima* 2.2.414a12–14). Taking as evident that "This individual human being understands" (*hic homo singularis intelligit*), Thomas questions how we could even inquire about the intellect if we ourselves did not understand.[47] Citing Aristotle's explicit statement (*De anima* 3.4.429a23) that it is the intellect by which the soul understands, Thomas takes him to conclude that if something is the first principle by which we understand, it must be the form of the body: each thing operates insofar as it is in act, and it is in act by reason of its form.[48]

Thomas now deftly points to the weak point in the psychology found in Averroes' long commentary on the *De anima*. He remarks that anyone who would deny that the principle of thinking or understanding is the form of the body must find some appropriate manner in which

46. *De unitate*, chap. 2, par. 60 (Leonine, p. 302b; Keeler, p. 38).

47. Historians have rightly underscored the central importance of the *hic homo intelligit* argument in Thomas's critique of Averroes. Van Steenberghen sees as "the fundamental argument" (*l'argument fondamental*) against Averroes and the Averroists the implications of "the undeniable affirmation of consciousness" (*l'indéniable affirmation de conscience*), namely, *hic homo intelligit* (*Siger de Brabant d'après ses oeuvres inédites*, 2: 635). Thomas demonstrates by this "principal argument" (*argument principal*), which is of the psychological order, that the explanations of Averroes and certain Averroists are insufficient to render an account of "this indisputable fact" (*ce fait inéluctable*). According to Van Steenberghen, Thomas thus adopts a method or tactic in his fight against Averroism of placing the problem of the intellect on the terrain of psychological experience, starting his argument from *ce fait de conscience inéluctable* (639; see also 640 and 646). Van Steenberghen credits Dominique Salman with having properly evaluated the decisive role of Thomas's appeal to *hic homo intelligit* in his struggle against Averroism (640, n. 1). Indeed Salman himself speaks of it as *ce principe fondamental* ("Albert le Grand et l'averroisme latin," *Revue des sciences philosophiques et théologiques* 24 [1935]: 53). Van Steenberghen again underscores in *La philosophie au XIIIe siècle* that Thomas's critique of Averroism rests on "an unimpeachable psychological datum" (*une donnée psychologique irrecusable*) (449). In his perceptive and carefully developed study, Verbeke cites *In I Sent.*, d. 1, q. 2, a. 1, ad 2; d. 10, q. 1, a. 5, ad 2; ST I, q. 76, a. 1; q. 77, a. 7; SCG II, chap. 75–76; and *De veritate*, q. 10, a. 8, in order to stress Thomas's appeal to "the immediate experience" (*l'expérience immédiate*) that we have of our own activity, especially intellectual activity ("L'unité," 246–47). In our knowing, we enjoy a continuous presence of ourselves as subjects to ourselves. That knowing and knowing that we know are correlatives is the "nerve" of Thomas's argument (*le nerf de l'argumentation*) against Averroes. What is surprising, however, is that Verbeke does not discuss Thomas's appeal to *hic homo intelligit* nor does he give any references to it in Thomas's writings. In contrast, Mazzarella is careful to trace it in various of Thomas's writings ("La critica," 263–64, 267–68, and 274). Nédoncelle ("Remarques") attempts to bring out the rhetorical and dialectical aspects of Thomas's argument from *hic homo intelligit*. The value of Thomas's appeals to self-knowledge in general and as an argument against Averroes in particular has been questioned by Anthony Kenny in his recent book, *Aquinas on Mind* (London and New York: Routledge, 1993), 119–25.

48. *De unitate*, par. 61–62 (Leonine, p. 303a; Keeler, pp. 38–40).

the activity of that principle becomes the activity of this individual human being (*hic homo*). Thomas's analysis and presentation of Averroes' attempt to solve the problem is much the same as that met in his earlier writings. For Averroes, we share the act of understanding of the separate possible intellect. That is to say, its act of understanding becomes my act of understanding or your act of understanding insofar as the possible intellect is joined (*copulatur*) to you or to me through our respective phantasms. The intelligible species that is the form and act of the separate possible intellect has two subjects (*subiecta*), namely, the phantasms in the individual human beings and the single possible intellect. It is by means of these phantasms that the possible intellect is joined (*continuatur*) to us. Only in this fashion can Averroes maintain that as long as the possible intellect understands, this human being also understands (*hic homo intelligit*).[49]

But this supposed explanation by Averroes is immediately dismissed by Thomas. The account of union (*coniunctio*) through intelligible species is once again judged to be unsatisfacory. Insofar as the intelligible species is present in the phantasms it is only potentially known or intelligible, whereas insofar as it is present in the possible intellect it has been abstracted from phantasms and is therefore actually known or understood. Consequently, the activity of the possible intellect cannot be attributed to this individual human being in such fashion that this human being would know or understand (*hic homo intelligeret*). Moreover, since phantasms themselves are not a cognitive power, they do not know or understand, though the possible intellect does understand by means of intelligible species of those phantasms. Thomas likens this situation to the colors in a wall that do not see but that the power of sight does see by means of a sensible species of those colors. The phantasms in the human being would *be understood* by the separate possible intellect rather than being the means by which the act of understanding belongs to that human being. In a word, Averroes' position cannot explain how this individual human being will actually know or understand (*hic homo intelligat*), that is, he cannot explain how universal cognition is individualized.[50] Thomas goes on to recount that some contemporary defenders of Averroes—presumably Siger of Brabant is meant—realized that Averroes' way of explaining the mode of union of the intellect with humans could not account for the fact that this individual human will understand (*hic homo intelligat*). Conse-

49. Ibid., chap. 3, par. 63 (Leonine, p. 303ab; Keeler, pp. 40–41).
50. Ibid., par. 64–65 (Leonine, pp. 303b–4a; Keeler, pp. 41–42).

quently, they shift to another way of explanation according to which the intellect is united to the body as its mover (*motor*).[51]

There are two further arguments that Thomas offers to prove that the intellect is united to the body as its form. The one is that that which provides a thing's species, for example, being able to understand (*intelligere*), must be its form.[52] The other argument deserves special attention. It is the "moral argument" already met in the *Summa contra gentiles*.[53] If the position holding that the intellect is united to the body only as its mover were correct, the principles of moral philosophy (*moralis philosophiae principia*) would be destroyed, since nothing would be within our own power. Since the will is in the intellect, if the intellect does not truly belong to this individual human being, the will will exist solely in the separate intellect and not in this human being. Accordingly, this individual human being will not be the master (*dominus*) of his own acts and no act will be either praiseworthy or blameworthy (*laudabilis vel vituperabilis*), which is to destroy the very principles of moral philosophy. But such an outcome is absurd and opposed to human life itself, since all moral counsels and laws would then be unnecessary. In Thomas's judgment, such a consideration indicates that reason itself and not merely revelation shows that the intellect is so united to us that we are one with it, namely, as the power of the soul that is united to us as form.[54]

In chapter 4, Thomas takes up the second of the two errors he discerns in Averroes' theory of the possible intellect. He is not concerned here with the question of the unity of the agent intellect, which can be maintained with some plausibility and which he admits many philosophers have set forth.[55] Whatever be the case regarding the

51. Ibid., par. 67–70 (Leonine, p. 304ab; Keeler, pp. 42–45). See n. 12 above. On Siger, the "mover" theory, and the theory of the *intrinsecum operans ad materiam* as "form," see Nardi, *Trattato*, 66–67, 76–77, and 143, n. 1; Van Steenberghen, *La philosophie*, 450–51; idem, *Maître Siger*, 369–70; Charles J. Ermatinger, "The Coalescent Soul in Post-Thomistic Debate" (Ph.D. diss., Saint Louis University, 1963), 20–40; Zdzislaw Kuksewicz, *De Siger de Brabant à Jacques de Plaisance: La théorie de l'intellect chez les averroïstes latins des XIIIe et XIVe siècles* (Wroclaw: Ossolineum, 1968), 27, 34–36, and 40; Mahoney, "Saint Thomas and Siger," 533–34 and 540–42; idem, "Sense, Intellect and Imagination," 611–12 and 617–18.

52. *De unitate*, par. 80 (Leonine, p. 306ab; Keeler, pp. 50–51).

53. See SCG II, chap. 60.

54. *De unitate*, par. 81 (Leonine, p. 306a; Keeler, pp. 51–52).

55. Ibid., par. 86 (Leonine, p. 307; Keeler, pp. 54–55). Thomas does not appear to consider the unity of the agent intellect to be the distinctive characteristic or danger of Averroes' doctrine. On the other hand, in various of his works he gives arguments against Avicenna's version of a single agent intellect for all humans. On Aquinas and Avicenna, see C. M. Joris Vansteenkiste, "Avicenna-citaten bij S. Thomas," *Tijdschrift*

unity of the agent intellect, the unity of the possible intellect is clearly impossible for many reasons. One argument offered is that if the individual human being who is actually thinking (*homo singularis intelligens*) were the possible intellect itself, then all humans will be numerically one human being (*omnes homines sint unus homo . . . secundum unum individuum*).[56]

Thomas now pursues more doggedly the hypothesis that the individual human being, for example, Socrates, understands by reason of the intellect being united to Socrates only as a mover. The first analysis to which Thomas subjects the hypothesis involves the conception of a prime mover or principal agent using many instruments. But he does so only to invoke once again a "moral argument" against the unity of the intellect. If there were one intellect for all humans, it necessarily follows that there would be one knower (*unus intelligens*) and consequently one "willer" (*unus volens*) and one user (*unus utens*), who would use according to the choice (*arbitrium*) of his will all the differences distinguishing humans one from the other. Humans would therefore in no way differ as regards the free election of their individual wills (*libera voluntatis electio*). On the contrary, their choices would be identical, which is obviously false and impossible. The result would be the destruction of all moral science (*scientia moralis*) and everything that concerns the social intercourse (*conversatio civilis*) natural to human beings.[57]

Yet another time Thomas brings out the epistemological consequence of the hypothesis that all humans know by means of one intellect. The intellectual operation (*intellectualis operatio*) that exists simultaneously and in regard to one intelligible (*unum intelligibile*) must be numerically one, namely, the act of knowing or understanding (*unum numero ipsum intelligere*). That is to say, if you and I know a stone, there must be one and the same intellectual operation that belongs to you and to me. Once again Thomas denies that phantasms

---

voor Philosophie 15 (1953): 457–507; Noriko Ushida, *Étude comparative de la psychologie d'Aristote, d'Avicenne et de St. Thomas d'Aquin*, Studies in the Humanities and Social Relations, vol. 11 (Tokyo: Keio Institute of Cultural and Linguistic Studies, 1968); Patrick Lee, "St. Thomas and Avicenna on the Agent Intellect," *The Thomist* 45 (1981): 41–61; Germaine Cromp, "Les sources de l'abstraction de l'intellect agent dans la 'Somme de théologie' de Thomas d'Aquin" (Ph.D. diss., l'Université de Montréal, 1980), 153–64. On Avicenna's doctrine of the agent intellect, see Herbert A. Davidson, *Alfarabi, Avicenna, and Averroes on Intellect: Their Cosmologies, Theories of the Active Intellect, and Theories of Human Intellect* (Oxford: Oxford University Press, 1992), 83–116.

56. *De unitate*, chap. 4, par. 87 (Leonine, p. 307b; Keeler, p. 55).
57. Ibid., par. 88–90 (Leonine, p. 308ab; Keeler, pp. 56–58).

suffice to individuate or to diversify the activity of the one intellect, especially as it regards one and the same intelligible (*intelligibile*).[58]

A further line of attack that Thomas adopts is to underscore that the hypothesis of the unity of the intellect is repugnant to the very words of Aristotle in *De anima* 3.4. Moreover, he points out that if there were only one intellect, then the separate possible intellect would already possess from the human beings who have lived before us the intelligible species that enable it to have the intellectual habit of science. As a result the separate possible intellect could not gain new intelligible species through my learning anything. But there are even more unhappy consequences. First, since, according to Aristotle, there have always been human beings, then there never was a first human being through whose phantasms the intellect gained intelligible species. Consequently, the intelligible species in the single possible intellect would be eternal. There was then no reason for Aristotle to have postulated an agent intellect.[59]

In chapter 5, Thomas turns directly to arguments purporting to show the impossibility of a plurality of human intellects. In doing so, he both reveals further his own understanding of Aristotle's cognitive psychology and also sets forth several of his own views on key philosophical topics, some of which he had adopted as long ago as his early work on the *Sentences*. Those views concern individuation, the status and function of the disembodied soul, and the nature of the *intellectum*, that is, the intelligible object and its relationships to the intellect (*intellectus*), to the intelligible species (*species intelligibilis*), and to the act of knowing or understanding (*intelligere*). There seems every reason to believe that Thomas had developed his philosophical positions on these key topics at least in part in order to answer the challenge of Averroes.[60]

The first argument is based on the nature of individuation and can be found in Averroes himself.[61] It is that since whatever is multiplied

58. Ibid., par. 90–91 (Leonine, p. 308b; Keeler, pp. 57–58).

59. Ibid., par. 92–95 (Leonine, pp. 308a–9b; Keeler, pp. 58–61).

60. The central role of the doctrine of intelligible species in Thomas's critique of Averroes is underscored by Wéber, *La controverse*, 221–90, and Bazán, "Le dialogue philosophique," 98–124, cited above in n. 4. It is significant to note that Siger himself appears to attribute intelligible species to Averroes in his own late questions on the *Liber de causis* and to accept Thomas's distinction between one *intellectum*, many intelligible species, and many intellects. See *Les quaestiones super librum 'De causis' de Siger de Brabant. Edition critique*, ed. Antonio Marlasca, Philosophes médiévaux, vol. 12 (Louvain: Publications Universitaires and Paris: Béatrice-Nauwelaerts, 1972), q. 27, pp. 108–17. Recent scholarship has demonstrated Thomas's influence on that work in regard to various doctrinal issues.

61. See Averroes, *Commentarium magnum in Aristotelis De anima libros*, Corpus com-

by the division of matter must itself be a material form (*forma materialis*), if there were many intellects in many human beings who differ numerically by reason of the division of matter, that is, their bodies, then the intellect must be a material form. Those using this argument, Thomas relates, then proceed to say that God could not make many intellects of the same kind in different human beings since that would involve a contradiction.[62] Thomas characterizes their mode of argumentation as very coarse (*valde ruditer argumentantur*). He notes that intellects could be multiplied by a supernatural cause (*supernaturalis causa*), namely God. Consequently, those presenting this argument could just as well argue that God could not make the dead rise or the blind see. Thomas would of course have considered such an outcome intolerable, since it contradicts the testimony of the New Testament.[63]

The next move made by those presenting this argument is to claim that no separate form is numerically one or anything individuated, that is, an individual. Thomas considers those who argue this way to have misunderstood Aristotle, who clearly allowed of separate substances that are individuals. Once again Thomas gives his own solution to the problem of how the intellect can be simultaneously separate from matter and also individuated. It is that the intellect is the power (*virtus*) of the soul, which itself is the act of a body (*actus corporis*). Consequently, there are many souls in many bodies and many intellectual powers that are called intellects.[64]

Another argument used as a defense of the unity of the intellect that Thomas had already recounted in earlier works and that he now presents again regards the nature of the intelligible (*intellectum*) and its relationship to the intellect and to the intelligible species. If there is only one intelligible object (*unum intellectum*) in us, then there will be only one intellect (*unus intellectus*) in the whole world. If there are two different intelligible objects (*intellecta*), then they themselves will need a single intelligible (*unum intellectum*). There is therefore only one intelligible object and numerically one intellect (*unus intellectus numero*) in all humans.[65] Thomas's immediate response is to retort that since the intelligible is known by all knowers, and not just by humans, then God must be the only intellect in the world. Their argument

mentariorum Averrois in Aristotelem, Versionum Latinarum, vol. 6, pt. 1 (Cambridge, Mass.: Medieval Academy of America, 1953), III, comm. 5, p. 402, ll. 432–38. On Averroes and individuation, see Joaquín Lomba, "El principio de individuación en Averroes," *Revista de filosofía* 22 (1963): 299–324.

62. *De unitate*, chap. 5, par. 99–100 (Leonine, p. 310ab; Keeler, pp. 63–64).
63. Ibid., par. 105 (Leonine, p. 311ab; Keeler, pp. 67–68).
64. Ibid., par. 100–103 (Leonine, pp. 310b–11a; Keeler, pp. 64–67).
65. Ibid., par. 106 (Leonine, p. 311; Keeler, pp. 68–69).

would mean both that our intellect is God's intellect and that all separate substances other than God, that is, angels and Intelligences, would be eliminated.[66]

In order to quash this line of reasoning completely, Thomas offers again the same theory regarding the nature of the intelligible (*intellectum*), its relation to the many intellects (*intellectus*) of individual human beings, and the individual intelligible species (*species intelligibiles*) in those numerically different human intellects that he had adopted in his earlier writings.[67] He first accuses the proponents of the argument just cited of maintaining something like Plato's theory of Forms in that they posit immaterial forms, namely, "intelligibles" (*intellecta*), in the separate intellect.[68] His retort is to insist that for Aristotle the intelligible object (*intellectum*) is the very nature or quiddity of a real thing (*ipsa natura vel quidditas rei*); it is not a species (*species*) in the intellect—that is, a representation—as these defenders of the unity of the intellect would have to say. If indeed the intelligible (*intellectum*) were an intelligible species of the stone as present in the intellect and not the very nature of the stone (*ipsa natura lapidis*) in the real order (*in rebus*), then we would know not the thing that is the stone but only an intention (*intentio*), that is, a representation abstracted from the stone.[69] Taking care to nuance further his notion of the intelligible species, Thomas notes that the intellect (*intellectus*) understands (*intelligit*) the universal nature by means of this abstraction of an intelligible species from individual principles. As a result, that which you and I understand is one (*unum*)—Thomas means, of course, the *intellectum*—although it is understood differently by you and by me, that is, by means of different intelligible species. My act of knowing or understanding (*intelligere*) is different from yours and my intellect (*intellectus*) is different from your intellect.[70]

Two other arguments put forth on behalf of the unity of the intellect involve the notion of disembodied human souls. The first is that if there were individual intellectual substances, that is, individual human souls that survived death, they would be without purpose, since they do not move bodies as do Intelligences. The other argument is that since Aristotle held both that the world is eternal and that there have always been human beings, the disembodied souls would now be infinite in number. Thomas tries to blunt the force of these arguments.

66. Ibid., par. 107 (Leonine, pp. 311b–12a; Keeler, pp. 69–70).
67. Ibid., par. 109–12 (Leonine, p. 312ab; Keeler, pp. 70–73).
68. Ibid., par. 109 (Leonine, p. 312a; Keeler, p. 70).
69. Ibid., par. 110 (Leonine, p. 312ab; Keeler, p. 71).
70. Ibid., par. 111–12 (Leonine, p. 312b; Keeler, pp. 71–73).

Although they are not to be found in Averroes' long commentary on the *De anima*, they will reappear in the later "Averroist" tradition.[71]

Returning now to a theme found at the beginning of the *De unitate intellectus*, Thomas presents the further objection that all who philosophize (*philosophantes*), both the Arabs (*Arabes*) and the "Peripatetics" (*Peripatetici*), that is, the ancient Greek commentators, hold that the intellect is not multiplied numerically (*non multiplicetur numeraliter*). According to Thomas, the upholders of the unity of the intellect—presumably his contemporaries—say that only the Latins (*Latini*) disagree. He considers their claims to be clearly false, pointing first of all to Algazel and Avicenna as Arabs who held to a plurality of human souls.[72] He then singles out Themistius among the Greeks (*Graeci*). Drawing once again on Moerbeke's translation of Themistius, he quotes the celebrated passage in which Themistius speaks of one illuminating intellect (*illustrans*) and many illuminated and illuminating intellects (*illustrati et illustrantes*). He takes this to mean that there is one principle of illumination that is a separate substance (*aliqua substantia separata*)—whether it be God, as Catholics hold, or the lowest Intelligence (*intelligentia ultima*), as Avicenna holds—but there are many agent and possible intellects. Thomas concludes that it is obvious that Averroes erroneously recounted the thought (*perverse refert sententiam*) of Themistius regarding the possible intellect and the agent intellect. He therefore repeats his earlier charge that Averroes is the depraver of peripatetic philosophy (*philosophiae peripateticae perversor*) and appears to challenge the defenders of Averroes to reply to his own critique, especially regarding Themistius. He declares his wonder that some who look only at the commentary of Averroes presume to state that what he said is what all philosophers thought, that is, both the Greeks and the Arabs, the Latins alone excluded.[73]

In the concluding lines of the *De unitate intellectus*, Thomas reaffirms that what he has written to refute the error of the unity of the intellect was set forth through the arguments and the words of philosophers, not through the teachings of the faith. He ends by challenging anyone who wishes to contradict what he has written not to speak in corners and before youths (*pueri*) but to write, if that person dares, against what he himself has written. And if that person does dare to do so, he will find not only Thomas but also many others who are zealous

71. Ibid., par. 114–17 (Leonine, p. 313ab; Keeler, pp. 73–76).
72. Ibid., par. 119 (Leonine, pp. 313b–14a; Keeler, pp. 76–77).
73. Ibid., par. 120–21 (Leonine, p. 314ab; Keeler, pp. 77–78). For further details regarding both Thomas's use of Themistius and also Siger's use of Themistius in the *De anima intellectiva*, which was his reply to the *De unitate intellectus*, see my article, "Themistius and the Agent Intellect," cited above in n. 30.

for the truth: they will oppose that person's error and cure his ignorance.[74]

We may in fact see Siger of Brabant as daring to reply in his *De intellectu* and again in his *De anima intellectiva*, but it is evident in the latter work that he has begun to shift away from Averroes. The arguments of Thomas's *De unitate intellectus* had presented an inescapable challenge to Siger that forced him both to rethink his position and also to abandon Averroes as an accurate interpreter of Aristotle.[75] Another contemporary of Thomas who studied his *De unitate intellectus* and shows its influence is Giles of Rome (ca. 1243/47–1316). But he criticizes not only Averroes' theory of the unity of the intellect but also Thomas's account of it in his own *De plurificatione intellectus*.[76] On the other hand, John of Jandun (ca. 1285/1289–1316) would defend Averroes' interpretation of Aristotle but he too shows that he had studied Thomas's analysis and arguments with care and respect. Most striking is that he follows Thomas in attributing to Averroes the doctrine of intelligible species.[77]

The impact of Thomas's *De unitate intellectus* was felt once again during the Italian Renaissance. A wide range of philosophers, such as Marsilio Ficino (1433–1499),[78] Nicoletto Vernia (d. 1499), Agostino

74. *De unitate*, par. 124 (Leonine, p. 314b; Keeler, p. 80).

75. There is a sizable literature on the evolution of Siger's thought. See for example Albert Zimmerman, "Dante hatte doch Recht," *Philosophisches Jahrbuch* 75 (1967–68): 206–17. For further bibliography on the topic, see my studies cited in nn. 28 and 30. For the text of Siger's *De anima intellectiva*, see *Siger de Brabant: Quaestiones in tertium de anima, De anima intellectiva, De aeternitate mundi*, 70–112 (cited above in n. 22). It has recently been translated into German by Wolf-Ulrich Klünker and Bruno Sandkühler, *Menschliche Seele und kosmischer Geist. Siger von Brabant in der Auseinandersetzung mit Thomas von Aquin* (Stuttgart: Verlag Freies Geistesleben, 1988), 37–77.

76. See Van Steenberghen, *Siger de Brabant d'après ses oeuvres inédites*, 2: 724–25; Bruno Nardi, "Note per una storia dell'averroismo latino, III: Egidio Romano e l'averroismo," *Rivista di storia della filosofia* 3 (1948): 8–29; Ermatinger, *The Coalescent Soul*, 41–109; idem, "Giles of Rome and Anthony of Parma in an Anonymous Question on the Intellect," *Manuscripta* 17 (1973): 91–94.

77. See my study, "Themes and Problems in the Psychology of John of Jandun," in *Studies in Medieval Philosophy*, ed. John F. Wippel, Studies in Philosophy and the History of Philosophy, vol. 17 (Washington, D.C.: The Catholic University of America Press, 1987), 273–88, and also Kuksewicz, *De Siger de Brabant à Jacques de Plaisance*, 202–43, esp. 220–26.

78. Ficino uses arguments against Averroes that he has clearly borrowed from Aquinas. He shows acquaintance with the *De unitate intellectus* in his *Theologia platonica*, Bk. 15, esp. chaps. 7, 14, and 19. See his *Opera omnia* (Basel, 1576; repr., Turin: Bottega d'Erasmo, 1962), 1:327–67. Raymond Marcel refers to Book 15 as a true *De unitate intellectus* whose Thomist resonances are undeniable (*Marsile Ficin: Théologie platonicienne de l'immortalité des âmes, Tome I—Livres I-VIII* [Paris: Societé d'edition "Les Belles Lettres," 1964], 16). And in the concluding pages of his *Marsile Ficin (1433–1499)* (Paris: Les Belles Lettres, 1958), he suggests that it would be difficult to discern what Ficino in fact owed to Thomas's *De unitate intellectus* (676). I hope to take up that task on another occasion.

Nifo (ca. 1470–1538) and Pietro Pomponazzi (1462–1524),[79] and even the Franciscan Antonio Trombetta (1436–1517),[80] all studied and made use of Thomas's *De unitate intellectus* and the discussions regarding Averroes' doctrine of the intellect to be found in his various writings. Regrettably, limits on this present study demand chronicling on another occasion the varied ways in which they used that work and Thomas's other writings in their approaches to Averroes' doctrine of the unity of the intellect.[81]

What simply remains to be underscored is that Thomas's understanding and critique of Averroes' doctrine remained rather constant throughout his career. He had determined as early as the commentary on the *Sentences* the basic weaknesses and errors of Averroes' theory of the unity of the intellect. The analysis and critique were simply expanded and sharpened in the *Summa contra gentiles*. When he returned to Paris and realized how influential Averroes' interpretation of Aristotle's *De anima* had become, he moved to save Aristotle and philosophy. It should hardly be surprising that he drew upon the arguments in his earlier discussions in order to weld together the powerful critique of Averroes and the challenge to his followers in the Arts Faculty that the *De unitate intellectus* represents. Nor should it be surprising that he would make use of the text itself of Aristotle and Moerbeke's translation of Themistius's paraphrases on the *De anima* to make that critique and challenge even more formidable.[82]

79. On Vernia, Nifo, and Pomponazzi, see my article, "Saint Thomas and the School of Padua at the End of the Fifteenth Century," *Proceedings of the American Catholic Philosophical Association* 48 (1974): 277–85. On Nifo, see my "Agostino Nifo and St. Thomas Aquinas," *Memorie domenicane* n.s. 7 (1976): 195–220, esp. 207–8.

80. On Trombetta's use of Thomas, see Antonino Poppi, *La filosofia nello studio francescano del Santo a Padova* (Padua: Antenore, 1989), 109–10.

81. For an introduction to the general debate at Padua on whether intelligible species are necessary in cognition and the particular issue whether Averroes had maintained them, see Antonino Poppi, *Saggi sul pensiero inedito di Pietro Pomponazzi* (Padua: Antenore, 1970), 139–94, and my study, "Antonio Trombetta and Agostino Nifo on Averroes and Intelligible Species: A Philosophical Dispute at the University of Padua," in *Storia e cultura al Santo di Padova fra il XII e il XX secolo*, ed. Antonino Poppi (Vicenza: N. Pozza, 1976), 289–301.

82. I am grateful to Thérèse Druart for helpful criticisms and to David Gallagher for his editorial advice. Once again I must express my indebtedness to the Duke University Research Council for the grants for travel and microfilms that made possible this and other studies.

After the completion of this essay in February 1992, two relevant studies were published. They are Ralph McInerny, *Aquinas against the Averroists: On There Being Only One Intellect* (West Lafayette, Ind.: Purdue University Press, 1992), and Deborah Black, "Consciousness and Self-Knowledge in Aquinas's Critique of Averroes' Psychology," *Journal of the History of Philosophy* 31 (1993), 349–85.

The Logic of Perfection in Aquinas

OLIVA BLANCHETTE

According to *The Oxford English Dictionary* the word "perfection" has two meanings which are still in common use.[1] First, "perfect" means to be fully accomplished, thoroughly versed and skilled in some activity. This is the meaning we might think of as technical in that it has to do with getting things done.

The second meaning has to do with "the state of complete excellence, free from any flaw or imperfection of quality." This is the meaning we associate with moral excellence or with divinity. It is the meaning which we tend to focus on in philosophy today, as Hartshorne does in his *Logic of Perfection,* where he simply equates perfection with divinity.[2]

But there is a third meaning of perfection which became obsolete in English after the nineteenth century and which still included some reference to the idea of process which is implied etymologically in the term *perfect* according to its derivation from the Latin *perfectum.* According to this meaning "perfect" qualifies something as "thoroughly made, formed, done, performed, carried out, accomplished." This is the meaning which perfection still had for Aquinas and from which his logic of perfection began, far from anything divine in his view.

It is this idea of perfection in its original and originating meaning as Aquinas saw it on which I would like to focus in order to show how it applied first to the universe before it could be applied to God and how, for Aquinas in contrast to Hartshorne, it could be applied to God only in a peculiar way by abandoning its original meaning.

THE ORIGINAL MEANING OF PERFECTION

Theologian though he was, St. Thomas did not think of perfection as applying to God in its original meaning. He brings this out even in

---

1. Vol. 7 (Oxford: Clarendon, 1970), 682–3.
2. Charles Hartshorne, *The Logic of Perfection and Other Essays in Neoclassical Metaphysics* (La Salle, Ill.: Open Court, 1962), 33.

speaking of the divine perfection by focusing on the etymological origin of the term. "It should be known," he writes, "that perfection
[*perfectio*] cannot fittingly be attributed to God if we attend to the
meaning of the word in relation to its origin: for it seems that what
has not been made [*factum*] cannot be said to be perfect [*perfectum*]."[3]
In its original sense, then, perfection presupposes a coming to be, a
fieri, which has arrived at some completion, some *factum esse*.

St. Thomas explains this in terms of act/potency theory. "Because
everything that comes to be [*quod fit*] is reduced from potency to act
and from not being to being when it has been made [*factum est*], it is
then rightly said to be perfect [*perfectum*], as totally made [*totaliter
factum*], when the potency has been totally reduced to act, so that it
retains nothing of not being [*nihil de non esse*], but has complete
being."[4] It is not becoming alone which gives us the idea of perfection
but a becoming that has reached a certain completion, where nothing
of the process remains to be done. Perfection implies a certain being
done with relative to a process of becoming.

This does not mean that every perfection has to be thought of as
absolute. When Aquinas says that what is perfect retains nothing of
not being, he does not mean that all perfection has to be thought of
as unlimited. A thing can be perfect when it retains nothing of the
not being of what pertains to its being, when its coming to be is completed. He speaks of retaining nothing of not being generally in order
to pass on quickly to the way we can come to think of God as perfect,
even though He is not thought of as coming to be in any sense. If we
prescind from coming to be altogether, we can still think of a being
that has nothing of not being in some unlimited way, that is, of an act
that is not educed from potency but that is somehow pure and lacking
in absolutely nothing, without having come to be. As he writes elsewhere, "Because among things that come to be something is then said
to be *perfect* [*perfectum*] when it is educed from potency to act, this
name perfect [*perfectum*] is transposed to signify every being in which
being is not lacking, whether by way of being made [*factionis*] or not."[5]

---

3. SCG I, chap. 28: "Sciendum tamen est quod perfectio Deo convenienter attribui
non potest, si nominis significatio quantum ad sui originem attendatur: quod enim
factum non est, nec *perfectum* posse dici videtur."

4. "Sed quia omne quod fit, de potentia in actum deductum est et de non esse in
esse quando factum est, tunc recte perfectum esse dicitur, quasi totaliter factum, quando
potentia totaliter est ad actum reducta, ut nihil de non esse retineat, sed habeat esse
completum" (ibid.).

5. ST I, q. 4, a. 4, ad 1: "Quia in his quae fiunt, tunc dicitur esse aliquid perfectum,
cum de potentia educitur in actum, transumitur hoc nomen *perfectum* ad significandum
omne illud cui non deest esse in actu, sive hoc habeat per modum factionis, sive non."

Our point here is not to dwell on this idea of pure act or how it relates to perfection as the completion of a process. We shall come back to this when we come to confront Hartshorne's logic of perfection with that of Aquinas. We must rather dwell on how the idea of perfection itself relates to coming to be (*fieri*) or being made (*factum*), where the Latin expresses the relation much more readily than modern English. For that is precisely what the expression of Aquinas, *totaliter factum*, means, something that has gone through its whole process of coming to be and has nothing more to go through or retains nothing of the not being from which it began.

St. Thomas illustrates this process of perfection with an act of walking in the perfect tense to which the intensifying prefix *per* is added. "According to the mode of signifying . . . perfect means completely done [*complete factum*], as we say we have walked [*perambulasse*] when we have completed a walk."[6] This suggests that when we read *perfectum* in Latin we should think, not just "perfect," but rather "perfected," since *perfectum* is formed from the perfect participle of the verb *facere* or *fieri*. In Latin it is more difficult to get away from this original meaning of per-fection than in English.

All this can be summed up in terms of nature or the form of things when they have reached their perfection, as St. Thomas does in this text where he speaks of having completed a walk. Again he is cautioning against applying the idea of *perfectum* or perfected according to the mode of signification of the word, in which "perfect" is meant as completely made (*complete factum*), to something that has not been made (*quod non est factum*). But this time he speaks of things attaining perfection according to their specific nature. "Because things that come to be arrive at the end of their perfection when they attain the nature and power of their species, it follows that this name perfect is taken over to signify every thing that attains its proper power and nature. And in this way Divinity is spoken of as perfect, inasmuch as it is most in its nature and power."[7] Thus it is only by extension that God is spoken of as perfect, since He is not thought of as coming or having come to be in any way. But for things that do come to be, it is

6. *In div nom.*, chap. 2, lect. 1, n. 114: "*Perfecta*, non est accipiendum secundum modum significationis vocabuli, quo perfectum dicitur quasi complete factum, sicut perambulasse nos dicimus, quando ambulationem complevimus" (Marietti, p. 39).

7. "Unde quod non est factum, non potest secundum hanc rationem dici perfectum; sed quia res quae fiunt, tunc ad finem suae perfectionis perveniunt, quando consequuntur naturam et virtutem propriae speciei, inde est quod hoc nomen perfectum assumptum est ad significandum omnem rem quae attingit propriam virtutem et naturam. Et hoc modo Divinitas dicitur perfecta, inquantum maxime est in sua natura et virtute" (ibid.).

said according to the mode of signification of the word "perfected," in which the perfection of a thing is seen as the attainment of the fullness of its nature and power according to its species.

This can be called its first perfection, in contrast to the second perfection of a thing which comes only through its action, as we shall see. But it is important to see it as the perfection of a process. The form attained at the end of the process is its perfection. Thus Aristotle spoke of the form of a thing as its *entelecheia*, as the thing having its *telos* within itself. He was thinking of it as in this way having its perfection, according to its nature and power to act. *Natura* in Latin, like *physis* in Greek, is associated with coming to be and birth. To speak of the nature of a thing is to speak of that for which it is born or comes to be, and to speak of its form is to speak of the end or *telos* of this process of per-fection. Form as such is the perfection of a thing.

Thus, in its original meaning as understood by Aristotle and Aquinas, perfection does not refer to any special excellence, but simply to a kind of expected completion at the end of a process, what they call the nature and the power of a thing as having come from such a process. "What we call the nature of each and every thing is what is fitting for it when its generation has been per-fected: as the nature of man is what he has after the per-fection of his generation; and similarly for the horse and for the house, as long as by the nature of the house is understood its form."[8]

It is interesting to note that this relation between perfection and the process by which it comes to be could be seen much more readily in Latin than it could even in Greek. In Greek the idea of perfection is associated with the idea of *telos,* from which the adjective *teleion,* meaning "perfect," and the substantive *teleiōsis,* meaning "perfection," were formed. Now the usual translation for *telos* is "end," but the more exact translation should include some idea of fulfillment or completion. *Telos* is not just any end or cessation of a process, which may or may not have achieved its purpose, but one that is a positive fulfillment of the process. But the Greek did not have the compact way of putting this idea of per-fection together with one verb as the Latin did with *facere* and *fieri*. In fact, the ideas expressed by these two forms of one and the same verb in Latin are usually expressed by two different verbs in Greek, *poiein* for *facere* and *genesthai* for *fieri*.

8. *In I Politicorum,* lect. 1, n. 32: "Illud dicimus esse naturam uniuscuiusque rei, quod convenit ei quando est eius generatio perfecta: sicut natura hominis est, quam habet post perfectionem generationis ipsius: et similiter et de equo, et de domo: ut tamen natura domus intelligatur forma ipsius" (Marietti, p. 10).

On the other hand, Latin does not have a precise equivalent for *telos*. The usual translation was *finis*. But this lent itself to some confusion, as the word "end" can in English. *Finis* is derived from the verb *finire*, from which we also have the adjective *finitum*, which is also formed from the perfect participle of the verb. Now *finitum* could have been used as a translation for the adjective *teleion*, as it was in some medieval translations, but this was seen as leading to a serious confusion. The verb *finire* did not suggest anything of the positive fulfillment implied in the idea of *telos* or the verb *teleiein* or *teleein*. It had only the idea of ceasing, as *finis* had only the idea of a boundary, which was expressed in Greek, not by *telos*, but by *terma* or *peras*. Thus the Latins had to come up with a better word to express the idea of *teleiōsis*, and in thinking of *perfectio* they hit upon a very good way of keeping the idea related to the process with which it is associated. It is this relation which St. Thomas exploits in his analysis of the original meaning of the name "perfect."

It is with this idea of perfection as positive completion of a process that the idea of act is associated in Aquinas, but the idea of act itself is first understood in connection with motion. In the commentary on the *Metaphysics* Aquinas writes:

This name act which is posited to signify entelechy and perfection, namely, form, and other names like that, as are operations of any sort, comes mainly from notions with regard to the origin of the word. For inasmuch as names are signs of intelligible conceptions, we first impose names on those things which we first understand, even though they are posterior according to the order of nature. Among other acts, however, motion, which is seen sensibly by us, is the most known and apparent to us. And therefore to it was the name act first imposed, and from motion it was derived to other things.[9]

Motion is thus the first kind of act we know, but it is a very peculiar kind of perfection. As motion it is still imperfect. It is an *actus imperfectus*, as the classical definition of Aristotle tries to say: the act of something existing in potency insofar as it is in potency. Potency denotes imperfection in this definition so that motion has to be viewed as a passage from imperfection to perfection. As act, motion is already

---

9. *In IX Metaph.*, lect. 3, n. 1805: "Hoc nomen actus, quod ponitur ad significandum endelechiam et perfectionem, scilicet formam, et alia huiusmodi, sicut sunt quaecumque operationes, veniunt maxime ex motibus quantum ad originem vocabuli. Cum enim nomina sint signa intelligibilium conceptionum, illis primo imponimus nomina, quae primo intelligimus, licet sint posteriora secundum ordinem naturae. Inter alios autem actus, maxime est nobis notus et apparens motus, qui sensibiliter a nobis videtur. Et ideo ei primo impositum fuit nomen actus, et a motu ad alia derivatum est" (Marietti, p. 432).

some perfection, but as only motion, that is, as still only in process to its completion, it is imperfect. Much as we may think of this act, it is still not complete fulfillment or the perfection of the process.

What this shows, however, is that the idea of perfection allows for degrees: degrees in the gradual passage from imperfection to perfection over time and degrees in various levels of perfection to which different kinds of motion can rise. This becomes an important aspect of the idea of perfection for elaborating the idea of the universe, as we shall see in a moment. But it is also an important aspect for keeping the idea of perfection itself positively open so that it can yield a positive idea of infinity, as we saw Aquinas do in transposing the idea of perfection, which initially presupposes a coming to be, to God, who does not come to be but who can still be thought of as act insofar as He has nothing of not being or imperfection. Such an act is not only pure act insofar as it is not from any coming to be, but also infinite in a positive way insofar as it transcends all finitude.

The idea of finitude can be very ambivalent without a proper understanding of Aquinas's logic of perfection. It is easy to see how a movement or a process can be terminated or *finished* without having reached its completion, that is, the perfection which such a process naturally leads to, as in the generation of an oak, a human being, or even the construction of a house. Without the positive perfection, however, we think of the finished motion as *unfinished,* like an unfinished symphony, since the per-fection of the process calls for something more, which is still lacking or left out when the process is cut short. Something is perfect or, better still, perfected, when it retains nothing of its not being or when it is all that it should be. Finitude can thus refer to the perfection of a thing, when it has reached its proper completion. But it can also refer to its imperfection, when its motion has been cut off before attaining its perfection.

Similarly infinity, or the negation of finitude, can also relate to perfection in two ways. There is an infinite we associate with imperfection, as when we speak of something as unfinished. But there is also an infinite we associate with perfection, in which case perfection is seen as without limitation, excluding even the limitation of deriving from any coming to be. This is completion of a kind different from any we know from experience, which always entails motion. It is a *supercompletion,* to borrow from Neoplatonic language, as we shall see Aquinas do at one point. But it is nevertheless positive completion, apart from any incompletion we may know in the realm of coming to be.

It is sometimes thought that the Greeks did not have this idea of infinity as perfection or positive completion. But that is perhaps because the precise meaning of *telos,* from which the idea of perfection of *teleiōsis* is taken, is not always kept clearly in mind. Liddell and Scott suggest that the strict sense of *telos* is not so much the ending of a past state as the arrival at a complete or perfect one. Aristotle confirms this interpretation in *Metaphysics,* Book 5, when he distinguishes *teleion,* or perfect, from *peras,* or boundary, which means either the last part (*to eschaton*) of something outside of which no part of it can be found or the end (*to telos*) of each thing in the sense of the point beyond which it does not seek to go.[10]

There is thus a sense in which perfection and finitude overlap, because things which have attained their end (*telos*) are called perfect (*teleia*). But this is only in the sense that the end is equivalent to something that is last (*to eschaton ti*). This is what allows us to speak of even a destructive action as perfect in that it leads to perfect destruction. Hence termination of anything (*teleutē*), as of a life in death, is called an end only by analogy. In the original meaning perfect refers to an end that is good or sought positively (*spoudaion*). The reason for the overlapping is that perfection, as the arrival of a complete or perfect state, is associated with movement and connotes a cessation or a termination of movement, a quiescence in the perfect state, though not a purely negative end as in the sense of termination or extermination.

The opposite of "the end" understood as boundary or as last is *to apeiron,* which is usually translated as "the infinite." In this sense the infinite has nothing to do with perfection. It only means indeterminate or a lack of limit. The opposite of "the end" understood as perfection, on the other hand, is *to atelēs,* which is better translated as "the unfinished" in the sense of incomplete or imperfect. This brings out an important difference of meanings which both terms, finite and infinite, can have. If we extend the meaning of perfection beyond movement, we can then include, not something negative like mere termination, but something positive that is no longer associated with movement, as in the case of divine perfection or even the perfection of pure forms.

In his commentary on the passage from the *Metaphysics* we have been referring to, St. Thomas clearly focuses on this distinction between "perfect" and "boundary", which in Latin comes out as the difference between *perfectum* and *terminus.* He speaks of *terminus,* or "boundary," as a "condition of the perfect," not perfection itself, a condition that is tied to its association with movement, as it was for Aristotle. In another "condition" the perfect could be without bound-

10. *Metaphysics* 5.17.1022a4–9.

ary. It is only in our experience, which is of things in movement, that the condition of the perfect coincides with boundary. But even under this condition perfection still transcends movement and time. For, as Aquinas writes in the *Summa theologiae,* "although to be moved toward perfection may not be totally simultaneous [*totum simul*], still to attain natural perfection is totally simultaneous."[11]

With this distinction between boundary, as only a condition of perfection, and perfection itself, it is easy to see how St. Thomas could agree with Aristotle in saying that "nothing infinite and unterminated is perfect,"[12] since it has not gone through to the end of its motion, and still go on to attribute some kind of infinity to the Unmoved Mover, with the claim, in opposition to Averroes, that Aristotle himself did this. In its first meaning the infinite is taken to apply to sensible things and is taken to mean "something whose nature is not to be gone through, for the infinite is the same as the intransible."[13] This is the bad infinite, as Hegel would say, since it does not allow for completion or perfection. It is shown not to be actual in *Physics* 3. This is also the infinite which cannot be defined as "that outside of which there is nothing," as some predecessors of Aristotle had claimed, since that is the definition of the whole or the perfect and, as we have seen, "nothing lacking an end is perfect."

But this is the infinite only in the *privative* sense, which is said of things whose nature is to have an end but don't have it and which is found only in quantities. There is also the infinite taken in a *negative* sense, that is, taken as "that which has no end." In this negative sense the infinite can be said of God with regard to all that is in Him, "since He is not Himself bounded [*non finitur*] by anything, nor is His essence, His wisdom, or His goodness, so that all things in Him are infinite."[14] In fact, as St. Thomas writes in the *Compendium theologiae,* "Since God is infinite by reason of [the fact] that He is only form or act, having no admixture of matter or potentiality, His infinity pertains to His

11. ST I-II, q. 31, a. 1, c.: "Quamvis moveri ad perfectionem non sit totum simul, tamen consequi naturalem perfectionem est totum simul."

12. *In III Physicorum,* lect. 11, n. 385: "Finis autem est terminus eius cuius est finis: nullum igitur infinitum et interminatum est perfectum" (Marietti, p. 189).

13. Ibid., lect. 7, n. 344: "Sic igitur et uno modo dicitur infinitum, quod non est natum transiri (nam infinitum idem est quod intransibile)" (Marietti, p. 170).

14. *De Potentia,* q. 1, a. 2, c.: "Infinitum dicitur dupliciter. Uno modo privative; et sic dicitur infinitum quod natum est habere finem et non habet: tale autem infinitum non invenitur nisi in quantitatibus. Alio modo dicitur infinitum negative, id est quod non habet finem. Infinitum primo modo acceptum Deo convenire non potest, tum quia Deus est absque quantitate, tum quia omnis privatio imperfectionem disignat, quae longe a Deo est. Infinitum autem dictum negative convenit Deo quantum ad omnia quae in ipso sunt. Quia nec ipse aliquo finitur, nec eius essentia, nec sapientia, nec potentia, nec bonitas; unde omnia in ipso sunt infinita" (Marietti, p. 11).

highest perfection."[15] In the commentary on *Physics* 8 he even goes so far as to argue, against Averroes, that infinity as understood by Aristotle should not be restricted to the material and quantifiable but that it could be understood as a highest perfection above time (*in non tempore*) applicable to the Unmoved Mover.[16]

All this is admirably summed up in a passage from the *Summa theologiae* which is well worth quoting at some length here:

Something is said to be infinite from [the fact] that it is not finite. However, both matter is somehow made finite [*finitur*] through form and form through matter. Matter through form, inasmuch as matter, before it receives form, is in potency to many forms, but when it receives one it is terminated [*terminatur*] through it. But form is made finite [*finitur*] through matter, inasmuch as form considered in itself is common to many, but through being received in matter it becomes determinately the form of this thing. Matter, however, is perfected [*perficitur*] through form, through which it is made finite [*finitur*]; and hence the infinite, as it is attributed to matter, has the idea of [something] imperfect; for it is like matter not having form. Form, however, is not perfected [*non perficitur*] through matter, but rather, through matter its amplitude is contracted; hence the infinite, according to the way it is held on the part of a form not determined through matter, has the idea of [something] perfect.[17]

With this we can see, not only how the infinite can pertain to the highest perfection, but also how the whole idea of perfection relates back to the idea of being in motion even when it is transposed to pure form and pure act.

To complete this first understanding of the logic of perfection let us add only one more distinction within the idea which will prove important for understanding both the perfection of individual beings and the perfection of the universe. I mean the distinction between second and first perfection which St. Thomas uses constantly and which sets him apart from any philosophy of mere process, where no such distinction is made.

15. *Comp. Theol.* I, chap. 20: "Cum igitur Deus ex hoc infinitus sit quia tantum forma uel actus, nullam materiae uel potentialitatis permixitionem habens, sua infinitas ad summam perfectionem ipsius pertinet" (Leonine, p. 88).

16. *In VIII Physicorum*, lect. 21 (Marietti, pp. 610–17).

17. ST I, q. 7, a. 1, c.: "Infinitum dicitur aliquid ex eo quod non est finitum. Finitur autem quodammodo et materia per formam, et forma per materiam. Materia quidem per formam, inquantum materia, antequam recipiat formam, est in potentia ad multas formas; sed cum recipit unam, terminatur per illam. Forma vero finitur per materiam, inquantum forma, in se considerata, communis est ad multa, sed per hoc quod recipitur in materia, fit forma determinate huius rei.—Materia autem perficitur per formam per quam finitur; et ideo infinitum secundum quod attribuitur materiae, habet rationem imperfecti; est enim quasi materia non habens formam. Forma autem non perficitur per materiam, sed magis per eam eius amplitudo contrahitur; unde infinitum secundum quod se tenet ex parte formae non determinatae per materiam, habet rationem perfecti."

This distinction is based on a twofold understanding of the end or the *telos* with regard to nature. First, there is the end of the process by which a thing comes to be, the *finis generationis,* in which a thing reaches the perfection of its substantial form. But then there is the end or the *telos* for which this thing itself has come to be in its first perfection, the *finis rei generatae,* which is to be achieved through its action, of which substantial form is the principle. "The imperfect is always for something more perfect: therefore, just as matter is for form, so also form, which is first act, is for its operation, which is second act; and so operation is the end of a created thing."[18] This is illustrated by Aquinas in the way a human being comes to be: "The end of the generation of a man is the human form; yet the end of man is not his form, but through form it is fitting for him to act toward an end."[19]

It is important to think of beings in their first perfection, if we are to think of them as whole beings in their substance. But it is no less important to think of them in their second perfection, since it is only through their action that they achieve their final perfection. This is part of St. Thomas's understanding of every being as active and it relates to perfection in that action itself is an act that comes to a being constituted in its first perfection as that being's second or ulterior perfection.

Moreover, this second perfection is something that pertains not only to things taken in isolation. Action is at the same time an interaction among beings which ties them together as a universe, for as St. Thomas argues against the occasionalists, to take away action from creatures is to take away from the order of the universe, which is to take away from the highest perfection in creation. "That which is the greatest good in created things is the good of the order of the universe, which is what is most perfect, as the Philosopher says, with whom Divine Scripture agrees [*consonat*] when it says, in Genesis 1:31, 'God saw all things which he had made, and they were very good', after it had said about each single work simply that 'they were good'."[20]

18. ST I, q. 105, a. 5, c.: "Semper enim imperfectum est propter perfectius; sicut igitur materia est propter formam, ita forma, quae est actus primus, est propter suam operationem, quae est actus secundus; et sic operatio est finis rei creatae."

19. *In II Physicorum,* lect. 11, n. 242: "Finis enim generationis hominis est forma humana; non tamen finis hominis est forma eius, sed per formam suam convenit sibi operari ad finem" (Marietti, p. 117).

20. SCG III, chap. 64: "Id autem quod est maxime bonum in rebus causatis, est bonum ordinis universi, quod est maxime perfectum, ut Philosophus dicit: cui etiam consonat Scriptura Divina, Gen. 1, cum dicitur, 31, 'Vidit Deus cuncta quae fecerat, et erant valde bona,' cum de singulis operibus dixisset simpliciter quod 'erant bona'."

PERFECTION AND THE UNIVERSE

Thus, with Aquinas, we pass spontaneously from the idea of perfection to the idea of the universe. In doing so, however, we should note that, unlike the infinite in the privative sense or as relating to matter and potency, which we saw earlier, the universe, even though it includes matter and potency, can be defined in the same way as perfection itself, namely, as that outside of which there is nothing. Prescinding from God, who is not numbered among created things, the universe is that which includes everything created. In saying this we are already saying that the universe is somehow perfect.

But to speak of perfection more precisely with regard to the universe we must think of perfection as some kind of wholeness or totality. "The perfect and the whole are the same or mean almost the same, as it is said in *Physics* 3."[21] In commenting on the text of the *Physics* he refers to, St. Thomas writes as follows: "Each whole is defined to be *that to which nothing is lacking*: as we say a man is whole or a box is whole when they lack nothing of what they should have." From this, however, Aquinas immediately leaps to the idea of the universe: "Just as we say this about any singular whole, as this particular thing or that, so also this idea applies to what is truly and properly whole, namely, the universe, outside of which there is simply nothing."[22] The universe is that which is most properly a whole and therefore what is most perfect in what is created. It is, as St. Thomas says, universally perfect.

The first thing which Aquinas thinks of as universally perfect is still God, the condition of whose perfection is to be lacking absolutely nothing at all, to be excelled by nothing whatsoever in goodness, and to need nothing from any external goodness. "In Him there is the most perfect goodness, lacking nothing of all the perfections to be found in particular genera."[23] But that is universal perfection in a being that is absolutely simple. There is also universal perfection for a whole made up of parts, and this is the universal perfection of the

21. *In V Metaph.*, lect. 18, n. 1033: "Perfectum enim et totum, aut sunt idem, aut fere idem significant, ut dicitur in tertio *Physicorum*" (Marietti, p. 271).

22. *In III Physicorum*, lect. 11, n. 385: "Definitur enim unumquodque totum esse *cui nihil deest*: sicut dicimus hominem totum aut arcam totam, quibus nihil deest eorum quae debent habere. Et sicut hoc dicimus in aliquo singulari toto, ut est hoc particulare vel illud, ita etiam haec ratio competit in eo quod est vere et proprie totum, scilicet in universo, extra quod simpliciter nihil est" (Marietti, p. 189).

23. *In V Metaph.*, lect. 18, n. 1040: "Et haec est conditio primi principii, scilicet Dei, in quo est perfectissima bonitas, cui nihil deest de omnibus perfectionibus in singulis generibus inventis" (Marietti, p. 272).

universe. "The world [*mundus*] is said to be perfect universally, because there is nothing entirely [*omnino nihil*] outside of it."[24]

To speak of perfection as totality, however, is to imply a certain relation between a whole, which is what is perfect, and its parts, which also have their perfection but only in relation to one another and to the whole. Parts as such are imperfect in relation to the whole. But more importantly for understanding the perfection of the universe, different degrees of perfection in the whole call for different degrees of diversity among the parts of the whole. Thus a body of water, which has a low degree of wholeness in comparison to, say, the body of an animal, allows for an almost complete similarity of its parts. But the body of an animal, on the other hand, does not allow for such similarity among its parts for its perfection. Its perfection requires a greater diversity and order among its parts. "More perfect forms have more operations that are more diverse than less perfect forms," and this in turn requires a "diversity of parts, and the more so the more the form is perfect. . . . Hence, since the rational soul is the most perfect of natural forms, in man is found the greatest distinction of parts because of the diverse operations."[25] This is the analogy which St. Thomas will use in speaking of diversity as a condition for the perfection of the universe, that is, the highest perfection in creation, since it includes that of the human being as well as that of all other creatures.

It is possible to think of each particular being in creation as somehow perfect in itself or in its genus. But as a particular being relative to or bounded by other particular beings, it remains imperfect. It is not all perfection or perfect in all respects. To paraphrase an argument which is given at the beginning of the commentary on *De caelo*, where it has to do only with bodies, the whole or the universe, whose parts are the particular beings or species of being, has to be necessarily perfect in all modes and, as the name "universe" itself signifies, perfect in every way (*omniquaque*), that is, in all modes, and not according to one mode in such a way that it is not in another, because it both has all perfections and comprehends all beings within itself.[26]

According to the analogy we saw a moment ago, this perfection of

24. Ibid., n. 1042: "Sed mundus dicitur perfectus universaliter, quia omnino nihil extra ipsum est."

25. *De anima*, q. 9, c.: "Unde formae perfectiores habent plures operationes et magis diversas quam formae minus perfectae. . . . in rebus autem magis perfectis requiritur ulterius diversitas partium, et tanto magis quanto forma fuerit perfectior. . . . Unde cum anima rationalis sit perfectissima formarum materialium, in homine invenitur maxima distinctio partium propter diversas operationes" (Robb, p. 148).

26. *In I De caelo*, lect. 2, n. 18 (Marietti, p. 11).

the universe, which is the highest in creation, requires the highest diversity. The greater the diversity, the higher will be the perfection, as we see in the progression of diversity and perfection among the beings found in nature, with the rational soul at the summit. This is a principle of perfection for St. Thomas which has a certain necessity about it, though it is not one that determines the Creator of the universe. It is a concrete necessity that presupposes the intention to create, which remains free, and to create the universe with this particular form or configuration, which is not necessitated in any way on the part of God. But given this intention to create this universe made manifest in the universe itself, the form of the universe shows a necessity for diversity that is greater than for any particular being, including the rational animal.

God could have made the universe better by adding parts to it or by making each part better still, as Aquinas argued in the commentary on the *Sentences*,[27] since no created perfection can ever manifest adequately the uncreated perfection of God or is ever required for the perfection of God. But the universe that He does create has its perfection in the diversity of the parts from which it is integrated (*ex quibus integratur*).

Be it said in passing that "parts" here refer primarily to the diversity of the species in the universe, and not to the individuals of the species. It is the species that pertain *per se* to the order of the universe. Individuals pertain to that order only *per accidens*, that is, insofar as they are required for the perpetuation of the species through time. For Aquinas, only the rational individual is in direct relation to the perfection of the whole and so pertains *per se* to the order and perfection of the whole. This is made clear in terms of the twofold perfection of things:

> The first perfection is found when a thing is perfect in its substance; and this perfection is the form of the whole, which arises from the integrity of the parts. The second perfection, however, is the end; but the end is either the action, as the end of the zitherist is to play the zither, or is something arrived at by action, as the end of the builder is the house, which he makes by building. The first perfection, however, is the cause of the second, because the form is the principle of action. But the ultimate perfection, which is the end of the whole universe, is the perfect happiness of the saints, which will take place in the final consummation of time [*saeculi*].[28]

27. *In I Sent.*, d. 44, q. 1, a. 2 (Mandonnet, pp. 1015–18).
28. ST I, q. 73, a. 1, c.: "Prima quidem perfectio est, secundum quod res in sua substantia est perfecta. Quae quidem perfectio est forma totius, quae ex integritate partium consurgit. Perfectio autem secunda est finis. Finis autem vel est operatio, sicut finis citharistae est citharizare; vel est aliquid ad quod per operationem pervenitur, sicut

To understand the ultimate perfection of the universe we must therefore understand its final consummation at the end of time which will
include the perfection of rational individuals, an idea which Aquinas
employed to argue for an end in time as more rational than Aristotle's
position with regard to the duration of the motion of the world.[29] But
to do so we must also understand the first perfection or the form of
the universe out of which this ultimate perfection has to flow. This
first perfection, "which is the integrity of the universe, was in the first
instauration of things."[30] Because this integrity entailed a diversity of
parts for St. Thomas, he never thought of creation merely as production of things in being. He always thought of it as a distinction and a
diversification of things as well, as we see in the organization of both
the *Summa contra gentiles* and the *Summa theologiae*, where the discussion
of the production of things is always followed by a discussion of their
distinction into diverse kinds of being.

Having said that diversity was essential to the perfection of the universe, we might ask what the essential parts of the universe were for
Aquinas in order to see how he represented this perfection of the
universe to himself. Nowhere does he draw up a complete list of essential parts as such, but we can infer what such a list would include
from his discussion of what would remain in the final state of the
universe after the consummation of time.

First on the list would be separate substances, since they are not
only superior parts, but also principal parts that participate most intimately in the order of the universe. "Each separate substance is much
more of a principal part of the universe than the sun or the moon,
since each one of them has its proper species and one more noble
than any species of bodily things."[31] Their immateriality notwithstand-
ing, these substances were seen as belonging to the same order as that
of material substances since "it is fitting for them to have been established together [*simul*] with corporeal substance."[32]

Among the corporeal substances there are two kinds which bear a

finis aedificatoris est domus, quam aedificando facit. Prima autem perfectio est causa
secundae, quia forma est principium operationis. Ultima autem perfectio, quae est finis
totius universi, est perfecta beatitudo Sanctorum, quae erit in ultima consummatione
saeculi."
29. *De potentia*, q. 5, a. 5, c. (Marietti, p. 143).
30. ST I, q. 73, a. 1, c.: "Prima autem perfectio, quae est in integritate universi, fuit
in prima rerum institutione."
31. SCG II, chap. 98: "Unaquaeque autem substantiarum separatarum est de prin-
cipalibus partibus universi multo amplius quam sol vel luna, cum unaquaeque earum
habeat propriam speciem et nobiliorem quam quaevis species corporalium rerum."
32. *De potentia*, q. 3, a. 18, c.: "Competit eis quod simul cum creatura corporali sint
conditi" (Marietti, p. 99).

special resemblance to separate substances and consequently are also parts of the universe in their own special way. First, there is the rational individual whose soul makes it an essential part of the universe. "Man is ordered to the perfection of the universe as an essential part of it since in man is something that is not contained in any power whether it be in the heavenly bodies or in the elements, namely, a rational soul."[33]

Then, according to the ancient cosmology, there are the heavenly bodies, which have no souls for Aquinas, but which resemble separate substances in that they are incorruptible and each unique in its species. This also entails a special affinity to the order of the universe, as it indicates a higher degree of perfection in bodily existence as such. Hence they too were viewed as "essential parts of the universe."[34]

Among the corruptible bodies here below, the four elements also had a special place in the order of the universe as such insofar as "the entire machine of the world had its consistence" from them as well as from the heavenly bodies.[35] Thus the elements, corruptible though they were, as well as the heavenly bodies, were destined to remain in the final state of the world along with the glorified bodies of the risen human beings. Needless to say, the scientific view which this represents has been superseded, but it is worth recalling here to show how Aquinas saw the physical world as essentially structured in a way that pertained to the perfection of the universe.

But what of all the other species of corporeal beings, the compounds, the minerals, the plants, the brute animals, in short, all the intermediate species between the elements and human bodies? Were they also considered essential parts of the universe? St. Thomas denied them a place in the definitive state of the universe on the grounds that they "were not ordered as existing *per se* and essentially pertaining to the perfection of the universe."[36]

At first glance this seems surprising, since St. Thomas did think of the natural order going from minerals to plants to animals to humans as an order of perfection *per se* among species which are properly parts of the universe. But he distinguished between two states of the universe: the final state, which is one of immobility, since the end has

33. Ibid., q. 5, a. 10, c.: "Homo ordinatur ad perfectionem universi ut essentialis pars ipsius, cum in homine sit aliquid quod non continetur virtute nec in elementis nec in caelestibus corporibus, scilicet anima rationalis" (Marietti, p. 156).

34. *Comp. Theol.* I, chap. 170: "Sunt autem partes eius essentiales corpora caelestia . . ." (Leonine, p. 147).

35. ". . . utpote ex quibus tota mundi machina consistit" (ibid.).

36. *De potentia*, q. 5, a. 9, c.:". . . non ordinantur sicut per se et essentialiter de perfectione universi existentes" (Marietti, p. 154).

been reached, and the present state, which is one of mobility. Some things which pertain to the perfection of the universe in its present state will no longer be required in its final state. What will remain in the final state will be only what is essential to the universe as such. This includes bodies that are part of the integral structure of the physical world, but not the intermediate species which pertain to the perfection of the universe only in its transitory state. In fact, these intermediate bodies are "particular effects of the universal causes, which are the essential parts of the universe; and therefore they belong to the perfection of the universe only inasmuch as they proceed from their causes, which happens through motion. Hence they pertain to the perfection of the universe as it exists in motion, not the perfection of the universe simply."[37] This is why these intermediate species will not be found in the final state of the universe though they do remain part of the *per se* order of perfection while the world is still in motion.

This distinction between the two states of the universe leads into an interesting question as to St. Thomas's understanding of how the universe as a whole is in motion. Could it be that he had some idea of evolution in mind? Clearly he did, if we think of evolution as a succession of individuals that perpetuate species and in this way contribute to the perfection of the universe in its state of motion. But did he think of an evolution of the species in the way we think of it today? This is far from clear, though he did suggest something that resembles such an evolutionary conception of perfection even for the order of species.

He does assert that "in its beginning the universe was perfect with regard to species."[38] By this he meant that the universe had all its essential species from the start. But then we must ask what was included among those original essential species in which the initial perfection of the universe consisted. For Aquinas did admit that a gradual formation of the universe would better manifest the order of divine wisdom in creation. "In order to demonstrate the order of divine wisdom in the institution of things, He who produced things in being from nothing did not institute them immediately after nothing in the ultimate perfection of nature, but first he made them in a certain imperfect being [*esse*], and afterward brought them to perfection, so

37. ". . . particulares effectus causarum universalium, quae sunt essentiales partes universi; et ideo de perfectione sunt universi secundum hoc tantum quod a suis causis progrediuntur, quod quidem fit per motum. Unde pertinent ad perfectionem universi sub motu existentis, non autem ad perfectionem universi simpliciter" (ibid.).

38. *De potentia*, q. 3, a. 10, ad 2: "Universum in sui principio fuit perfectum quantum ad species . . ." (Marietti, p. 71).

that the world would thus gradually proceed from nothing to its ultimate perfection."[39] In fact, even on the hypothesis of instantaneous formation of the universe from the beginning, with all species present, St. Thomas did not think that the world was created from the start as it was actually in his day, but that some evolution had in fact taken place as he explains in terms of causes. In the beginning the world was perfect, he writes, "with regard to the causes of natural things, from which afterward other things can be propagated, but not with regard to all the effects."[40]

This could be read as referring only to the propagation of individuals within the species given in the initial perfection of the universe. Yet it did not positively exclude the possibility of adding new species which, according to another text, would not be an everyday affair, as was the addition of individuals,[41] but could still be seen as compatible with the initial perfection of the universe, as St. Thomas had to recognize when he observed the appearance of what seemed to him new species. "Even if there do appear new species, they pre-existed in certain active powers, as in the case of animals generated from putrefaction; they are produced from the powers of the stars and the elements which they received from the beginning, even though new species of such animals are produced. There are also certain animals that arise sometimes according to a new species from intercourse between animals that differ according to species, as when a mule is generated from an ass and a mare, but these also came before causally in the works of the six days [of creation according to Genesis]."[42]

This is surely far from any general theory of the evolution of species, but it shows how St. Thomas could accommodate what little evidence he had that some such evolution might take place in what remained for him rare cases with his understanding of the initial

---

39. *De potentia*, q. 4, a. 2, c.: ". . . ut ordo divinae sapientiae in rerum institutione demonstraretur, qui res ex nihilo in esse producens non statim post nihilum in ultima perfectione naturae eas instituit, sed primo fecit eas in quodam esse imperfecto, et postea eas ad perfectum adduxit, ut sic gradatim ex nihilo ad ultimam perfectionem mundus perveniret" (Marietti, pp. 115–16).

40. *De potentia*, q. 3, a. 10, ad 2: ". . . quantum ad causas rerum naturalium, ex quibus possunt postmodum alia propagari, non quantum ad omnes effectus" (Marietti, p. 71).

41. ST I, q. 118, a. 3, ad 2.

42. ST I, q. 73, a. 1, ad 3: "Species etiam novae, si quae apparent, praeexistiterunt in quibusdam activis virtutibus, sicut et animalia ex putrefactione generata producuntur ex virtutibus stellarum et elementorum quas a principio acceperunt, etiamsi novae species talium animalium producantur. Animalia etiam quaedam secundum novam speciem aliquando oriuntur ex commixtione animalium diversorum secundum speciem, sicut cum ex asino et equa generatur mulus; et haec etiam praecesserunt causaliter in operibus sex dierum."

perfection of the universe. In fact, in his reading of Genesis he could even distinguish between some parts, like the fishes of the sea, the birds of the air, and the animals of the land as adornments of the various parts of the universe, adornments which came after the *opus creationis* itself, through which he understood the heaven and the earth to have been produced, though still unformed (*informia*), and after the *opus distinctionis*, through which the heaven and the earth are perfected or fully formed. "To these two works," he writes, "is added adornment: and adornment differs from perfection for the perfection of heaven and earth seems to pertain to those things that are intrinsic to heaven and earth, whereas adornment pertains to things distinct from heaven and earth; for example, man is made perfect by his proper parts and forms, but he is adorned by clothes or anything like that."[43]

In this text, "the heaven and the earth" refer to the essential structure of the physical world in the mind of Aquinas and the adornment stands for the intermediate species we spoke of earlier as pertaining to the perfection of the universe only while it is in its present state of motion. In the commentary on *De caelo* these intermediate species are referred to "as secondary parts [of the universe] which pertain more to its well-being [*bene esse*] than to its first integrity."[44] "Bodies of this kind which come to be and cease to be, such as animals and plants and stones, are not properly parts of the world (otherwise the world would never be perfect, since it does not have all such things at once); but they are rather certain effects of the world."[45] In other words, they are particular effects of the universal causes of the world, as we saw earlier, while it exists in motion.

Given the scientific cosmological model with which he was working, St. Thomas could not have come to a theory of the evolution of species as we understand it today. But even within such a model we see how his idea of perfection as found in the universe existing in motion was almost straining toward such a theory. Had he been presented with the evidence we now have for such a theory of evolution, not only

---

43. ST I, q. 70, a. 1, c.: ". . . et his duobus operibus additur ornatus; et differt ornatus a perfectione, nam perfectio caeli et terrae ad ea pertinere videtur quae caelo et terrae sunt intrinseca; ornatur vero ad ea quae sunt a caelo et terra distincta; sicut homo perficitur per proprias partes et formas; ornatur autem per vestimenta, vel aliquid huiusmodi."

44. *In I De caelo*, lect. 3, n. 19: ". . . secundariae partes eius, quae magis pertinent ad bene esse ipsius quam ad primam eius integritatem" (Marietti, p. 14).

45. *In II De caelo*, lect. 1, n. 289: ". . . huiusmodi corpora quae sunt generabilia et corruptibilia, sicut animalia et plantae et lapides, non proprie sunt partes mundi (alioquin mundus nunquam perfectus esset, cum non habeat omnia huiusmodi simul): sed huiusmodi sunt quidem effectus partium mundi" (Marietti, p. 144).

would he have found no contradiction between it and his understanding of the initial production and distinction of things in creation as presented in the Bible, but he would rather have found in it another way of showing the wisdom and the power of God, who not only produces beings perfect in their nature but gives them power to act on their own and to produce or cause other beings as parts of the universe on its way to ultimate perfection. For the action of creatures was for Aquinas an essential feature of the perfection of the universe.

NEOCLASSICAL AND CLASSICAL LOGIC OF PERFECTION

It remains for us to compare this logic of perfection with that of Hartshorne, who, speaking of his version as neoclassical, both underlines a certain continuity with the classical logic of perfection as found, say, in Anselm and Descartes, and signals a departure from certain basic suppositions about God which this logic shared with other logics that did not admit the ontological argument based on the idea of perfection, suppositions about God as *Ens perfectissimum* and as pure Act above and beyond all becoming. Hartshorne's metaphysics is resolutely a metaphysics of becoming as opposed to a metaphysics of being or, more exactly, of substance; and this metaphysics, which has its logic of perfection, tries to include God in its becoming.

Hartshorne, like Anselm, whose influence he readily admits, starts from a *total* religious commitment and then reasons to the existence of the *perfection* which such a commitment implies, but in a way that differs from Anselm. His intention is to reinstate the ontological argument, albeit in a new mode. He argues that "perfection cannot be of one type with ordinary predicates, and this for at least ten reasons."[46] Moreover, as we mentioned at the outset, he identifies this perfection, which is definable *a priori* for him, with the divine.[47]

What is new about this neoclassical idea of perfection, according to Hartshorne, is that it now includes potentiality as well as actuality in the divine perfection, so that it can properly be "conceived as open to embodiments, states, which are contingent—save only in the logical exclusion of no-embodiment."[48] In other words, the *a priori* argument based on the definition of perfection does arrive at a "necessary existence," but one which "is not actuality, plus something, some necessity or other. It is nothing actual at all, but an essence, embodied in any and every *total* state of contingent actuality."[49]

46. Hartshorne, *The Logic of Perfection*, 31.
47. Ibid., 33–34.   48. Ibid., 65.
49. Ibid., 102 (emphasis added).

Actualities include the possibility of not having existed and exclude some possibilities, as any reflection on the concrete state of the universe will show. But divine perfection is not to be separated from such contingent things, since that would make it poorer than the actualities are. Rather, actualities are to be conceived as embodiments of divine perfection, conceived on the one hand as necessary, in that some concrete instance of an otherwise abstract divine perfection is necessary, and on the other hand as contingent, in that no particular instance is similarly necessary. The supposedly divine perfection can be and is in fact embodied in any particular state of affairs.

It will be noted that this logic of perfection is rather like that of Aquinas in that it associates the idea of perfection with potentiality and coming to be and sees perfection as having to be embodied in the universe. Hartshorne is operating with an idea of universal perfection which is quite similar to that of Aquinas, except that he has collapsed what were two very distinct ideas of universal perfection in Aquinas into one, or perhaps more exactly, he has reduced the divine perfection to the perfection of the universe. For everything which Hartshorne says about divine perfection could be said about what Aquinas refers to as the perfection of the universe. Perfection of itself, that is, apart from the actual parts of the universe, is only an abstraction. But as the perfection of the universe it is an abstraction that has to be thought of as embodied in some concrete order of actualities.

Hartshorne's ontological argument flows from a very fundamental distinction "between an individual (a) in its abstract identity and (b) in its concrete actual states."[50] Thus, all one has to do to meet the conditions of his ontological argument is to show that the idea of perfection, which is unlike all other predicates, does in fact apply to an individual, that is, to one that will of course be unique but one that will also be open to a plurality of states of contingent actuality. The question for us then is to identify this unique individual. Is it the divine as such or is it the universe understood as this individual totality, which is what comes closest to the divine in creation but which is still to be distinguished from the divine? Hartshorne speaks of his position as a sort of panentheism, as distinct from straight pantheism, but it is not one which St. Thomas would readily endorse even though it uses an idea of universal perfection which he made much of.

Aquinas does distinguish between the abstract and the concrete as Hartshorne does in terms of perfection, but his distinction turns out somewhat differently when it comes to speaking about God and creatures:

50. Ibid., 65.

For in all things that are below the first cause some are found to be perfectly existing or complete, others imperfect or diminished: the perfect indeed are seen to be those that subsist *per se* in nature, and they are signified by us through concrete names such as wise man and that sort of thing; the imperfect, however, are those that do not subsist *per se* like forms such as humanity, wisdom and that sort of thing, which are signified among us by abstract names.[51]

In this we see how the concrete has to be seen as more perfect than the abstract, as Hartshorne claims. But Aquinas makes the point more emphatically by saying that the imperfect is what "cannot bring an operation to perfection; for it is not heat that heats, but what is hot; nor is wisdom wise, but one who is wise—*neque sapientia sapit, sed sapiens*."[52] The same connection between perfection and concretion can be made in terms of the composition between form and matter: "The form in things around us is found to be simple, but imperfect, insofar as it does not subsist: what has the form, however, is found to be subsistent, but not simple, indeed as having concretion."[53]

We can see here the point of insertion for St. Thomas's metaphysics of *esse* or the act of being, which is "the actuality of acts and hence the perfection of all perfections."[54] The composite itself, which has its own form or act, is at the same time in potency to or finds its completion in a further act, that of *esse*, in which it participates concretely. But we can see also how this metaphysics of being is not in opposition to a metaphysics of becoming. It simply complements it in its understanding of being as the perfection of perfection, that is, as a perfection which transcends the perfection which is still associated with becoming. The reason why St. Thomas thinks of the concrete as more perfect than the abstract is not only that it has reached a certain level of completion but also that it has *esse*, which for him is "signified through the mode of concretion" and from which, as found in the things around us, he will take his science to rise to the One he refers to concretely as *Esse subsistens* or, more abstractly, as *Esse per essentiam*.[55]

51. *In De causis*, 22: "In omnibus enim quae sunt infra causam primam, quaedam inveniuntur perfecte existentia sive completa, quaedam imperfecta sive diminuta. Perfecta quidem videntur esse ea quae per se subsistunt in natura, quae a nobis significantur per nomina concreta ut homo, sapiens et huiusmodi; imperfecta autem sunt illa quae per se non subsistunt, sicut formae ut humanitas, sapientia et huiusmodi, quae significantur apud nos nominibus abstractis" (Saffrey, p. 115).

52. ". . . non potest perficere operationem; non enim calor calefacit, sed calidum, neque sapientia sapit, sed sapiens" (ibid.).

53. SCG I, chap. 30: "Forma vero in his rebus invenitur quidem simplex, sed imperfecta, utpote non subsistens: habens autem formam invenitur quidem subsistens, sed non simplex, immo concretionem habens."

54. *De potentia*, q. 7, a. 7, ad 9: ". . . *esse* est actualitas omnium actuum, et propter hoc est perfectio omnium perfectionum" (Marietti, p. 192).

55. ST I, q. 3, a. 4, c.

It is this same metaphysics of being which enables Aquinas to make a further distinction between two ontological modes of perfection, the created and the uncreated, a distinction which Hartshorne cannot make with his metaphysics only of becoming. *Non est unius modi perfectio Dei et perfectio creaturae.*[56] Hartshorne can be satisfied with speaking of "'divinity' or its equivalent [as] the sole property definable abstractly which but one individual can have."[57] But then in recognizing that the abstract is still imperfect, he is forced to speak of divine perfection as concrete only in some "particular actuality not deducible from our idea,"[58] which seems contrary to the point of any ontological argument having to do with necessity. Aquinas cannot be satisfied with such one-sided abstract speech about God. To speak less inadequately of God, according to him, one has to adopt both the concrete and the abstract modes of speech at the same time, though not in a way that confuses the two modes of ontological or universal perfection which he distinguishes between the Creator and the created.

That which is complete among us, although it be *per se* subsistent, is in a way sufficient unto itself in the sense that it does not need another in which to adhere as in a subject; however, because the form which is the principle of action is in it limited and participated, it cannot act through the mode of creation or outpouring, as that which is wholly form acts, which by participation in itself, is according to itself wholly productive of other things.

Since therefore it is so among us in these things which are diminished and concrete, it follows that God is neither diminished nor simply complete, but rather supercomplete. For He does not lack action, like diminished things [things as taken in the abstract, such as wisdom or humanity], and he acts in the mode of one creating and pouring out, which those things that are complete among us cannot do.[59]

In short, like things in the concrete among us, God is perfect in such a way that he can bring his own operation to perfection. But this operation, which is that of creation itself, is something radically different from any operation in which any creature can participate. Adopting the Neoplatonic language of the text he is commenting on, St. Thomas characterizes the divine perfection not just as complete,

56. *De potentia*, q. 5, a. 10, ad 5 (Marietti, p. 156).
57. *The Logic of Perfection*, 66.   58. Ibid., 94.
59. *In De causis*, 22: "Illud autem quod est completum apud nos, quamvis sit per se subsistens, in hoc sibi quodammodo sufficiens quod non indiget alio cui innitatur sicut subiecto, tamen, quia forma quae est principium actionis est in ipso limitata et participata, non potest agere per modum creationis aut influxus, sicut agit id quod totum est forma, quod sui participatione secundum se totum est aliorum productivum. Cum ergo ita sit apud nos in his quae sunt diminuta et concreta, sequitur quod Deus neque sit diminutus neque completus simpliciter, sed magis supercompletus. Non enim caret actione sicut diminuta, et agit per modum creantis et influentis, quod non possunt ea quae sunt completa apud nos . . ." (Saffrey, pp. 115–16).

but as supercomplete. In another text, however, he even goes so far as to speak of this supercompletion as a kind of imperfection, not in the sense that Hartshorne posits potentiality or imperfection in divinity, but rather in the sense that God is "perfect above all things and before all things,"[60] that is, without undergoing any change whatsoever even in His action. He is imperfect in the sense that He does not need to be perfected.

Our way of signifying *esse* starts from a mode of concretion in that we think of the concrete as more perfect than the abstract. "Still in attributing *esse* to God the intellect transcends the mode of signifying, attributing to God what is signified, not, however, the mode of signifying."[61] This implies that to speak less inadequately of God we have to use both concrete and abstract names at the same time. We have to say both God and deity. "The name God signifies divinity, but in a supposit and concretely; but the name deity signifies deity in the abstract, and absolutely."[62]

The concrete name, God, contains more of an existential reference. But taken alone it tends to reduce God, as Hartshorne does, to the level of things which are diminished in comparison to the first Cause. The concrete name has to be corrected or complemented by the more abstract name, deity, because the mode of abstraction in a way rises above concretion and speaks more absolutely, as we must in speaking about God or the first Cause.

On the other hand, the abstract name taken alone seems to take away from the perfection of God, as it does when we use such abstract names as humanity or entity for the things we know concretely and as Hartshorne saw quite rightly, though he drew the wrong conclusion from this in attributing potentiality and imperfection to God. Aquinas saw in the greater perfection of concretion rather a need to correct and to complement the mode of abstraction with the mode of concretion, which he did with his idea of *Esse per essentiam* and *Esse subsistens.* In God the two modes coincide perfectly, while in the things around us they do not, so that our language about God can never be anything more than a remote convergence of two irreducible modes of naming, that of concretion and that of abstraction, a convergence which can

60. *In div. nom.*, chap. 7, lect. 3, n. 721: ". . . attribuimus Ei *imperfectionem*, in quantum est perfectus super omnia et ante omnia . . ." (Marietti, p. 271).

61. *De potentia*, q. 7, a. 7, ad 7: ". . . intellectus attribuens esse Deo transcendit modum significandi, attribuens Deo id quod significatur, non autem modum significandi" (Marietti, p. 192).

62. *In Ioan.*, chap. 1, lect. 1, n. 44: "Hoc nomen Deus significat divinitatem, sed in supposito and concrete; hoc vero nomen *deitas* significat deitatem in abstracto, et absolute" (Marietti, p. 11).

be mediated through the idea of perfection in its two radically distinct modes, the created and the Uncreated.

In fact, we might think of the ways to prove the existence of God as ways of articulating this mediation between the two modes of perfection and the two modes of naming. St. Thomas's objection to the Anselmian argument was not so much that it did not work, but rather that it worked only if we already had the idea of absolute perfection. The problem of a proof for the existence of God for Aquinas was to bring someone to such an idea, which could not be done *a priori*, given the imperfection endemic to any of our abstract names. It had to be done *a posteriori*, which means adding concretion, in order to arrive at an idea of a more positive completion or perfection.

We see this most clearly in the Fourth Way, which starts from the different degrees of perfection found in things and rises to a most perfect which is "the cause of *esse* and goodness and whatever perfection for all beings, and this we call God."[63] The whole point of the argument is to show how the perfection of the universe is relative to the perfection of God. The other Ways rely less on the idea of perfection as such, but they still ride on the order of the universe, which is an order of *per se* ordered causes, or on its radical potentiality to not be as well as be, in order to arrive at the first Cause or the necessary Being, whose perfection can only be supereminent in comparison to the perfection of things in the universe and of the universe itself.

In conclusion, then, one gets the sense that Aquinas would have agreed with most of what Hartshorne says in his logic of perfection. But he would not have seen it as applying to God or to deity. He would have seen it as applying only to the universe in its perfection. At the same time, however, he would also have insisted on the necessity of understanding this perfection of the universe to arrive at a better sense of the perfection of God himself, as he shows in his theology by using philosophy, which brings out the perfection of the universe, to make the truth of Sacred Teaching more manifest. The logic of perfection which we have tried to sketch here underlies his method in both philosophy and theology as it ties them together in a single unified teaching.

---

63. ST I, q. 2, a. 3, c.: "Ergo est aliquid quod omnibus entibus est causa esse et bonitatis et cuiuslibet perfectionis, et hoc dicimus Deum" (*Quarta via*).

7   Aquinas and the Principle of Plenitude
ALEJANDRO LLANO

In 1933 Arthur Lovejoy delivered the William James Lectures at Harvard University. In 1936, these lectures were published in a book entitled *The Great Chain of Being*.[1] If books can be said to have a fate as people can, then the fate of this book is paradoxical. On the one hand, it has been considered by some in the United States as one of the greatest books of this century; on the other hand, while the author was a professor of philosophy, the book became influential chiefly in the province of literary criticism and in the largely undetermined field called the history of ideas.[2]

In the last few years, however, the poor reception of Lovejoy's book in its original philosophical home seems to have improved. The Finnish philosophers Jaakko Hintikka and Simo Knuuttila discovered the relevance to modal ontology of the principle called by Lovejoy "the principle of plenitude"; that is, the principle according to which no authentic possibility is left unrealized, or, more succinctly, the principle that if something is possible, then it occurs.

Reference to the principle of plenitude has become a commonplace in contemporary discussions about modal notions. Nonetheless, the paradoxical nature of the history of this idea has not disappeared. In the last chapter of his book, "The Outcome of the History and Its Moral," Lovejoy drew the conclusion that the history of the idea of the Chain of Being is the history of a failure, insofar as that idea presupposed that the world was completely intelligible.[3] "Rationality, when conceived as complete, as excluding all arbitrariness, becomes

---

1. Arthur O. Lovejoy, *The Great Chain of Being: A Study of the History of an Idea* (Cambridge: Harvard University Press, 1970).

2. Cf. Jaakko Hintikka, "Gaps in the Great Chain of Being: An Exercise in the Methodology of the History of Ideas," in *Reforging the Great Chain of Being: Studies of the History of Modal Theories*, ed. Simo Knuuttila (Dordrecht and Boston: Reidel, 1980), 1–3.

3. Lovejoy, *The Great Chain of Being*, 329.

itself a kind of irrationality."[4] Hintikka and Knuuttila permit themselves the paradoxical claim that they have understood Lovejoy's principle better than Lovejoy himself, and maintain that the principle of plenitude, according to their peculiar interpretation of it, is valid.

The purpose of this paper is not that of narrating the strange destiny of a book and the equivocal effects of its reception. Rather, its concern is with Hintikka and Knuuttila's understanding of the principle of plenitude, and, still more, with their claim that they find this principle in Aristotle and Aquinas. For example, Hintikka thinks that the *tertia via* which Aquinas gives for proving God's existence coincides with some modern formulations of the principle of plenitude. Hintikka believes that the phrase of the third way "that which can not-be at some time is not"[5] constitutes a clear use of the principle of plenitude and that this therefore implies that Aquinas held the "assumption that whatever *can* happen *will* happen in the long run, i.e., that no genuine possibility can remain unfulfilled through an infinity of time."[6]

What is being offered here is a new mode of understanding—or misunderstanding—of the notion of possibility employed by Aristotle and St. Thomas. This is not a mere piece of historical scholarship. It has to do with the understanding of shifts in modal metaphysics which have given rise to modern ways of thinking, ways of thinking that hearken back to certain pre-Aristotelian and Neoplatonic positions.

"The principle of plenitude," writes Lovejoy, "had latent in it a sort of absolute cosmic determinism which attains its final systematic formulation and practical application in the *Ethics* of Spinoza."[7] Lovejoy is aware, then, that the principle of plenitude cannot be endorsed by orthodox Christian thinkers, since it implies denying both human freedom and God's freedom. Nevertheless, Lovejoy believes that "the dominant philosophy of the Middle Ages" found itself in a practical dilemma: it could not admit this principle, on the one hand, but on the other, it could not manage without it.[8] While medieval thought had to maintain the freedom of divine creation and providence, according to the Christian faith, nevertheless, an increasing rationalism during that period, and the rational optimism of Scholastic philosophy, committed the medievals to accepting a kind of principle of sufficient reason, a principle which openly contradicted the freedom of God. The tension between these opposing ideas can be seen "in the

4. Ibid., 331.
5. ST I, q. 2, a. 3, c.
6. Hintikka, "Gaps in the Great Chain," 2.
7. Lovejoy, *The Great Chain of Being*, 54.
8. Ibid., 73.

form of an inner opposition of tendencies in the minds of individual thinkers."[9]

Lovejoy believes that this opposition can be seen in Aquinas. According to Lovejoy, Aquinas freely employs the principle of plenitude whenever it suits his purpose, but he evades its consequences "by means of subtle but spurious or irrelevant distinctions" when it seems "to be on the point of leading him into the heresy of admitting the complete correspondence of the realms of the possible and the actual, with the cosmic determinism that this implies."[10]

An example of the way in which Lovejoy comes to his wrong interpretation can be seen in the use he makes of the most important text which has to do with this problem: *Summa theologiae* I, q. 25, a. 6. This question is devoted to the power of God, and the article asks "Whether God can do better than what he does." The only literal quotation that Lovejoy makes from this discussion is Thomas's reply to the third objection. He clearly thinks that this passage makes obvious the open conflict in Thomas's mind between his rational approval of the principle of plenitude and his dogmatic rejection of it.[11]

First, according to Lovejoy, comes Thomas's acceptance of the principle of plenitude: "It is to be maintained that, these things being supposed, the universe cannot be better than it is, because of the supremely befitting order which God has assigned to things, wherein the good of the universe consists. If one of these things were [separately] better, the proportion which constitutes the order of the whole would be vitiated" (Lovejoy's translation). Then Lovejoy goes on immediately to quote what he alleges is the contradiction of the principle of plenitude, at the end of the reply: "Nevertheless, God could make other things than he has, or could add others to the things he has made; and this other universe would be better."[12]

The key to this passage is the interpretation of the clause that occurs at the beginning. The original Latin reads as follows: "Ad tertium dicendum quod universum, suppositis istis rebus, non potest esse melius." Lovejoy translates "suppositis istis rebus" literally, as "these things being supposed." Translated in this literal and unspecific way, it is possible to suppose that the phrase refers to some doctrines that have previously been presented. The real meaning, however, of Aquinas's text is better rendered by the Benziger translation: "The universe, the present creation being supposed, cannot be better."[13]

9. Ibid. 10. Ibid., 81.
11. Ibid., 78–79. 12. ST I, q. 25, a. 6, ad 3.
13. *Summa Theologica*, 3 vols. (New York: Benziger Brothers, 1947), 1:141. Cf. the translation in the *Great Books of the Western World* (Chicago: Encyclopaedia Britannica, 1952), 19:149: "The universe, the things that exist now being supposed, cannot be better, . . ."

There is a crucial difference between these renderings of the text. Lovejoy's literal translation suggests that the universe cannot be better, in accordance with the principle of plenitude, whereas the true sense is that *this* universe cannot be better. According to the first interpretation, Aquinas would be asserting an absolute necessity: the universe cannot be better than it is. According to the second interpretation, we have a hypothetical necessity: given that the universe is as it is—which it certainly is, but need not have been—it cannot be improved by the modification of any one thing, because to modify any one thing would destroy the proportion of order that the universe in fact has. If we do not confine ourselves to the single reply that Lovejoy quotes, and look at the whole of the article, we can see that it is not self-contradictory, but a coherent whole that throughout rejects the notion of the world's being an optimum totality.

The core of this article is of metaphysical importance because it shows us Aquinas's conception of the fundamental structure of reality as such; that is, we find in reality a double order of participation. The first order is what Cornelio Fabro calls "categorial" or "predicamental" participation.[14] This is the participation that each individual has in the essence that corresponds to its kind. In this sort of participation, the perfection that is possessed by each one of the participating substances is *completely* possessed by each one, and does not exist outside the participants. The participated form does not admit of different degrees and hence, insofar as it is the form that it is, cannot be made better by God. Thomas appeals to Aristotle's doctrine that essences are like numbers,[15] and "just as a number does not admit of variations of degree, so neither does substance in the sense of form." There is a kind of good "which is of the essence of the thing. Thus, for instance, to be rational pertains to the essence of human being. As regards this good, God cannot make a thing better than it is itself . . . , even as he cannot make the number four greater than it is; because if it were greater it would no longer be four, but another number."[16]

The second kind of participation is "transcendental" participation. On this level the participated perfection is *never* completely possessed by the participants, and does exist outside the participants. This is a participation at a level beyond the order of the predicamental essences, at the level of pure perfections. Possession of this sort of perfection *does* admit of different grades. "Another kind of goodness,"

14. Cornelio Fabro, *La nozione metafisica di partecipazione*, 3d ed. (Turin: Societá Editrice Internazionale, 1963); *Partecipazione e causalitá secondo S.Tommaso d'Aquino* (Turin: Societá Editrice Internazionale, 1960).

15. *Metaphysics* 8.3.1043b32–1044a2.   16. ST I, q. 25, a. 6, c.

writes Aquinas, "is that which is over and above the essence. . . . As regards this kind of goodness God can make better the things he has made."[17] As Thomas suggests,[18] this gradation applies to perfections that are possessed accidentally by some things: for example, the virtue or wisdom participated in by a human being. The chief instance, though, which is also crucial, is ontological perfection: that is, being as actuality (*actus essendi*), which is the primary and original source of the real value and nobility of a thing.[19] The conclusion of this article, then, is clear: "Absolutely speaking, God can make something better than each thing made by him."[20]

We can now see the connection between the principle of plenitude and essentialism. According to an essentialist metaphysics, the ultimate perfection of a thing consists in its essence, which is its absolute possibility. If the perfection of things, and hence, we might say, their dignity and ontological value, lies in their essences, then the activity of the Creator must be in some way subject to a principle of convenience, a principle of fittingness, and is in some way constrained to bring about the best of all possible worlds.

If, on the other hand, the ultimate perfection of things consists in being as actuality, then possibility, on the transcendental level, has to be understood as a potentiality relative to being (*potentia essendi*), that is, as a greater or lesser capacity of partaking in the actuality of being. Hence a world better than the world which actually exists is always possible. Even the expression "the best of all possible worlds" makes no sense, because everything that can possibly exist can only exist in a limited manner. Thus every possible being necessarily falls short of infinite perfection (*Esse subsistens*), and thus always leaves room for a more perfect being.

While Lovejoy has clearly read Thomas incorrectly, his interpretation of Aristotle does seem basically correct. He holds that the principle of plenitude is incompatible with Aristotle's fundamental position on modality and, consequently, that "That principle is, in fact, formally rejected by Aristotle in the *Metaphysics*."[21] Lovejoy offers two texts as proof: "It is not necessary that everything that is possible should exist in actuality" and "It is possible for that which has a potency not to realize it."[22]

Lovejoy is aware that other passages of the *Metaphysics* seem at first to contradict this interpretation.[23] He refers to a text that apparently

17. Ibid.   18. ST I, q. 25, a. 6, ad 1.
19. SCG I, chap. 28.   20. ST I, q. 25, a. 6, c.
21. Lovejoy, *The Great Chain of Being*, 55.
22. *Metaphysics* 3.6.1003a2; 12.6.1071b13.
23. Lovejoy, *The Great Chain of Being*, 340.

involves acceptance of the principle of plenitude: "Obviously it cannot be true to say so-and-so is possible but will not be; this view entirely loses sight of the instances of impossibility."[24] Now comes one of the most remarkable paradoxes of a paradoxical story. Lovejoy thinks that this text does not imply a conflict with the Aristotelian rejection of the principle of plenitude; but Jaakko Hintikka, the philosopher who rediscovered the philosophical relevance of Lovejoy's book, believes that "this passage offers us strong evidence for Aristotle's adherence to the principle that each genuine possibility is sometimes realized."[25] According to Hintikka, "In the passage under consideration Aristotle is warning us against a mistake. . . . The mistake Aristotle is worried about is assuming that a possibility can remain for ever unrealized."[26]

It is clear that Aristotle warns us against the utterance "Something is possible but will never be." But to hold that this utterance is never true is by no means the same thing as to maintain that whatever is possible will be the case. Aristotle does not wish to exclude there being a real potentiality which will never be realized. What he rejects, as Klaus Jacobi has pointed out,[27] is only the prognostical or predictive utterance "Something is possible but will never be," since, when it is applied to the whole of time, it involves us in the contradiction of saying that something is at one and the same time both possible and impossible.

Hintikka does not notice that Aristotle is not speaking here about a real possibility, a possibility which attaches to the thing itself. He is dealing here with a possibility which attaches to the truth of a proposition. The subject of the modality is not a thing (*res*), but a statement (*dictum*). The contradiction against which Aristotle warns us is a pragmatic contradiction, not a semantical one. We should recall that truth has two dimensions: an "adequative" and a "reflective" dimension. As Aquinas says, only the intellect which reflects on itself knows the truth.[28] The semantical dimension of truth—its adequative aspect—has to do with the conformity of the proposition with the thing, while the pragmatic dimension of the truth—its reflective aspect—has to do with the logical and linguistic utterance of the proposition itself. If I

24. *Metaphysics* 10.4.1047b2–6.
25. Jaakko Hintikka, *Time and Necessity* (Oxford: Clarendon, 1973), 109.
26. Ibid., 108.
27. Klaus Jacobi, "Aussagen über Ereignisse: Modal- und zeitlogische Analysen in der mittelalterischen Logik," *Anuario Filosófico* 16, no. 1 (1983): 95.
28. *In VI Metaph.*, lect. 4, n. 1236 (Marietti, p. 311). Cf. Fernando Inciarte, "El problema de la verdad en la filosofía actual y en Santo Tomás," *Veritas et Sapientia*, ed. Juan J. R. Rosado and Pedro Rodríguez (Pamplona: EUNSA, 1975), 43–59; and Carmen Segura, "La dimensión reflexiva de la verdad en Tomás de Aquino," *Anuario Filosófico* 15, no. 2 (1982): 271–79.

know that something will not happen, I cannot truly say that it is possible.

Lovejoy himself grasped this point when, in commenting on this text, he understood Aristotle to mean that we are not *entitled to assert* that something is possible but will never in fact exist.[29] Lovejoy sees that this text of Aristotle does not imply the principle of plenitude, precisely because the text is about an utterance and not directly about reality. But it seems that Lovejoy is not prepared to draw the consequences of this distinction.

We now arrive at the conceptual key to our problem: the fact that the notion of possibility is an *analogous* one. "Potentiality" and "possibility" are said in many ways, as Aquinas says again and again. And the two main modes of possibility are in fact the two we have already mentioned, possibility according to truth and possibility according to reality. All formulations of the principle of plenitude can be seen to rest on an inattention to, or a misunderstanding of, this distinction.

Aquinas distinguishes between analogous possibility and equivocal possibility.[30] Analogous possibility has to do with things which have a real potentiality in themselves, while in the case of equivocal possibility there is no principle of potentiality, no real possibility in things themselves. Analogous possibility is a proper and real possibility: it has to do with analogous reality in itself, with motions and changes in natural things. Equivocal possibility, on the other hand, is a propositional or veritative possibility: it has to do with propositions and their truth. That which is analogously possible is that which can exist; that which is equivocally possible is that which can be true, that which is not necessarily false.[31]

This distinction reveals a feature of the doctrine of Aristotle and Thomas on the analogy of being which is frequently overlooked. This analogy embraces four classifications or divisions, each of which corresponds to a different logical or ontological approach: (1) being in itself as opposed to coincidental being (*ens per se* and *ens per accidens*); (2) proper being as opposed to veritative being (*ens proprium* and *ens ut verum*); (3) being according to the ten categories (*substantia* and *accidentia*); and (4) being as actuality as opposed to being as potentiality (*ens ut actus* and *ens ut potentia*).[32] The most interesting aspect of this multiple classification is the complex interaction of the four orders,

29. Lovejoy, *The Great Chain of Being*, 340.
30. *In IX Metaph.*, lect. 1, n. 1773 (Marietti, p. 424); cf. *Metaphysics* 9.1.1046aff.
31. Cf. *Metaphysics* 5.12.1019b30–32.
32. *Metaphysics* 6.2.1026a33–b2; 5.7.1017a7–b2. Cf. *In VI Metaph.*, lect. 2, nn. 1171–90 (Marietti, pp. 301–3); *In V Metaph.*, lect. 9, nn. 885–87 (pp. 237–40).

the way in which each of them can be found to work within the others. Especially relevant for our present discussion is the interaction of the second distinction and the fourth distinction.

Since possibility is said in relation to being, writes Aquinas, what applies to being also applies to possibility. Now, being is found not only in natural things, in one sense, but also in another, in the composition and division of propositions. Therefore, possibility is not only that which can exist according to the real possibility of the thing, but also that which can be, not according to real potentiality, but according to the putting together and taking apart of subject and predicate in propositions; that is, according to the truth.[33] To sum up, possibility according to potentiality (*possibilitas secundum potentiam*) is analogical or real possibility, while possibility not according to potentiality (*possibilitas non secundum potentiam*) is equivocal or veritative possibility.

The richness and rigor of this account was to be lost when, in late medieval philosophy and in the modern way of thinking, the doctrine of the analogy of being collapses, and the only distinction which remains is that which is put forward as a mental contraposition between being as something thought and being as fact. In such a philosophical framework, there is born the essentialist idea of logical possibility. What is called the logically possible (*possibile logicum*) is what happens when we reify and formalize the kind of possibility which, according to Aquinas, does not occur in concepts but in judgments. This misunderstanding leads to the rejection of any analogy within the notion of possibility, and to the proposal of a sole kind of possibility that is at once logical and physical.

Such is the position of Hintikka and Knuuttila. Despite the logical and philological sophistication of their discussions,[34] the only ontologically relevant distinction they admit in this context is that between partial possibilities and total possibilities, a distinction already proposed by Bärthlein.[35] They think that partial possibilities can remain unrealized; but this is precisely because they are not genuine possibilities. Total possibilities must be realized because all the necessary conditions for actualization are present in them.[36]

---

33. *In V Metaph.*, lect. 14, n. 971 (Marietti, p. 258).
34. Cf. Jaakko Hintikka, Unto Remes, and Simo Knuuttila, *Aristotle on Modality and Determinism*, Acta Philosophica Fennica, vol. 29, no. 1 (Amsterdam: North-Holland, 1977); and Jaakko Hintikka, "Aristotle's Different Possibilities," in *Time and Necessity*, 27–40.
35. Karl Bärthlein, "Untersuchungen zur aristotelischen Modaltheorie," *Archiv für Geschichte der Philosophie* 45 (1963): 43–67; cf. Leonor Gómez Cabranes, *El poder y lo posible: Sus sentidos en Aristóteles* (Pamplona: EUNSA, 1989).
36. Simo Knuuttila, "Introduction" to *Reforging the Great Chain of Being*, xi.

I think that what Hintikka and Knuuttila call "total possibility" is what Aristotle calls "actuality." So it is tautological that "no genuine possibility," in this sense, can remain unrealized. The reader of the *Metaphysics* is astonished when he sees that—in a very complicated way—Hintikka and Knuuttila present Aristotle as assuming the very modal theory that he sharply criticizes in 9.3.[37] I mean by this the Megaric conception of possibility, according to which a thing only has potentiality when it is actualized, and when it is not actualized it does not have potentiality.[38]

The strange fate of Lovejoy's book attains its ironic climax when the principle of plenitude is twisted by Hintikka and Knuuttila into its own mirror image: a sort of principle of scarcity. Hintikka claims that this version of the principle of plenitude "is only an ontological balance sheet, not an entry into one column rather than into another. It does not assert the plenitude of actual realizations, but only an equation between possibilities and their realizations. It is as much or as little a Principle of Paucity of Possibilities as a Principle of Plenitude of their Realizations. . . . The reason why a thinker adopts the so-called Principle of Plenitude may be his belief in the richness of the real world. But it may also be his narrow view of the hidden possibilities that lurk behind the ontological backdrop of our actual world, hoping to enter the limelight of actuality."[39]

The principle of plenitude always implies determinism, but it may be either a rationalistic or a materialistic determinism. The school of Helsinki offers a refined, positivistic version of materialistic determinism. Hintikka and Knuuttila propose a statistical interpretation of modality, "according to which a temporally indefinite sentence is necessarily true if it is true whenever uttered, possibly true if it is true sometimes, and impossible if it is always false."[40] They recognize that such a model for modality implies giving a reductionistic account of modalities into extensional terms. The relationship between time and truth is here the sole ontological framework. The rich and complex horizon of modal metaphysics boils down to the actual sequence of "nows," to the factual succession of homogeneous moments. This is, claims Hintikka, "the only forum on which a possibility can prove its mettle."[41]

---

37. *Metaphysics*, 9.3.1046b29–1047a24.
38. Martin Heidegger, *Aristoteles, Metaphysik IX 1–3*, Gesamtausgabe, vol. 33 (Frankfurt a. M.: Vittorio Klostermann, 1981), 166–77.
39. Hintikka, "Gaps in the Great Chain of Being," 6.
40. Simo Knuuttila, "Time and Modality in Scholasticism," in *Reforging the Great Chain of Being*, 163; cf. Hintikka, "Gaps in the Great Chain of Being," 9.
41. Hintikka, "Gaps in the Great Chain of Being," 8.

Simo Knuuttila has tried to demonstrate that the statistical interpretation of modalities was adopted by most medieval philosophers, from the time of Boethius until the late thirteenth century. A typical example of his intricate arguments is his discussion of a famous problem that comes from Aristotle's *Sophistical Refutations*.[42] When Socrates is sitting, he can walk and, therefore, he can be not sitting. That seems to imply the contradiction of saying that Socrates can be sitting and not sitting at once. But such a contradiction only occurs if we consider the possibility as applying to the proposition as a whole. There is however no contradiction at all if we consider "possibility" as applying separately to each of the opposed predicates "sitting" and "not sitting." On this second reading, while Socrates is sitting, obviously he can be sitting; but he can also be not sitting, because he can stand up.

Many medieval thinkers gave the same solution as Aristotle. They said that the proposition "Socrates can be sitting and not sitting" is false in the composite sense (*in sensu composito*), but it is true in the divided sense (*in sensu diviso*).

Knuuttila considers that this Aristotelian and Scholastic solution implies that its authors held the statistical model of possibility, and therefore that it can be interpreted exclusively in terms of time and truth. "The distinction is, in the last analysis, reduced to a temporal distinction between the simultaneity and non-simultaneity of actualization of predicates."[43] Hence the composite sense means "at the same time," whereas the divided sense means "at different times." Thus it is false to say "Socrates can be sitting and not sitting" if we mean that Socrates can be sitting and not sitting at one and the same time; but it is true if we mean that he can be sitting now—just because he is sitting now—and that he can be not sitting, because obviously he can stand up a moment later.

Knuuttila's account only deals with diachronic possibilities, possibilities that can be rendered in extensional terms.[44] But the whole meaning of the Aristotelian and medieval solution implies a reference to synchronic alternatives that should be rendered in non-extensional terms. A more natural, nonreductionist interpretation of the traditional example is the following: *in sensu diviso*, it is true to say that "Socrates can be sitting and can be not sitting," because he could be not sitting *now*, although he is in fact sitting now. Socrates had and

42. *Sophistici Elenchi* 166a23–30.
43. Knuuttila, "Time and Modality in Scholasticism," 168.
44. Simo Knuuttila, "Varieties of Natural Necessity in Medieval Thought," in *Estudios de Historia de la Lógica*, ed. Ignacio Angelelli and Angel d'Ors, Actas del II Simposio de Historia de la Lógica (Pamplona: Eunate, 1990), 307–8.

has the possibility of being seated and the possibility of being standing. The possibility that is realized now is, even now, a possibility; and therefore its actualization does not eliminate the opposite possibility as a possibility. In things composed of potentiality and actuality, the actualization of some possibility does not remove the relevant potentiality: this remains, and remains open to the opposite possibility. Otherwise we would have to endorse the Megarian theories that, as Aristotle says, "make potentiality and actuality identical" and "do away with both motion and generation."[45] While sitting, Socrates can be standing, precisely because his being seated is not necessary but contingent. The foundation of the possibility of being seated, and the foundation of the possibility of being standing are one and the same: that is, the real potentiality of sitting down and standing up. In the *Summa contra gentiles,* Aquinas offers a metaphysical rationale for this nonreductionistic interpretation: "All of the substances in which potentiality is mixed, in so far as they have potentiality, can not be; because what can be, can not be."[46]

Knuuttila seems to forget the metaphysical basis of the issue, and thus gives an account which is clearly partial. The statistical model for modalities is a conceptual framework which explains some logical and epistemological consequences of the ontological structure of things, but it is not to be confused with this real structure.[47] Such a model has to be located on the level of being as true. On this level, the possibility we find is only "the possibility according to truth": the possibility that has to do with the being together of subject and predicate in a proposition. This being together of subject and predicate is not to be identified with the real states of things, though it in some way corresponds to it. This "being united" or "being together" admits of different modalities,[48] which are reflected in the relationship between truth and time. A text of Aristotle expresses this aspect of the interaction that we have referred to above, between the second and the fourth classifications of the different senses of being: "Now, if whereas some things are always united and cannot be divided, and others are always divided and cannot be united, others again admit of both contrary states, then 'to be' is to be united, *i.e.* a unity; and 'not to be' is to be not united, but a plurality. Therefore as regards the class of things which admit of both contrary states, the same opinion or the same statement comes to be false and true, and it is possible at one

---

45. *Metaphysics* 9.3.1047a20; 1047a15.
46. SCG I, chap. 16.
47. I am indebted to Christopher Martin (University of Glasgow) for this remark.
48. Cf. Heidegger, *Aristoteles, Metaphysik IX 1–3,* 61–66.

time to be right and at another wrong; but as regards things which cannot be otherwise the same opinion is not sometimes true and sometimes false. . . ."[49] In his commentary on this text, Aquinas establishes the fact that the real modalities are the foundation of the veritative modalities which must be understood as qualifications of the putting together and taking apart in propositions, that is to say, as modalities of being as true and not-being as false.[50]

In his commentary on *De Interpretatione,* Thomas points out the *a posteriori* character of temporal considerations about modalities; for instance, it is not that something is necessary because it will always be: rather, it will always be because it is necessary.[51] The statistical model is, to be sure, present in Aristotle, in Aquinas, and in most of the Aristotelian thinkers. There is no evidence, however, that any of them has been tempted to confuse this epistemological model with the real modalities.

This distinction between the level of the veritative and the level of the real is even more explicit when medieval thinkers make it by means of the semantical expressions *de dicto* and *de re,* rather than by the syntactical expressions *in sensu composito* and *in sensu diviso.*[52] *De dicto* modality has to do with a proposition; *de re* modality has to do with a real thing. For instance, it is true *de dicto* to say "Socrates is necessarily sitting," while Socrates is sitting. The same statement is false *de re,* because his being seated is not necessary but contingent, although it is *necessary for us to say* that Socrates is sitting.

This scholastic distinction is often used to break important links of "the great chain of being." Nonetheless, Hintikka and Knuuttila think that the distinction simply carries on Aristotle's own conceptual strategy, in which he tries to dodge the deterministic implications of his assumptions by shifting the focus of attention from temporally qualified to temporally unqualified events and sentences. But it leaves unmodified, they claim, the fact that there are no alternatives, or counterfactual possibilities, at a given moment to the state of affairs that obtains at that moment.[53]

The crucial and most famous case is Aristotle's example of the sea-battle.[54] In the utterance "There will be a sea-battle tomorrow" we have an instance of a temporally qualified sentence, referring to a

49. *Metaphysics* 9.10.1051b9–17 (trans. Hugh Tredennick [Cambridge: Harvard University Press, 1933]).
50. *In IX Metaph.,* lect. 11, n. 1899 (Marietti, p. 456).
51. *In I Periherm.,* lect. 14 (Leonine, p. 80).
52. Cf. Jacobi, "Aussagen über Ereignisse."
53. Knuuttila, "Time and Modality in Scholasticism," 167.
54. *De Interpretatione* 9.19a23–b4.

temporally qualified event which is a future contingent. Hintikka has discussed the traditional interpretation, according to which such a sentence is neither true nor false, and has concluded that Aristotle executes the simple-minded maneuver of (in effect) denying that there is a genuine problem with future contingents, "by insisting that an attribution of modal status to a future event is but to compare it with other similar events."[55] In my opinion, Hintikka's interpretation of this and other related passages is colored by his anxiety to attribute to Aristotle a determinism that Aristotle rejects again and again. In any case it is very clear that Aquinas's reading, at least, of the sea-battle passage constitutes one of the best instances of the traditional antideterministic interpretation.

Thomas explicitly distinguishes between approaching the problem from the aspect of the truth about things (*veritas circa res*) and approaching it from the aspect of the truth about utterances (*veritas circa enuntiationes*).[56] Since the truth about things is the foundation of the truth about utterances, epistemological considerations of the relationship between time and truth are always secondary to ontological considerations about the internal and real states of things in themselves. So the necessity of the past and the present is only necessity *ex suppositione*, not necessity *absoluta*. It should not be said, then, that everything that happens has to happen *simpliciter et absolute*.[57] *De dicto* necessity is a *per accidens* necessity, because to be truly known and said is something that merely happens to occur, or is coincidental (*per accidens*) to the thing itself;[58] but *de re* necessity is a *per se* necessity, because it belongs to the thing itself, in itself, and in its own right (*per se*).

What Aristotelians are trying to do here—what Hintikka and Knuuttila consider as no more than a strategy to shift the attention from the temporally qualified to the temporally unqualified—is actually something much more serious. It follows from an account in which the temporal relationship between the event and the knower does not modify the real modality of the event. A contingent event is *really* a nonnecessary event, no matter whether it has already come about, in the past or in the present, or whether it remains to come about (perhaps) in the future. In the case of the past or present contingent event, however, *de dicto* necessity applies, because the cognitive relationship

---

55. Jaakko Hintikka, "The Once and Future Sea Fight: Aristotle's Discussion of Future Contingents in *De Interpretatione* 9," in *Time and Necessity*, 175; cf. 147–78.
56. *In I Periherm.*, lect. 15 (Leonine, p. 80).
57. Ibid. (Leonine, p. 81).
58. *In V. Metaph.*, lect. 9, n. 896 (Marietti, p. 239).

between the contingent event and the knower has already been deter-mined. In contrast, in the case of the *future* contingent such a relation is still open to opposed alternative extremes, whose foundation is the thing's real potentiality of being and not being. The veritative neces-sity, then, which applies separately to each of the contrary possibilities, is not yet available: we do not have what we require for it to be avail-able, neither the semantical requirement of a real thing as the object of the adequative relation, nor the pragmatic requirement of a knower who could reflect on his own knowledge. Thus, the only necessity available is the *in sensu composito* necessity, according to which one of the two opposed possibilities must occur. As Aquinas says, what is not *in se necessarium absolute* becomes necessary by the disjunction of the opposed predicates,[59] although each one of them taken separately (*in sensu diviso*) is not *absolutely* necessary but contingent.[60]

That is indeed what Aristotle's example shows: it is necessary that there will be a sea-battle or will not be a sea-battle tomorrow. But it is not necessary that there will be a sea-battle tomorrow; nor is it necessary that there will not be a sea-battle; because this *in sensu diviso* necessity is absolute necessity, that is to say, *de re* necessity. To say that there necessarily will be or not be a sea-battle tomorrow, on the other hand, is an *in sensu composito*, that is, *de dicto* necessity.[61]

According to Aquinas, the veritative possibility of each one of the contradictory sentences concerning the future contingent is an epis-temological and linguistic feature which derives from the indetermi-nacy or real contingency of the future event; and it so derives just because the being of things is the foundation of the truth of propo-sitions.[62] Hence, a determinate assertion about one of these possibili-ties—the occurrence *or* the nonoccurrence of a sea-battle tomorrow—is neither true nor false.[63] By this argument, concludes Aquinas, Ar-istotle has attained his purpose: that of demonstrating that, of given opposite affirmations and negations, it is not always necessary that one of them is true and the other false.[64]

In her excellent book on *ens per accidens*, Amalia Quevedo has shown that, according to Aristotle, the coincidental is found throughout the world: the world is one in which there are plenty of coincidences that do not derive from any internal necessity.[65] But Aquinas has to face a difficulty in reconciling this indeterminacy of the world with the Chris-

59. *In I Periherm.*, lect. 15 (Leonine, p. 81).
60. Ibid.   61. Ibid.
62. Ibid.   63. Ibid. (Leonine, p. 82).
64. Ibid.
65. Amalia Quevedo, *Ens per accidens: Contingencia y determinación en Aristóteles* (Pam-plona: EUNSA, 1989).

tian doctrine of God's universal providence; as he says in the context of such a discussion, "Sed de providentia maiorem habet difficultatem."[66]

Aquinas wants to show that the existence of divine providence and the real existence of chance (*casus et fortuna*) are compatible. His solution presupposes, from a semantical point of view, the distinction between *necessitas de re* and *necessitas de dicto*; and, from a metaphysical point of view, the transcendental character of the creative and provident Cause—a transcendental character which Aristotle could not admit. Divine providence cannot fail: it is not possible that God should foresee something as existent and that this event should not happen. Therefore, every effect, insofar as it is under the order of providence, is necessary. This necessity, though, is merely an external or *de dicto* necessity. The conditional "Si aliquid est a Deo provisum, hoc erit," is true, and every true conditional is necessary.[67] Nonetheless, the transcendental causality of the Creation does not interfere with the action of created causes. "Second causes" determine whether their effect is contingent or necessary. Such contingency and necessity are internal, they have to do with things in themselves, and are therefore *de re* modalities. The necessity of the conditional "If God foresees something, then it will be," does not affect the alternative of the contingency or necessity of the effect itself. This account does not diminish the infallible character of the forecast; rather it recognizes it. As Aquinas argues, it is not only being as such that is subject to divine providence; the modes of being, including contingency and necessity, are subject too.[68] If God foresees that something will be, it is necessary that this thing will be, and it is necessary that it will be contingent, if it is contingent, and necessary if it is necessary.[69] No event, however casual it may be, falls outside God's providence: but this providence does not make *entia per accidens* not to be what they are, coincidental.

According to the principle of plenitude, the necessity of the divine knowledge carries through to the things that God knows. Since God knows everything, everything is necessary: only what must happen does happen, and everything that does happen must. So necessity, possibility, and actuality blend into a single modality.

The solution to difficulties of this kind demands the richest resources of Thomas's thought. In the case of human knowledge, we should clearly be able to distinguish the epistemological aspect from the ontological aspect; thus we can use the distinction between *de dicto*

66. *In VI Metaph.*, lect. 3, n. 1218 (Marietti, p. 308).
67. *In XI Metaph.*, lect. 5, n. 2218 (Marietti, p. 526).
68. *In VI Metaph.*, lect. 3, n. 1222 (Marietti, p. 308).
69. Ibid.

interpretation and *de re* interpretation to solve puzzles about modal propositions concerning present and future contingents. It seems, however, that we cannot have recourse to such a distinction in the case of divine knowledge, because "to be known by God is inseparable from the thing; for what is known by God cannot be not known."[70] This objection is a difficult one for Thomas, since he maintains that the divine mind is the measure and creative cause of everything. He replies that the objection would hold if the fact of being known implied any property or disposition of the created thing. Since the only actuality implied by this being known is God's act of knowledge, the thing can be considered in itself as contingent, although it is necessary in so far as it is the object of the divine knowledge.[71]

Aquinas does not hesitate to apply the distinction between the epistemological modality (*de dicto*) and the ontological modality (*de re*), even in the extreme case of divine knowledge. So he is able to admit both that many things are contingent in themselves, and that such things are necessarily known by God's creative intellect.[72]

In Thomas's metaphysics of creation, real possibility as well as veritative possibility find their transcendental foundation in an absolute possibility, which defines the realm of what can be created by God. Now, every kind of possibility must be referred to an actuality. Absolute possibility is not absolute in itself, but by reference to the absolute actuality of the Subsistent Being, of God. Absolute possibility is absolute because of God's absolute power. God is omnipotent because he has the absolute ability to produce all absolutely possible things, that is, all things that do not imply any contradiction.[73]

Nevertheless, this realm of the essentially possible, of the absolutely thinkable, does not have any autonomous existence, any free hypostatic being. It intrinsically depends on God's creative intellect. These essences or ideas are possible only on the foundation of the absolute Being.[74] The eternity of eternal truths is the very eternity of God.[75]

The principle of plenitude involves a world of pure possibilities independent of any eternal reality. In Thomas's metaphysics there is no room for such a world. As he says, the fact that God can create something is not equivalent to the fact that something can be created by him. If the possibility of creating and the possibility of being created were equivalent, the potentiality of the creature must pre-

70. ST I, q. 14, a. 13, ad 3.   71. Ibid.
72. *De veritate*, q. 2, a. 12, ad 4 (Leonine, pp. 84–85).
73. ST I, q. 25, a. 3, c.
74. Cf. Bernhard Lakebrink, *Hegels dialektische Ontologie und die Thomistische Analektik* (Ratingen: A. Hehn, 1968), 187.
75. ST I, q. 16, a. 7, c.

exist; otherwise God could not create anything. But the hypothesis of an eternal matter contradicts the very concept of *creatio ex nihilo*.[76]

Absolute possibility transcends the realm of the logical, the mere objectivity of the modern *possibile logicum*, because it has an ontological scope. Absolute possibilities are rooted in the Subsistent Being, and they are in themselves an ordering towards the being they can acquire in reality. To be possible is to be *feasible*. The *ratio possibilis* implies the *ratio factibilis*.[77] Absolute possibility—even as idea—includes a reference to the thing, insofar as its existence can be brought about in reality.[78]

In this difficult subject, we have to try to avoid both intellectualism and voluntarism. The history of late medieval and modern philosophy manifests that both extremes here lead to the conceptual confusions that are at the basis of the principle of plenitude. Knuuttila believes that Duns Scotus's voluntarism makes it impossible for him to accept the statistical interpretation of modalities. Hence, according to Knuuttila, the principle of plenitude is not to be found in late medieval thought.[79] As a matter of historical fact, however, we find rather that a one-sided assertion of the freedom of God leads to the nominalistic idea of the *potentia Dei absoluta,* which involves the principle of scarcity, and later still to the rationalist triumph of the principle of plenitude in Spinoza, Leibniz, and Hegel.

Hintikka and Knuuttila think that one of the most conspicuous medieval examples of the statistical interpretation of possibility occurs in the *tertia via,* in Thomas's third proof of God's existence. The remark which, according to their understanding, implies the principle of plenitude is the following: "That which can not-be at some time is not" ("quod possibile est non esse quandoque non est"). "Therefore," Aquinas continues, "if everything could not-be, then at one time there was nothing in existence."[80] It seems that, according to Aquinas, things that have the possibility of not-being must, in the long run, not-be; otherwise this possibility would not be a real possibility.

But the meaning of Thomas's argument is not at all that given by the Helsinki school. Aquinas does not attribute any complete plenitude to contingent things. The possibility of not-being is not simply one possibility among all the other possibilities that a contingent being has. Contingent things, in virtue of their own being, are not eternal: "they

---

76. *De veritate,* q. 2, a. 10, ad 2 sed contra (Leonine, p. 77).
77. ST I, q. 25, a. 3, c.
78. *De veritate,* q. 3, a. 5, c. (Leonine, p. 122).
79. Knuuttila, "Time and Modality in Scholasticism," 217–34; "Varieties of Natural Necessity in Medieval Thought," 311–13.
80. ST I, q. 2, a. 3, c.

do not have the power to exist forever."[81] From this ontological feature, from the impossibility of being forever, it follows that they cannot realize all their possibilities. When, at some moment, they cease to exist by natural corruption, they always leave some real possibilities unrealized. Their natural necessity of realizing their possibility of not-being any longer does not imply that every other possibility that they have must also, like this one, be realized: on the contrary, it implies precisely the opposite, that since such things must cease to be, it is impossible that all their possibilities should be realized.

Thomas develops his argument from this starting point, from a very familiar experience of the contingency of physical beings. We cannot suppose that there is only a world which is thus exclusively contingent: such a world would lack all consistency, it would have no plenitude at all, and would therefore vanish into not-being. Thus, the nerve of the proof is the following: if the contingent exists, the necessary must exist also.[82]

The principle of plenitude would apply to these necessary beings, if it applied to anything at all, but it would apply to them only insofar as they are necessary, not insofar as they are contingent. Nothing is completely contingent, yet at the same time nothing is fully necessary except the Necessary Being. All things have a certain degree of plenitude, in different proportions, a plenitude which derives from their essences, that is to say, the ways of being which are necessary to them. So, too, all things have a certain degree of non-plenitude. They are not fully what they are, since they have the internal possibility of becoming what they are not.

Propositional or veritative possibility is one-directional (*ad unum*). On the other hand, real possibility is two-directional (*ad utrumque*): it is open to being and not-being. The possible, says Aristotle, can exist and can not exist, because every real possibility is a potentiality that has reference to its fulfilment and to the contradiction of its fulfilment.[83] Such a "dialectical possibility" makes for a dynamic and open world, a world teleologically oriented to a plenitude that is never completely accomplished. Aquinas's world is not a block without fissures, a complete and univocal unity. It is a cosmos, an order: an order that does not completely exclude disorder, discontinuity, opposition or indeterminacy. The order of the cosmos is the limit of disorder.

81. J. H. Walgrave, "Tertia via," in *Quinque sunt viae*, ed. Leo Elders (Rome: Libreria Editrice Vaticana, 1980), 69.

82. ST I, q. 2, a. 3, c.

83. *Metaphysics* 9.8.1050b10–11; 30–33. I thank Thomas Cavanaugh for all the help he has extended to me in the preparation of this paper.

8 Jacques Maritain and Yves R. Simon's Use of Thomas Aquinas in Their Defense of Liberal Democracy

JOHN P. HITTINGER

Although his writings on the topic are sparse, St. Thomas left a rich legacy for political philosophy.[1] Some of the great themes of Aristotelian political philosophy were transmitted and developed by Aquinas, such as the social and political nature of man, the importance of the common good, and the role of virtue. In addition, Thomas developed the classic formulations of natural law philosophy by which human reason could appeal to a standard higher than positive human law. Finally, mention must be made of the development of Catholic social teaching which owes much to the theology of Aquinas.[2] This rich legacy has been appropriated and transformed by two of the chief Thomist philosophers of the twentieth century, Jacques Maritain (1882–1973) and Yves R. Simon (1903–61). These two French philosophers, who spent much time in the United States, developed a very persuasive and influential philosophy of democratic government. Their work helped to shift the axis of Catholic social and political thought away from tradition and monarchy to support for liberal democratic regimes.[3] Because the development and exposition of the political thought of Thomas Aquinas has been virtually identified with

1. The chief writings are the unfinished commentary on Aristotle's *Politics*, the treatise *On Kingship*, portions of theological writings pertaining explicitly to politics and law, and remarks scattered throughout his works related to matters of metaphysics, ethics, and so forth. For judicious selections of key texts see Saint Thomas Aquinas, *On Law, Morality and Politics*, ed. William P. Baumgarth and Richard J. Regan (Indianapolis: Hackett, 1988); Saint Thomas Aquinas, *On Politics and Ethics*, ed. Paul E. Sigmund (New York: Norton, 1988).

2. See Janko Zagar, "Aquinas and the Social Teaching of the Catholic Church," *The Thomist* 38 (October 1974): 826–55.

3. See Paul Sigmund, "Maritain on Politics," *Understanding Maritain*, ed. Deal W. Hudson and Matthew J. Mancini (Macon, Ga.: Mercer University Press, 1987), 153–55; idem, *Natural Law in Political Thought* (Cambridge, Mass.: Winthrop Press, 1971); Heinrich A. Rommen, *The State in Catholic Thought* (St. Louis: Herder, 1947).

the work of these two authors, it is important to examine the use that they make of Aquinas in their justification of democracy. We propose in this paper, therefore, to outline the case that Maritain and Simon make for liberal democracy and to examine the warrants they claim for it in the legacy of St. Thomas. We hope to draw some conclusions about the continued relevance of the political legacy of St. Thomas.[4]

THE MARITAIN/SIMON CASE FOR DEMOCRACY

The case for liberal democracy made by Maritain and Simon relies on four clusters of themes and texts. These are (1) political rule and the problem of universal suffrage, (2) the transmission theory and the problem of consent, (3) subsidiarity and the problem of liberty, and (4) equality and human rights. We must examine these four themes and the relevant texts of St. Thomas, and attempt to determine in what manner the legacy of Aquinas does indeed warrant an endorsement of liberal democracy.

1. Political Rule and the Problem of Universal Suffrage

Universal suffrage is an essential element of the western liberal democratic regimes that Maritain and Simon sought to defend. On what basis can this feature of democracy be justified from within the legacy of St. Thomas? Simon makes a very interesting case for universal suffrage on the basis of a classic distinction between despotic and political rule; it is a distinction that Thomas derives from Aristotle's *Politics*.[5] In his treatment of the sensual powers of human beings, Thomas queries whether the appetites obey reason. It is objected that the appetites resist reason, and therefore they are not subject to reason. Thomas replies to the objection as follows:

For a power is called despotic whereby a man rules his slaves, who have not the right to resist in any way the orders of the one that commands them, since they have nothing of their own. But that power is called political or royal by

---

4. The success of this achievement I have evaluated in the following articles and reviews: "Approaches to Democratic Equality," in *Freedom in the Modern World*, ed. Michael Torre (Notre Dame: American Maritain/Notre Dame Press, 1989), 237–52; review of *Natural Law and the Rights of Man*, by Jacques Maritain, *Crisis* 5 (July/August 1987): 51–52; review of *Theology of Freedom*, by John Cooper, *Crisis* 4 (December 1986): 32–33; "Maritain and the Intellectuals," *This World* 5 (Spring 1983): 164–68; and "Maritain and America," *This World* 3 (Fall 1982): 113–23. I have taken leads from Leo Strauss, review of *Philosophy of Democratic Government*, by Yves Simon, in *What is Political Philosophy* (New York: Free Press, 1959), 306–11, and Ernest Fortin, "The New Rights Theory and the Natural Law," *Review of Politics* 44 (October 1982): 590–612. See also Brian Benested, "Rights, Virtue and the Common Good," *Crisis* 1 (December 1983): 28–32.

5. Aristotle, *Politics*, 1.2.1252a1–1253a38.

which a man rules over free subjects, who, though subject to the government of the ruler, have nevertheless something of their own, by reason of which they can resist the orders of him who commands.[6]

Thomas concludes that reason rules the body despotically, but that reason rules the appetites with a royal or political rule because the appetites can resist the rule of reason. In a similar text, Thomas asks whether in the state of innocence man would have been master over man.[7] Thomas explains a twofold meaning of the term *master*: the first meaning entails mastery of slaves, the second, rule over free men. The essential difference between a slave and a free man is that a free man has "disposal of himself " whereas "a slave is ordered to another." Thomas concludes that in a state of innocence there would be no rule of master over slave; however, there would be rule of one over others on the basis of acting for the unity of the common good and on the basis of superior knowledge and virtue.

Now Simon understands that political rule, and the presence of resistance, does not warrant democracy alone; democracy is one form of political rule, exercising its peculiar form of resistance to unjust rule, but there are other means available to other types of regimes. Democracy, therefore, insofar as it helps to establish conditions of political rule, and avoids tyranny, is a regime justified by the Thomistic text. Simon seeks to go beyond this legitimation, however, to a recommendation of democracy as the best regime available. What is the feature that goes beyond political rule and what is its warrant? Simon defines that feature as follows: "When the political idea assumes the democratic form, the people asserts, over and above its freedom from abusive power, its freedom to govern itself. Keeping the government confined within a definite field is no longer held sufficient; the government has been taken over by the people. Such is democratic freedom, the defining feature of democracy."[8] In order to justify this feature of democratic government Simon recapitulates the partisan dialogue of Aristotle's *Politics* 3.9–13. Simon weighs very carefully the

6. ST I, q. 81, a. 3, ad 2: "Dicitur enim despoticus principatus, quo aliquis principatur servis, qui non habent facultatem in aliquo resistendo imperio praecipientis, quia nihil sui habent. Principatus autem politicus et regalis dicitur, quo aliquis principatur liberis, qui, etsi subdantur regimini praesidentis, tamen habent aliquid proprium, ex quo possunt reniti praecipientis imperio." See James M. Blythe, "The Mixed Constitution and the Distinction Between Regal and Political Power in the Work of Thomas Aquinas," *Journal of the History of Ideas* 47 (October/December 1986): 547–65.

7. ST I, q. 96, a. 4: "Utrum homo in statu innocentiae homini dominabatur?" Thomas says "Cuius ratio est, quia servus in hoc differt a libero, quod 'liber est causa sui' . . . servus autem ordinatur ad alium."

8. Yves R. Simon, *Philosophy of Democratic Government* (Chicago: University of Chicago Press, 1951), 76.

arguments for and against the practice of universal suffrage. He classifies these arguments into three types—the statistical, the sociological, and the romantic. Thus, the objections to universal suffrage (the many) and in favor of aristocracy (the few) are, first, the statistical fact that the qualifications for good government cannot be possessed by a very great number of people: "good government is the work of excellent wisdom; it demands unusual virtue, intelligence, some education, a great deal of experience, and many other qualifications which cannot be expected to be possessed by any great number of men."[9] Second, the rule of the few is preferred because of the sociological fact that the upper class of society produces a "comparatively high rate of excellence." Third, an argument is sometimes made based upon the romantic conception that the upper class is capable of lofty pursuits and disinterested service to society. On the other hand, Simon makes a case for what he calls democratic "optimism." First, from a statistical perspective there is less evil in a large group: "evil may have a selective affinity for this minority and saturate it, while remaining infrequent in mankind at large." Similar arguments are made in favor of rule by a larger group rather than a smaller group by Aristotle and Madison.[10] A second reason for democratic optimism is the sociological consideration that the many can produce an aggregate virtue and wisdom through the pooling of their many talents and perspectives. Aristotle again makes a similar argument in *Politics* 3.11 with respect to the feast and the drama critic; in addition, he mentions the judgment of the patient over the physician. Finally, the romantic conception of the many deems the poor as intrinsically good. Surprisingly, Simon finally recommends none of the three arguments for democratic optimism. Universal suffrage, he says, is rooted in pessimism and the requirement in the present age for political rule. Simply put, the common man "will be crushed unless the constitution of society attaches some power to the only distinction that he certainly possesses, viz., that of having numbers on his side." It is protection of the people from despotism then that finally justifies universal suffrage; it is the Thomistic distinction between despotic and political rule that provides Simon's warrant for democracy. But what is it about the present conditions that does so? At this point in his argument Simon does not

9. Ibid., 78, 81; for subsequent references: 94, 93, 79.
10. Aristotle, *Politics* 3.15.1286a30ff.: A large volume dilutes poison. James Madison, *Federalist* #10: A large republic is more likely to frustrate evil schemes. Cf. Alexis de Tocqueville, *Democracy in America*, ed. J. P. Mayer and trans. George Lawrence (New York: Doubleday, 1969), 167.

elaborate other than to say that an elite cannot be trusted with rule: "there was a time when it was possible to believe that the destiny of the common man was safely intrusted to the wisdom of the upper class. That time is apparently gone forever."[11] It is the conditions of contemporary society, at least in the menace posed by elites, which justify democracy, not the intrinsic claims of the many to rule.

Maritain, on the other hand, sets out to justify universal suffrage from an axiom of the authority of the people. That is, Maritain merely asserts the sociological argument in favor of the rule of the many.[12] He does not engage the dialectical argument as to who should rule. It is an axiom of Maritain's thought that the people should rule. That axiom is given some defense by Maritain and Simon through another cluster of texts and themes entitled the transmission theory of authority.

2. The Transmission Theory and the Problem of Consent

The problem of universal suffrage points to a more original problem, that of the origin of the right to rule and the role of popular consent. As we have seen, Maritain bypasses the question of limited government as a means to justify universal suffrage and proceeds directly to the transmission theory of authority. This somewhat arcane debate about a theory which developed around issues pertaining to the temporal and spiritual powers of the supreme pontiff and the divine right of kings is developed by Maritain and Simon into a centerpiece of their Thomistic justification of liberal democracy.[13] In an important article entitled "The Doctrinal Issues Between the Church and Democracy," Simon outlines three issues of major significance: the general relation between the state and religion; freedom of belief and expression; and the origin and ultimate meaning of temporal power.[14] The third issue is the most important because it is most specific to democracy; and further, Church leaders had singled out an interpretation of democracy as inconsistent with Church doctrine and sound political principles. Both Leo XIII and Pius X condemned a theory that asserts men are bound only by laws to which they consent. Simon believes that democracy does not in fact rest upon such a view.

---

11. Simon, *Philosophy of Democratic Government*, 98–99.

12. Jacques Maritain, *Man and the State* (Chicago: University of Chicago Press, 1951), 53, 65.

13. On the transmission theory, see Rommen, *The State in Catholic Thought*, chaps. 19–20.

14. Yves R. Simon, "The Doctrinal Issue Between the Church and Democracy," in *The Catholic Church in World Affairs,* ed. Waldemar Gurian and M. A. Fitzsimons (Notre Dame: University of Notre Dame Press, 1954), 87–114.

To get at this issue Simon constructs his famous typology of theories of authority: the "coach driver" theory, the "divine right" theory, and the "transmission" theory of authority.

The coach-driver theory accords no authority to statesmen or officials of government. The rulers are but "pure instruments" of prior decisions of the people. This theory seems to justify the democratic practices whereby representatives are seen as hired servants, public opinion and lobby groups form decisions of these representatives, and it honors the autonomy of the individual. Simon argues that this theory is a "masked anarchy." His proof is that a majority must rule the minority lest there be chaos and inability to act. Real authority is required by the need for united action. The coach-driver theory mistakes the final cause (for the good of the whole) and the efficient cause (by the whole). Thus, this doctrine is condemned.

In reaction to the coach-driver theory, some have resorted to the divine right theory: God gives authority to the ruler. In part, this theory arose as a seventeenth-century problematic concerning the Christian prince. The disturbing implications of the theory are that the ruler holds a power with no accountability. Maritain describes the same position as the theory of absolute sovereignty, which he rightly rejects. It places the ruler as separate from the political body and without limit or accountability.[15]

As a solution to the extremes, Maritain and Simon propose to develop the "transmission theory" of authority. According to this theory authority resides in the people, in the civil community as a whole, and not in distinct persons. The civil community designates its rulers and thereby transmits power to the ruler. There are many ways in which such power is transmitted, but the clearest form is universal suffrage. It is argued that there is a genuine transmission, and therefore real authority and integrity of rule in the governing officials. The ruler must be granted the power of judgment and decision.

The Thomistic warrant for this theory is quite slim; there is an intriguing but ambiguous passage in the *Treatise on Law*. In response to "whether the reason of any man is competent to make laws," St. Thomas states that:

A law properly speaking, regards first and foremost the order to the common good. Now to order anything to the common good, belongs either to the whole people, or to someone who is the vicegerent of the whole people. And therefore the making of a law belongs either to the whole people or to a public

15. Maritain, *Man and the State*, 28–53.

personage who has care of the whole people: since in all other matters the directing of anything to the end concerns him to whom the end belongs.[16]

This text is construed to mean that authority resides in the civil community and not in distinct persons; and that the governing person would rule as a substitute or representative of the people. Simon and Maritain both compare the spiritual authority of the Pope as the vicar of Christ and the temporal authorities who serve as vicars of the people. The temporal ruler is said by Maritain to be the "image and deputy of the people." He represents the "majesty of the people" in their collective life. Simon and Maritain are following the lead of the great Thomistic commentators Cajetan, Bellarmine, and Suarez, all of whom use this text to solve disputes surrounding temporal and spiritual power. For example, Cajetan argues that while the Pope cannot be deposed by the people, the king may be so deposed. Similarly, Bellarmine argues that because authority is given to no particular man it belongs to the multitude. Finally Suarez claims that democracy is the most natural form of government because it requires no institution, whereas all other forms require a conventional institution. Maritain and Simon follow this tradition of interpretation. Now, Simon admits that the text itself warrants nothing like a full justification of democracy; at most it points out the role of consent in political order and perhaps does grant a power to depose in extreme circumstances. It is a development from the text of Thomas to make it serve the purpose of democratic theory.

Accordingly, as part of democratic theory, Simon continues in this vein: when the power of rule is not transmitted, there is direct democracy; when the power is transmitted, this is done through periodic exercise of consent through election. But power is never completely transmitted, thus in some way every democracy is a direct democracy or a deliberative assembly. Elections, referenda, and public opinion are the means whereby such authority is exercised and transmitted. Simon insists that the transmission is genuine, which vouchsafes the integrity and judgment of the designated personnel in command.

Thus, from the debate on temporal and spiritual powers that gave rise to the transmission theory of temporal authority, Simon develops a very rich analysis of the various meanings of the phrase "consent of the governed." He carefully distinguishes and elaborates on seven meanings, and so provides a nice summary of the issue and its sig-

16. ST I-II, q. 90, a. 3, c.: "Respondeo dicendum quod lex proprie, primo et principaliter respicit ordinem ad bonum commune. Ordinare autem aliquid in bonum commune est vel totius multitudinis, vel alicuius gerentis vicem totius multitudinis."

nificance for political philosophy.[17] For example, the consent of the people reflects the fact that politics should be an act of reason and will and not instinct or blind force; or that persuasion is a better instrument of rule than is coercion. These are propositions pertaining to political order in general. The phrase may mean that the rulers are not self-appointed, nor do they receive their power directly from God; rather, the people designate their rulers at least through popular approval and thereby "transmit" the authority to the rulers. On this reading of consent, a regime need not be democratic as such; but the rulers must acknowledge their limited claim to rule and the proper end of rule. The transmission theory demands at least a properly political regime, but it is surely implicitly democratic. The other meanings of "consent of the governed" are explicitly democratic. It may "imply a demand for periodic exercise of popular consent" such as through elections of representatives. An even more specifically democratic meaning is what Simon calls the "incomplete transmission" of authority which is proper to democracy: the people retain the character of a deliberative body. The final meaning of "consent of the governed," which Simon emphatically rejects as the real error of some democratic theories, is that the people are bound only by laws to which they give their consent. With this analysis, Simon hopes to have settled the doctrinal dispute between the Church and democracy and to develop Thomas's implicit concern with the role and consent of the people into an explicit defense of democratic principles.

Maritain, for his part, follows a more axiomatic approach to the issue and arrives at a pithy conclusion. He declares that the people have a right to rule by essence, and the ruler a right only by participation in the people's original right.[18] Authority derives from the will or consensus of the people and their "basic right of self-governance." This right he says is inherent and permanent. The recognition of this right, he says, is a "basic verity" and a "conquest of democratic philosophy." Therefore, "whatever the political regime may be, monarchical, aristocratic, or democratic, democratic philosophy appears as the only true political philosophy." As a warrant for this claim, Maritain refers the reader to the text of Thomas cited above and its medieval developments by Suarez and Bellarmine. From the Thomistic reference to the whole multitude as a law maker and the ruler as its "vicegerent," Maritain and Simon derive a full-blown justification of liberal democracy.

17. Simon, *Philosophy of Democratic Government*, 190–94.
18. Maritain, *Man and the State*, 35, 127.

3. Subsidiarity and the Problem of Liberty

One of the key elements in Maritain's and Simon's social-political philosophy is the principle of subsidiarity or autonomy. They formulate this principle in slightly different ways. Simon formulates the "principle of autonomy": "No task which can be satisfactorily fulfilled by the smaller unit should ever be assumed by the larger unit. . . . It is perfectly obvious that there is more life and unqualifiedly greater perfection in a community whose parts are full of initiative than in a community whose parts act merely as instruments transmitting the initiative as the whole."[19] Maritain, who cites Simon's work on this principle, formulates the "principle of pluralism": "Everything in the body politic which can be brought about by particular organs or societies inferior in degree to the State and born out of the free initiative of the people *should* be brought about by those particular organs or societies."[20]

The Thomistic warrants for this principle of subsidiarity are found in unlikely places. In the *Summa theologiae* Thomas queries "whether it be necessary for the human will in order to be good to be conformed to the Divine will as regards the thing willed?" and again "whether all things are governed immediately by God?"[21] In the former text, Thomas argues that the wife of a thief condemned to death rightly wills that he be spared, whereas the judge rightly will that he be punished. The wife wills a private good, the judge wills a good for the whole, a common good. Thomas explains that not everyone must will the common good, or even the divine will, in a material way; they must will the divine good formally, but they do not always perceive the universal good to be willed materially.[22] In the latter text Thomas explains that "As to the design of government, God governs all things immediately; whereas in its execution, He governs some things by means of others. . . . God so governs things that He makes some of them to be causes of others in government; as a master, who not only imparts knowledge to his pupils, but gives them also the faculty of teaching others."[23]

19. Simon, *Philosophy of Democratic Government*, 129–30.
20. Maritain, *Man and the State*, 67.
21. ST I-II, q. 19, a. 10: "Utrum necessarium sit voluntatem humanam conformari voluntati divinae in volito, ad hoc quod sit bona." ST I, q. 103, a. 6: "Utrum omnia immediate gubernentur a Deo."
22. ST I-II, q. 19, a. 10, c.: "Voluntas igitur humana tenetur conformari divinae voluntati in volito formaliter, tenetur enim velle bonum divinum et commune: sed non materialiter."
23. ST I, q. 103, a. 6, c.: "Quantum autem pertinet ad executionem gubernationis,

The first text is said by Simon to be "the most profound thing ever written on the foundation of authority" and "the most precise exposition ever made of the principle commanding the theory of government."[24] With these texts he builds a very intricate theory of authority. Authority is required, as we have seen, for unity of action, but also for the direction of the community to the common good materially willed. And the same argument for authority establishes the principle of autonomy; that is, insofar as the authorities will the material good of the common good, it is up to particular people and particular groups to will the material good of the particular person or group. Simon states that "that particular goods be properly defended by particular persons matters greatly for the common good." Simon sees himself making common cause with Aristotle against the excessive unity of the state posited by Plato in the *Republic*. Accordingly, it is the modern democratic state that protects and encourages particular groups as opposed to the totalitarian attempts to control all sectors and activities of the citizens.

The principle of autonomy is also invoked to justify those institutions and practices which check the power of the state. Simon says that it is our duty to keep the state confined within its function and hold in check its threatening tendency to trespass.[25] Therefore, he says that the salvation of society depends upon an array of institutions provided with "the power of resistance"—private property, churches, press, private schools, labor unions, and free economic enterprise. In effect, then, Simon now combines the principle of political rule with the principle of autonomy to defend the structural pluralism of modern democracy.[26]

Maritain similarly applies his principle of pluralism to defend the existence of intermediate groups: The body politic must include a "multiplicity of particular societies which proceed from the free initiative of citizens and they should be as autonomous as possible" and be granted institutional recognition.[27] The state, he observes, is "inevitably dull and awkward—and as a result, easily oppressive and

---

Deus gubernat quaedam mediantibus aliis. . . . Et ideo sic Deus gubernat res, ut quasdam aliarum in gubernando causas instituat: sicut si aliquis magister discipulos suos non solum scientes faceret, sed etiam aliorum doctores."

24. Simon, "The Doctrinal Issue," 104; *Philosophy of Democratic Government*, 40.

25. Simon, *Philosophy of Democratic Government*, 134.

26. See David T. Koyzis, "Yves R. Simon's Contribution to a Structural Political Pluralism," in *Freedom in the Modern World*, 131–40.

27. Maritain, *Man and the State*, 11, 23. See Joseph W. Evans, "Jacques Maritain and the Problem of Pluralism in Political Life," in *Jacques Maritain: The Man and His Achievement*, ed. Joseph W. Evans (New York: Sheed and Ward, 1963), 215–36.

injudicious" in the fields of industry, culture, science, and the like. He concludes that the pluralist principle is even more vital to democracy than is universal suffrage: "vital energy should unendingly rise from the people within the body politic. In other words the program of the people should not be offered from above to the people . . . it should be the work of the people." Maritain bases his argument more on the second text cited above, concerning God's governance through intermediates or secondary causes. The pluralist principle demands a democratic regime if the people are to be free to exercise initiative.

4. Equality and Human Rights

Universal suffrage, popular consent, and private initiative are formal and material conditions for democracy. But it is the goal or end that most properly shows the nature of the regime. Democracy is classically defined by liberty; but liberty is traceable to the principle of equality against the claims to superiority made by aristocrats or monarchs. It is the ideal of equality which arguably animates contemporary democratic convictions. From the ideal of equality, democracy finds its goal of social justice and the defense of human rights. Indeed, one may well argue that the development of a natural rights doctrine is the distinguishing characteristic of modern political philosophy as distinguished from the ancient and medieval traditions. Maritain and Simon develop a notion of equality in which they combine the modern concern for rights with the natural law tradition. It also provides a ready defense of liberal democracy. Their notion of equality is derived from Thomas's metaphysics and epistemology.[28] Equality is founded on the real unity in nature of the essence of the human. By sharing the same nature, all human beings are accorded the same fundamental rights.

The basic text upon which both ground the democratic ideal of equality is from *On Being and Essence*.[29] Thomas explains that a nature or essence may be considered in two ways: one in individual things and one in the mind. In the former case it exists in an individual; in

28. See Jacques Maritain, "Human Equality," in *Ransoming the Time*, trans. Harry Lorin Binesse (New York: Scribner's, 1941), 1–31; Yves R. Simon, "Democratic Equality," in *Philosophy of Democratic Government*, 195–259. See my "Approaches to Democratic Equality."

29. *De ente*, chap. 3: "Natura autem uel essentia sic accepta potest dupliciter considerari. Uno modo secundum rationem propriam, et hec est absoluta consideratio ipsius. . . . Alio modo consideratur, secundum esse quod habet in hoc uel in illo. . . . Ergo patet quod natura hominis absolute considerata abstrahit a quolibet esse, ita tamen quod non fiat precisio alicuius eorum. Et hec natura sic considerata est que praedicatur de indiuiduis omnibus" (Leonine, p. 374). *On Being and Essence*, trans. Armand Maurer, 2d ed. (Toronto: Pontifical Institute of Mediaeval Studies, 1968), 46–47.

the latter, as a universal. The essence abstracts from individual differences but is open to such individual determination; the nature considered absolutely is truly predicated of each individual. Accordingly, there is one human nature that is the same in each. Simon concludes therefore, "It is highly proper that they should be described as created equal for in each of them the same system of intelligible features supplies individual reality with ability to exist."[30] Further, this metaphysical explanation allows one, he says, to make sense of the notions of brotherhood, natural rights, and rights belonging to all men. Nominalism is blamed for the racist and fascist totalitarian ideologies, for on sheer empirical grounds it is possible to deny the equality of individuals or races. There exists no real foundation for unity in essence or nature. Both men claim that it is a quirk of history that natural rights doctrines arose within a climate of nominalistic thought, and they see nominalism tending towards denial of equality. They believe that the modern notion of rights can be purged of its nominalist trappings and put on the proper grounding of natural law and a realistic metaphysics. By the same token, Maritain rejects an idealist denial of factual inequality and its role in social order. Rather, the idea of equality as unity in nature establishes the social solidarity to include all within the good of the civic community. It is not as such a justification for democracy; it imposes an obligation upon all to respect the fundamental dignity and good of each human being. Here is the link to natural law:

[T]here is no right unless a certain order ... is inviolably required by *what things are* in their intelligible type or their essence, or by what the nature of man is, and is cut out for: an order by virtue of which certain things like life, work, freedom are due to the human person. ... [S]uch an order ... which imposes itself upon our minds to the point of binding us in conscience, exists in things in a certain way, as a requirement of their essence.[31]

Maritain's grounding of rights is different from the modern nominalist and self-interested grounding; and it is not simply a theological grounding in the brotherhood of men, God's workmanship in all men, or the like. Rights embody the conditions necessary to promote the good human life; rights are telic, communal, and conditional. Maritain claims that all human beings possess certain rights; a minimum array of rights must be respected absolutely; but most rights are conditioned by the social and political conditions. That is, he says their exercise depends upon social conditions. He opposes the tendency to inflate

30. Simon, *Philosophy of Democratic Government*, 201.
31. Maritain, *Man and the State*, 96–97.

and make "absolute and limitless" individual rights. Yet on the other hand, he sets a dynamic goal for human society which is properly democratic; that is, the failure to realize and have all men exercise their rights is a sign of an "inhuman element that remains in the social structure of each period."[32] Thus the metaphysical doctrine as a shared nature justifies the goal of liberal democracy. Modern democracy is the most progressive attempt to realize the latent rights of all human beings, which rights are implicit in the shared unity of human nature.

Simon adopts a similar dynamic, but with his usual greater precision and political sobriety. He distinguishes the strict equality accorded to all by the minimum precepts, such as do not kill and fairness in exchange. But he says that many social goods are capable of a dynamic egalitarian tendency to be realized in time. Education, health, and welfare are goods that society must aim at establishing in greater equality. The true notion of equality demands social progress. But then Simon says that the egalitarian dynamic is legitimately delayed when its claim would infringe upon real human goods and in particular when it destroys subsidiarity and the autonomy of persons and institutions like family. It is this reading of equality in nature as establishing a dynamic or tendency towards greater and greater social progress that leads to the eventual transformation of the political philosophy of St. Thomas.

ST. THOMAS, DEMOCRACY, AND THE BEST REGIME

Do these texts indeed establish a justification of democracy? They may prove that democracy is a legitimate political regime consistent with fundamental principles of St. Thomas or they may be construed as recommending democracy as the best regime. The best regime may be qualified or absolute; qualified if best as a limited achievement and best under certain conditions; absolute if best under any conditions or best as the model in ideal conditions. It is clear that Maritain and Simon have developed a justification for liberal democracy that goes beyond the first option. They do not argue, however, that democracy is the best regime under any conditions; Simon for one is adamant in avoiding this excess of "democratic faith." They are recommending democracy as the best regime; in what sense do they do so? And how does it fit with the political philosophy of Thomas Aquinas? An examination of the texts of St. Thomas will help us to answer these questions.

32. Ibid., 102–3.

1. Thomistic Warrants for Democracy

The first cluster of texts relies upon the distinction between the political and the despotic regime. These texts certainly permit the justification of democracy as a means to resist tyranny and unjust rule. Specifically, the practice of universal suffrage is indeed an effective means to resist despotic rule. Democracy is therefore consistent with the Thomistic texts. But as Simon points out, democracy is not the only "political" regime. Other forms of regimes have effective means for resisting despotic rule; and indeed, he says that democracy may well consider some of these as well. Hence, the texts do not recommend democracy as the absolutely best regime or even the ideal regime. However, given the circumstances of the contemporary world, such as the tendency toward centralization, technical control, and new elites, democracy may be judged the best available regime to resist tyranny.

The second cluster of texts, the basis for the transmission theory of authority, again seems to legitimate democracy as one form of decent government. The power to depose in extreme circumstances and the role of consent in normal circumstances lend weight to the claims of popular authority. But again, it is not clear that the texts are exclusively democratic in nature. Simon acknowledges that the transmission theory was never meant to be an unqualified endorsement of democracy, nor does the text in the *Summa* warrant such.[33] Thomas says that either the people or the representative may make laws. The representative may legitimately make laws; the text does not imply that he must consult with the people through election or referendum, or that he derives power through transmission. He is said to represent and to care for the whole community. Thomas Gilby provides some interesting commentary on this text. First, he points out that the term *vicegerent* derives from "*gerere vicem*," to act on behalf of: hence the term designates "the public personage, the figure who personifies the community, and is its guardian and, in the fullest sense, its caretaker, 'qui curam habet'."[34] This description does not contain a hypothesis about the origin of temporal power; the implications for the meaning of temporal power are simply that it must serve the common good. Again, it does not exclusively endorse one or the other (multitude or

---

33. Simon, "The Doctrinal Issue," 112; *Philosophy of Democratic Government*, 177. See Wilfrid Parsons, "Saint Thomas Aquinas and Popular Sovereignty," *Thought* 16 (Spring 1941): 473–92.

34. Saint Thomas Aquinas, *Summa Theologiae, Law and Political Theory*. (IaIIae.90–97), ed. and trans. Thomas Gilby, Blackfriars vol. 28 (New York: McGraw-Hill, 1966), 13, n. c.

ruler), or derive one from the other, but affirms both as legitimate when commensurate to the common good.[35]

This problem of interpretation points to an ambiguity and possible equivocation in Maritain and Simon's case for liberal democracy. Maritain speaks of the "democratic philosophy" being the only true philosophy and that this philosophy legitimates any form of regime, aristocratic, monarchical, or other.[36] We seem to have two meanings of democracy. Democracy$_1$ means a political regime, as opposed to a despotic regime, which aims at the common good, and gives due consideration to popular consent and custom; Democracy$_2$ means a regime which includes popular elections, referenda, and the like. Of course, Democracy$_1$ does not automatically entail Democracy$_2$. The Thomistic texts establish Democracy$_1$ and not Democracy$_2$. How do the authors make the transition from Democracy$_1$ to Democracy$_2$? There are additional elements in their account. This is in part due to the historical conditions which make Democracy$_2$ the best approximation or embodiment of Democracy$_1$; but there is also a partisan argument for Democracy$_2$ that may well put them at odds with the spirit and text of their mentor. Further, it is strange to claim that there is a properly democratic body prior to the establishment of a regime, which is the fundamental political phenomenon according to the Aristotelian political science followed by Thomas Aquinas.

But the ambiguity is further compounded in the text at hand. What does Thomas mean by the "*multitudo*"? Gilby explains that "this does not mean the multitude, the masses, the populace, but the entire people, the whole body of citizens."[37] Similarly, Strauss points out that multitude does not necessarily designate a "democratically ordered multitude."[38] Indeed, Thomas at other times indicates that a multitude, by definition, must have an order of rule, and that rule must be by the best element in the whole.[39] His idea of the ordered multitude

---

35. "He does not touch on the hypothesis of a legal act by the people transferring the power of governing and legislating to the ruler, but leaves the matter as a general principle, that the people or their guardian are the only power under God commensurate with the common good"; ibid., 75.

36. See Maritain, *Man and the State*, 129.

37. Gilby, *Summa*, vol. 28, 14.

38. Strauss, *What is Political Philosophy?* 308.

39. *De regno*, chap. 1: "Wherefore also in all things that are ordained towards one end, one thing is found to rule the rest. Thus in the corporeal universe, by the first body, i.e., the celestial body, the other bodies are regulated according to the order of divine providence; and all bodies are ruled by a rational creature. So, too, in the individual man, the soul rules the body; and among the parts of the soul, the irascible and the concupiscible are ruled by reason. Likewise among the members of a body, one such as the heart or the head, is the principal and moves all the others. Therefore, in

is more inclined to monarchy or aristocracy, as we shall see below, and not democracy, which is the rule of a part over the whole. The ambiguity of the "multitude" repeats that of "democracy" insofar as multitude could mean an ordered whole (Democracy$_1$), or the majoritarian part of the whole (Democracy$_2$). These texts do not endorse the latter.

The third cluster of texts used to justify democracy pertains to the principle of subsidiarity, called pluralism or autonomy, derived from the metaphysics of divine governance. Maritain and Simon show the importance of freedom and particularity in Thomistic metaphysics. Again, it does not as such justify democracy; the principle calls for the political power to respect the integrity and prerogatives of the prepolitical associations such as family, business, and so forth. This respect for the less perfect society may be found in any number of regime forms. Modern liberal democracy is one such form, and perhaps it is an especially suitable form to allow for individual initiative. Perhaps it is the best regime available today to guarantee the integrity of intermediate groups; the problem of centralization is best resisted by the granting of political freedom. Tocqueville argues this case for political freedom as the buttress of intermediate groups. But this reading and justification of democracy runs into conflict with the reading of the fourth justification for democracy, the tendency towards greater equality. That is, the principle of subsidiarity, pluralism, or autonomy sets up a principled resistance to monarchical or oligarchical arrangements, but also to the encroachment of the state for liberal goals.

The basis for equality in the metaphysics of St. Thomas, the shared unity of human nature, provides an interpretation of rights as correlated with duties of natural law. The Thomistic account of rights allows for a minimum of natural precepts to be turned into the formulation of rights. But not only are other possible regimes consistent with respect for fundamental human rights, that is, fundamental precepts of natural law, there are serious doubts as to whether the Thomistic account is consistent with the interpretation given them by the jurisprudence of liberal democratic regimes. The Thomistic account

---

every multitude there must be some governing power." In St. Thomas Aquinas, *On Kingship*, trans. Gerald B. Phelan (Toronto: Pontifical Institute of Mediaeval Studies, 1949), 6. ". . . oportet igitur, preter id quod mouet ad proprium bonum uniuscuiusque, esse aliquid quod mouet ad bonum commune multorum. Propter quod et in omnibus que in unum ordinantur, aliquid inuenitur alterius regitium. In uniuersitate enim corporum per primum corpus, scilicet celeste, alia corpora ordine quodam diuine Prouidentie reguntur, omniaque corpora per creaturam rationalem. In uno etiam homine anime regit corpus, atque inter anime partes irascibilis et concupiscibilis ratione reguntur. Itemque inter membra corporis unum est principale, quod omnia mouet, ut cor, aut caput. Oportet igitur esse in omni multitudine aliquod regitiuum" (Leonine, p. 450).

is communally based and aims at a substantive notion of the good life; the contemporary democratic one is individually based and neutral towards questions of the good; it is a procedural notion of rights.[40] The contemporary notion is a development of the one proffered by the founders of modern political philosophy, Hobbes and Locke. There are equivocations in identifying the rights language of a Maritain with that of a Nozick, Rawls, or Dworkin. Simon and Maritain both admit that the theory of rights emerged in a climate of philosophical nominalism, but they consider this accidental and in some way a distortion of true rights theory. To what degree rights theories depend essentially on nominalist and voluntarist interpretations of natural law is a historical philosophical question of great import.[41] It is a question barely treated by Maritain and Simon. Further, the identification and endorsement of the goal of liberal democracy as the tendency to a greater realization of equality requires a theory of progress. And this conflicts with the principle of autonomy, as Simon himself admits.[42] Therefore, their justification of liberal democracy is not fully consistent within itself, nor is it fully warranted by the texts of Thomas Aquinas.

The texts cited by Simon and Maritain warrant democracy as a good regime to the extent that democracy embodies the conditions of a good regime—that it offers means of resistance to tyranny, serves the common good, protects intermediate groups, and protects the rights of its citizens in accord with the minimalistic precepts of natural law. The texts may even warrant a justification of democracy as the best available under contemporary circumstances of centralized power, and modern economic and educational conditions. This is a qualified acceptance of democracy. Additional texts of Thomas Aquinas, the explicitly political works, establish even greater qualifications on any Thomistic endorsement of democracy.

2. *Democracy and the Best Regime in St. Thomas*

As classically defined, democracy, as rule by the many, is not the best regime according to St. Thomas. In his treatise *On Kingship* Thomas outlines the major problems with democracy. As the rule of

40. See Michael Sandel, *Liberalism and the Limits of Justice* (Cambridge: Cambridge University Press, 1982); Christopher Wolfe and John Hittinger, *Liberalism at the Crossroads: Contemporary Liberal Political Theory and Its Critics* (Savage, Md.: Rowman and Littlefield, 1994); and John P. Hittinger, "Three Philosophies of Human Rights," in *Towards a National Morality,* ed. W. B. Ball (San Francisco: Ignatius Press, 1992), 246–57.

41. See Richard Tuck, *Natural Rights Theories: Their Origin and Development* (Cambridge: Cambridge University Press, 1979).

42. *Philosophy of Democratic Government,* 226–29. I treat this problematic in "Approaches to Democratic Equality."

a part over the whole, it is an unjust regime: "An unjust government exercised by the many is called a democracy, that is, 'rule by the people,' which occurs when the common people use the force of numbers to oppress the rich. In this case, the whole people acts like a tyrant."[43] Second, government by one person is better than government by many because one can better promote "unity in peace." From experience he argues we may learn that "provinces and cities that are not ruled by one person are torn by dissension." Continual dissension leads to civil war, as was evident in the Roman Republic. In addition, Thomas believes, following Aristotle, that the majority are not capable of a high or perfect virtue; accordingly, law must seek a moderate goal.[44] If virtue is the major qualification of rule, then it would follow that democracy is not the best form of government.

The argument for the best regime follows along these lines. Monarchy is best from the standpoint of unity in peace. Further, Thomas argues that a multitude is not a flat multitude, assuming egalitarian sameness; there is diversity of achievement, virtue, and function. The best should rule; and such a principle could justify monarchy, aristocracy, or polity, which Thomas defines as rule by the warriors. Virtue and character are mentioned as a basis for kingly rule. Thomas also sees the need for some limit on the king's power, lest it become tyrannical. He recommends legal constraints, and therefore something like constitutional monarchy.

One of the most succinct and comprehensive statements of political philosophy may be found in the *Treatise on Law* in conjunction with his analysis of the judicial precepts of the old law. In addressing "Whether the Old Law Enjoined Fitting Precepts Concerning Rulers?" Thomas argues that divine law provided for a mixed regime, combining monarchy, aristocracy, and democracy.[45] Combining unity, rarity

43. *De regno,* chap. 1 (Leonine, p. 450; Phelan, p. 8).

44. These arguments are from *De regno,* chap. 2 (Leonine, pp. 451–52; Phelan, pp. 11–13) and ST I-II, q. 96, a. 2, c.: "Lex autem humana ponitur multitudini hominum, in qua maior pars est hominum non perfectorum virtute. Et ideo lege humana non prohibentur omnia vitia, a quibus virtuosi abstinent, sed solum graviora, a quibus possibile est maiorem partem multitudinis abstinere; et praecipue quae sunt in nocumentum aliorum, sine quorum prohibitione societas humana conservari non posset, sicut prohibentur lege humana homicidia et furta et huiusmodi."

45. ST I-II, q. 105, a. 1, c.: "Unde optima ordinatio principum est in aliqua civitate vel regno, in qua unus praeficitur secundum virtutem qui omnibus praesit; et sub ipso sunt aliqui principantes secundum virtutem; et tamen talis principatus ad omnes pertinet, tum quia ex omnibus eligi possunt, tum quia etiam ab omnibus eliguntur. Talis enim est optima polita, bene commixta ex regno, inquantum unus praeest; et aristocratia, inquantum multi principantur secundum virtutem; et ex democratia, idest po-

of virtue, and popular consent is the great challenge of political form. The mixed regime does it best, not democracy.

Thomas's legacy in political philosophy, therefore, does not provide an unqualified endorsement of democracy. It actually provides grounds for a strong case against democracy and in favor of monarchy. The best regime is a mixture of the various regimes. Maritain and Simon go beyond claims of the legitimacy of democratic government; they endorse what Simon calls the "democratic spirit" and what Maritain calls the "democratic faith."

3. Thomism and the Democratic Spirit

How can one account for the differences between Thomas Aquinas and his twentieth-century interpreters? I believe that it is to be found in their sense of the historical situation and the possibility of progress. Their perspective raises some serious questions regarding the substance, as well as the rhetoric and method, of contemporary Thomistic political philosophy.

In order to appreciate the depth of commitment to the democratic ideal found in Maritain and Simon we have to look at some of the passages which preface and intertwine the actual deployment of texts and which reveal the convictions which animate their works. For example, Maritain claims that democracy is "the highest terrestrial achievement of which the rational animal is capable here below."[46] He believes that humanity is progressing to a definitive moral rationalization of political life and that we are at the early stages of that process; democracy is now "the only way through which the progressive energies in human history do pass." This is due in great part to the need for the "human energies of free men," thus reflecting his use of the principle of subsidiarity. But this is also due to the fact that democracy is the true "gospel regime"—democracy relies upon the inspiration of the gospel for its origins and true success and it best reflects the terrestrial hope of the gospel.[47] In a very important passage in *The Rights of Man and Natural Law*, Maritain explains his interpretation of Aristotle's typology of regimes. Monarchy produces unity and strength, aristocracy produces a differentiation of value and cultivates the high-

---

testate populi, inquantum ex popularibus possunt eligi principes, et ad populum pertinet electio principum." See John R. Kayser, "Aquinas's 'Regimen Bene Commixtum' and the Medieval Critique of Classical Republicanism," *The Thomist* 46 (April 1982): 195–220.

46. Maritain, *Man and the State*, 59.

47. Ibid., 61ff. See also *Christianity and Democracy* (San Francisco: Ignatius Press, 1986), passim.

est and rarest virtues, and the democratic or republican regime tends
toward freedom.[48] Furthermore, the best regime is a mixed regime
combining all three values. But then he goes on to say that monarchy
and aristocracy are stages on the road to the mixed republican regime
which assimilates the values of unity and excellence, and it thereby
transcends them. In order to develop the progressive tendency of
mankind Maritain is wont to praise what he calls "prophetic shock
minorities," self-appointed elites who will awaken the people and lead
them to the deeper realization of democracy. In particular he praises
John Brown, Thomas Paine, and French Revolutionaries.[49] This sur-
plus of democratic conviction goes well beyond the philosophy of
Thomas Aquinas.

Similarly, Simon exhibits the deeper convictions in favor of democracy in a number of significant passages in *Philosophy of Democratic
Government*.[50] In a sarcastic tone uncharacteristic of the book as a
whole, Simon accuses the conservatives of advocating paternal authority of the few over the many because they view the many on par
with an inferior race or no better than children, criminals, and the
feeble-minded. He says that an elite of "leaders trained and educated
by men of rare knowledge and superior virtue" may not be "a perverse
ideal," but it is not democratic. Further, he admits that some conditions
tending toward anarchy or tyranny may rule out democracy in favor
of nondemocratic measures. What characterizes the democratic spirit
is an "audacity" and a willingness to take risks in granting full autonomy to individuals. The risks, he says, require "new forms of discipline" and "new and costly forms of heroism" if democracy is to
maintain itself. In the argument for universal suffrage he makes the
case on the basis of checks and balances; then he concludes by saying
that gone forever is the belief that the destiny of the common man
could be entrusted to the wisdom of the upper classes. He makes the
argument more pointed in a lengthy discussion and critique of the
upper class as unable to be in communion with the people and therefore apt to seek their own advantage.[51] Social conservation in the face
of egalitarian progress he describes as "maintenance of advantages
traditionally enjoyed by small minorities." Although he gives very se-

48. Jacques Maritain, *Rights of Man and Natural Law*, trans. Doris C. Anson (San
Francisco: Ignatius Press, 1986), 131–33.
    49. Maritain, *Man and the State*, 139–40.
    50. See Simon, *Philosophy of Democratic Government*: on paternalism, 13–18; on uni-
versal suffrage, 98–99; on progress towards greater equality, 207; on the blindness of
the upper class, 215–22; on unequal exchange, 234.
    51. Tocqueville makes a similar argument for the justice of the democratic claim
against aristocracy; *Democracy in America*, 231–35.

rious consideration to the claim of excellence and virtue put forward by nondemocrats, Simon advocates a democratic spirit, a liberal attitude, as opposed to the conservative one historically characterized at best by paternalism and at worst by selfishness, indifference, or exploitation. Simon acknowledges many problems of democracy posed by Aristotle, Thomas, and contemporary writers, and scrutinizes many of them very closely, but others are left virtually untouched.

The advocacy of the democratic spirit and the sense of historical progress take Simon and Maritain well beyond the political philosophy of St. Thomas. The justification of democracy and the differences from Thomas raise some important substantive, as well as methodological and rhetorical issues.

The substantive issues are at least two. First, have Maritain and Simon done an adequate analysis of political regimes? Second, can the liberal notion of rights be so readily assimilated to traditional natural law? We have seen how Maritain speaks of a democratic philosophy which precedes the form of regime; in addition, he speaks of democracy as the term of progress incorporating the values of monarchy and aristocracy. Although he speaks of the analogous realization of the values of unity and excellence in a democracy, it is not clear that he admits the trade-off and possible loss of the strong or definitive sense of those values within democracy. This makes him either too blind to its shortcomings, or too expectant in the prospects for progress.[52] In the final analysis, Maritain makes appeal to Christian inspiration as a means to realize the heights of democracy. Simon makes a much more careful attempt to weigh the various claims to rule. His account relies more on the classical notion of the mixed regime as the way to ensure its success and excellence. Part of the difference between Thomas and Simon is simply due to the change in historical conditions. Many have pointed out that Aristotle's critique of democracy is premised upon the lack of education and development in the many due to primitive economic and technological conditions. With a majority who are educated, the prospects and claims for democracy take on a persuasive validity. But in Simon's case the problem is that he has not quite successfully merged the democratic spirit with the goods which he seeks to preserve from his Thomistic position, such as virtue and family. The difficulty in maintaining new forms of discipline or new forms of heroism in the contemporary situation is due in part to the very democratic spirit and conditions of a democratic regime which he so ardently advocates. Strauss has pointed out that Simon

52. See my "Maritain and America."

assumes that the conditions of modern technology, and therefore of modern democracy, are the normal or natural conditions; Strauss indicates that there is a certain audacity and lack of moderation in the technology which conditions modern democracy.[53] Is it a feature of the democratic spirit to push its audacity to immoderate measures?

The second substantive issue deals with the problem of human rights. We cannot begin to treat this very important issue of the relation of natural law and natural rights.[54] It is curious that both Maritain and Simon minimize the historical origins of the doctrine of rights. Maritain considers the nominalistic philosophy as an accidental error which preys upon the truth, and Simon believes that it was accidental that the doctrine arose in a nominalistic climate. Their account of human rights, based on natural law, is telic and communal. Rights are conditions which insure and promote human excellence and flourishing. Maritain would distinguish his "personalist" account from the "individualist" account given by modern philosophy.[55] But the doctrine of human rights as it unfolds in western theory and practice of democracy is increasingly neutral with respect to the good and individualistic in orientation. Are Maritain and Simon now in a situation of serious equivocation in their advocacy of rights? Ironically, the two authors are now classified as natural law theorists and conservatives, despite their best effort, as we have seen, to be positioned on the left and in the progressive spirit of democracy.

This in turn raises an issue about the rhetoric of their political philosophy. What are the possibilities of a common democratic faith and cooperation in a divided world given the development of the liberal notion of rights found in Dworkin or Rawls? We find attempts to free the public from any demand for virtue, pushed to extremes of decriminalization of the most serious vices and practices, all in the name of natural rights. Maritain and Simon would of course denounce such accounts as perversions of the true idea of natural rights. But they can do this only to the extent that they cling to the natural law account of morality and politics, which the modern account explicitly rejects. Perhaps Thomistic political philosophy must reverse the fields

53. *What is Political Philosophy?* 310–11.

54. John Finnis, *Natural Law and Natural Rights* (New York: Oxford University Press, 1978); Henry Veatch, *Human Rights: Fact or Fancy* (Baton Rouge: Louisiana State University Press, 1985); idem, *Swimming Against the Current in Contemporary Philosophy,* Studies in Philosophy and the History of Philosophy, vol. 20 (Washington, D.C.: The Catholic University of America Press, 1990); Alasdair MacIntyre, *After Virtue,* 2d ed. (Notre Dame: University of Notre Dame Press, 1984).

55. Jacques Maritain, "The Human Person and Society," in *Scholasticism and Politics,* ed. and trans. Mortimer J. Adler (New York: Doubleday, 1940), 61–90.

of rhetorical emphasis. Rather than highlight the promise of democracy and progress and then bring out the conservative constraints of pluralism and virtue, perhaps their account now must be presented with an emphasis upon the promise and prospects of the good life as traditionally understood, and then praise the democratic approximations to this standard.

This brings us finally to the question as to the method for appropriating the legacy of Thomas Aquinas. Maritain and Simon are concerned lest Thomism become irrelevant (a "paleo-Thomism") by an excessive attention to historical and textual study. Of course they strive to be faithful to the texts and spirit of Thomas. But as Simon states in the opening of his article "Thomism and Democracy":

A discussion of Thomism and democracy might have the character of an historical investigation; the question would be to disentangle, from many texts scattered in the works of St. Thomas, what he actually thought about the democratic regime such as he knew it. Now, if Thomism enjoys, as we believe it does, a vitality which is not by any means confined within the limits of St. Thomas's short life, it should be possible to give a Thomistic treatment of the problem of democracy such as it appears to us. The latter point of view will prevail in this study.[56]

Accordingly, Simon does two things; he focuses on the metaphysical texts and not the political texts of Thomas; and he takes his bearings by the dispute between democracy and totalitarianism. This methodological decision helps to explain the rhetorical and substantive issues mentioned above. Rhetorically, there was the fear that a critique of liberalism would feed into the nihilism of the right wing in Europe.[57] Today, of course, the problem of nihilism is posed from the left, not the right. Any attempt to put forward standards of natural justice and virtue are decried as impositions on the freedom of individuals. Substantively, it tends to obscure other sets of problems that may give a better analysis of the political regimes. For example, one may make thematic the problem of ancients versus moderns in the method of Leo Strauss; this yields a very different reading of the problem of regime both in terms of emphasis and in terms of analysis.[58] As an example, the problem of consent and universal suffrage

56. Yves R. Simon, "Thomism and Democracy," in *Science, Philosophy and Religion*, ed. Louis Finkelstein and Lyman Bryson (New York: The Conference on Science, Philosophy and Religion in Their Relation to the Democratic Way of Life, 1942), 258.

57. See Yves R. Simon, "Beyond the Crisis of Liberalism," in *Essays in Thomism*, ed. Robert E. Brennan (New York: Sheed and Ward, 1942), 265.

58. See Charles N. R. McCoy, *The Structure of Political Thought* (New York: McGraw-Hill, 1963); James V. Schall, "Metaphysics, Theology, and Political Theory," *Political Science Reviewer* 11 (Fall 1981): 1–26; Ernest Fortin, "Thomas Aquinas," in *History of*

takes on a different light when removed from the awkward problematic of the transmission theory; the tension of wisdom versus consent is actually a more directly political perspective on the problem of rule and the right to rule.[59] Simon may have set up an unnecessary methodological division between historical reading and the contemporary problematic. Closer attention to the text and intention in light of the challenge of modern philosophy may actually yield more insight than approaching the text from the contemporary problematic prior defined. One might also consider the problematic of traditions or communities of discourse and the breakdown of contemporary moral language, as does Alasdair MacIntyre. Again, this would allow one to approach Thomas on terms closer to his own and perhaps allow a more natural unfolding of political themes; for example, the natural law and virtue ethics of St. Thomas would not be rushed up so quickly into the terms of modern natural rights. This may actually offer much-needed alternatives to the stalemate of contemporary moral and political philosophy.

In conclusion, I would offer this summary evaluation of the legacy of St. Thomas and that of his disciples, Jacques Maritain and Yves R. Simon. The legacy of St. Thomas is rich and diverse; it is found throughout his writings; in particular, the explicit writings on political philosophy, but also in his metaphysics of liberty and order which Maritain and Simon developed so well. They developed a very significant and timely defense of liberal democracy and it is of deep Thomistic inspiration and influence. To be fully successful, their justification requires further development and broadening. The basis for natural rights and the prospects for virtue in democracy are important areas for a sharpened analysis. Simon's own account of the various claims to rule is a very important contribution and an item to be developed; so too is Maritain's critique of modern individualist democracy. The legacy of St. Thomas is the legacy of political philosophy itself: how to mix freedom (democracy) with unity (kingship) and virtue (aristocracy). One needs a perspective outside of modern liberal democracy to assess its strengths and weakness. Tocqueville had this, as did Maritain and Simon. How Thomas Aquinas, a premodern, a theologian, and an advocate of monarchy could inspire a modern, secular account of democracy is testimony to his rich legacy. Such is the fruitful tension we find in Maritain and Simon in their use of Aquinas in the justification of democracy.

Political Philosophy, ed. Leo Strauss and Joseph Cropsey, 3d ed. (Chicago: University of Chicago Press, 1987), 248–75.

59. See Leo Strauss, *Natural Right and History* (Chicago: University of Chicago Press, 1952), chap. 4, "Classic Natural Right."

9

Aquinas's Legacy on Individuation, Cogitation, and Hominization

—————————————————————————————————

WILLIAM A. WALLACE

One of the invaluable legacies bequeathed to us by St. Thomas Aquinas is the close connection he perceived between the speculative sciences, such as the science of nature, and the practical sciences, such as medicine and ethics. Not only in his *Summa theologiae,* wherein he made the strong claim that sacred theology as a science is itself both speculative and practical,[1] but also in his many other writings he urged a close union between *theoria* and *praxis,* between *esse* and *agere,* between *l'être et l'agir.* It might be interesting to count how many times Aquinas invokes in his writings the axiom *Agere sequitur esse,* action follows on existence, or a thing acts as it is, that is, according to its nature. But oddly enough this link he saw between nature and activity, and eventually the idea that human nature provides a norm for human activity, is much overlooked in the present day. Even Catholic moralists, including those who pay homage to his "natural law" doctrine, do their dialectics and casuistry in almost total disregard of his teachings in natural philosophy, metaphysics, and systematic or speculative theology.

In this essay I wish to call attention to some aspects of the latter teachings that impact on present-day problems in bioethics or medical ethics, particularly those relating to the origins of, and then the demise of, the human person. This explains the "hominization" part of the title. This term refers to the completion of the process whereby a human person is procreated, and God, according to Thomas's teaching, creates a human soul *ex nihilo* and infuses it into an incipient organism.[2] Aquinas's teaching on this process is referred to as "delayed hominization," for he did not think that God creates and infuses the human soul at the moment of conception, what is called today

1. ST I, q. 1, a. 4, c.
2. This is a constant refrain in St. Thomas's writings: e.g., see ST I, q. 79, a. 4; q. 90, a. 2. See also the texts referenced in n. 8 and those cited in n. 16 below.

"immediate hominization," but only after the genetic materials have developed to the point where they can support a human life. Related to this process, and actually the obverse of it, is what now may be called "dehominization," the process that terminates in the human soul's departing the body and beginning a new life as a separated substance—becoming, as we say, one of the "souls of the faithful departed." Aquinas himself did not speculate about the time at which this occurs, but consistent with his teachings one might hold that it can occur well before all the signs of physical death are apparent. The Polish Dominican who has pioneered this teaching, Mierczyslaw Krapiec, refers to physical death as death "accepted passively" and distinguishes it from death "understood actively," that is, death as a real experience of the human spirit.[3] Thus far we have no term to designate this active type of dehominization (the reverse of "delayed hominization"), but let us propose "psychic dehominization" as catching its essential element, for reasons to be explained shortly.

The two other terms in the title of this essay are "individuation" and "cogitation." The first has an obvious connection with delayed hominization, for the problem we are there addressing is the time of origin of the human person, of an individual human being, accepting Boethius's definition of a person as an individual of the human species. St. Thomas has his own teaching as to how individuation occurs, and this becomes important in light of new findings about the early development of the human zygote. The other term, cogitation, figures importantly in psychic dehominization. It does so through Thomas's teaching on the cogitative sense, particularly on how the human intellect is dependent on the phantasm or the percept for its thought processes. Cogitation, in this understanding, can take place only when the proper organs are present and functioning in the human body, at

3. In an abridged version of his *I-Man: An Outline of Philosophical Anthropology*, trans. Marie Lesco et al., and ed. Francis J. Lescoe and Roger B. Duncan (New Britain, Conn.: Mariel Publications, 1985), 177–78. In this work Krapiec does not cite any texts in which St. Thomas explicitly refers to dehominization, but David Gallagher has pointed out a text in his exposition of Proposition 1 of the *Liber de Causis* in which Aquinas does so. There the Angelic Doctor compares what happens in the generation of a human being with what happens at corruption. He writes: "For it is obvious that in the generation of an individual human being one finds in the material subject first existence, then a living thing, and after that a human. . . . And again, in the process of corruption, first [the individual] loses the use of reason and remains alive and breathing, then it loses life and remains a being, because it does not corrupt into nothingness" ("Manifestum est autem in generatione unius particularis hominis quod in materiali subiecto primo invenitur esse, deinde invenitur vivum, postmodum autem est homo. . . . Rursumque in via corruptionis primo amittit usum rationis et remanet vivum et spirans, secundo amittit ⟨vitam⟩ et remanet ipsum ens, quia non corrumpitur in nihilm" [Saffrey, p. 6]).

a minimum, the cerebral cortex and at least some portions of the brain. In their absence human thought becomes impossible and the ultimate decision that characterizes the natural completion of a human life, and thus death as "understood actively," can no longer take place, even though life-signs continue to persist in the body.

Now both of these terms, individuation and cogitation, stand for technical concepts that are difficult to comprehend, and so I cannot pretend to explain them adequately in an essay of this length. With the aid of two diagrams, however, I will attempt to convey the general idea behind them, and thus make clear the relevance of St. Thomas's teachings to present-day problems in bioethics.

NATURES AND POWERS

Let us begin with delayed hominization. Its discussion will ultimately center on the problem of individuation, but there are many other concepts that are presupposed for its understanding, and we must first review these. Among them the most fundamental are the concepts of protomatter (the *prōtē hulē* of Aristotle or the *materia prima* of Aquinas), of substantial form (the correlate of protomatter), and of bodily natures and the powers through which they act. All of these have their roots in Aquinas, and in Aristotle before him, but they also require updating in light of modern science, as we shall see. Such updating will also require us to take up some ideas relating to natural generation, to creation and evolution, to God's *concursus*, and to the little-heard notion of "transient nature," or *ens viale* in the language of the Schools, which is to assume key importance in what follows.

The schema of Figure 1 will serve to introduce the first set of concepts. Actually it is a composite of several diagrams I have used over many years, to explain what I call the "life powers model of human nature" in a Philosophy of Science course for graduate nursing students.[4] It is the closest one can get to providing a picture of the human soul. A human being, in the Catholic view, is said to be a composite of body and soul. To be technically correct, it is better to say that man is a composite of matter and form, for a human being is a natural substance, and all natural substances are composites of matter and form. The matter referred to here is not the matter of ordinary ex-

4. See my essay "Computers and the Modeling of Man," in *From a Realist Point of View: Essays on the Philosophy of Science,* 2d ed. (Lanham, Md.: University Press of America, 1983), 245–71. The original essay was based on Newman Lectures given at the Massachusetts Institute of Technology in 1961. A fuller development of the life-powers model sketched there will be found in my "Nature as Animating: The Soul in the Human Sciences," *The Thomist* 49 (1985): 612–48.

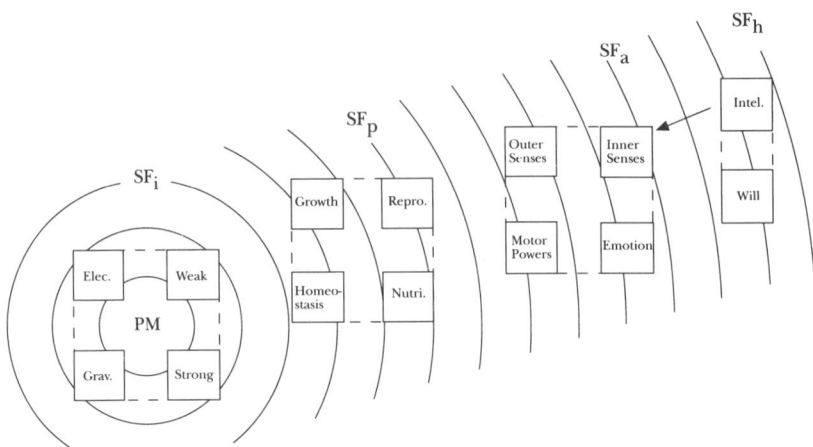

FIG. 1. A LIFE POWERS MODEL OF HUMAN NATURE

perience; rather, it is that out of which ordinary matter is formed, never itself existing in an unformed state, and hence called primordial matter or protomatter. It is hard to conceive this, but one way of doing so is to see it as a conservation principle, say, what is measured by mass-energy in the present day. Protomatter is designated by the letters PM enclosed by the small circle in the first box to the left of the diagram.

The activating or forming principle that is the correlate of protomatter is substantial form, designated by the letters SF at four places along the top of the diagram, for it is the form that energizes protomatter, as it were, and makes of it a natural substance. SF stands for "substantial form," but the letters can also be taken to stand for "specifying form" or "stabilizing form," for it determines the substance to be of a particular species and stabilizes or conserves it in the determined type. To make this clear we should note that there are four kinds of substantial form, designated by the different subscripts attached to the letters SF across the top of the diagram. The lowest order, indicated by SF_i, with the subscript i standing for inorganic, determines the protomatter to be a substance with an inorganic nature; that next to the right, indicated by SF_p, with the subscript p standing for plant, determines the protomatter to be a substance with a plant nature; that to the right of it, indicated by SF_a, with the subscript a standing for animal, determines the protomatter to be a substance with an animal nature; and the last to the right, indicated by

SF$_h$, with the subscript h standing for human, determines the proto-matter to be a substance with a human nature. Within each of these types, with the exception of the last, there is the possibility of many different species. Thus, among inorganic substances we might have copper or sulphur; among plants, geraniums or oaks; among animals, squirrels or cows, and so on. The substantial form is said to be a specifying form because it determines the substance to have a partic-ular nature, that of copper or sulphur, geranium or oak, squirrel or cow. In fact, the substantial form itself may be referred to as the nature of the substance it determines. And we recognize this when we observe a particular substance and note its nature, saying this is copper, and that is an oak, and the animal running there is a squirrel. A nature, moreover, is a durable thing, and that is why we can speak of a sub-stantial form as a stabilizing form. If a substance is copper, or oak, or a squirrel, it is not a transient entity but tends to stay that way—copper perhaps for years or centuries, the oak and the squirrel over their life spans.

Apart from surface appearance, we should add that we further categorize natures on the basis of the powers from which the activities or reactivities of various substances originate.[5] These are indicated in our diagram by the little boxes grouped under the four SF's. For the inorganic, note that Aquinas's four elements and their qualities have been updated by the four forces of modern physics: gravitational force, electromagnetic force, the weak force, and the strong force. Plant powers include those of nutrition, growth, and reproduction, all noted by Aquinas, to which homeostasis has been added as the basic power of life control. Animal powers are those of sensation, both ex-ternal and internal, those that originate movement, and those that activate the sense appetites or the emotions, all of which were likewise known to St. Thomas. And finally there are the two distinctively hu-man powers about which St. Thomas knew the most, those of thought and personal decision, known as the intellect and the will, respec-tively.[6]

It is important to note that all these powers, except the last two, require bodily parts or organs for their operation. That is why plants and animals are called organisms, for their bodies are differentiated into organs with which they perform their various life functions. The

5. A more complete description of these powers and their perfectibility is given in "Nature as Animating," 615–43.

6. Aquinas provides his view of the powers in some detail in ST I, first in general in qq. 77–78, then the intellective powers in detail in q. 79, and finally the appetitive powers in qq. 80–82.

organs are parts of their bodies; the powers that activate or energize them may be thought of as parts of their souls, so let us call them "power parts" to distinguish them from bodily parts. Inorganic substances, of course, do not have organs properly speaking, and so we do not refer to their forms as souls, though we speak of plant souls, and animal souls, and human souls. Yet we now know something that St. Thomas did not, namely, that inorganic substances likewise have bodily parts: molecules, atoms, nuclei, electrons, all controlled by the four basic forces that we might say "energize" the world of the non-living.

Notice now a curious feature of the diagram in Figure 1. It may be viewed as picturing four different kinds of natural substance, or it may be seen as picturing only one particular kind of substance, depending on how much of the diagram is taken into account. But, when considering any one kind of natural substance, note this further fact: one can disregard the powers that are found on its right, but one is forced to take into account the powers that are found on its left. A plant, for example, shown as SF_p, does not have the powers of sensation, movement, and reasoning that are found in animals and humans, and so these are not required for its understanding. Yet, as biochemistry has taught us, it cannot exercise its own powers of nutrition and growth if it is not a physico-chemical composite endowed with the basic forces of the inorganic. Similarly, a brute animal, shown as SF_a, does not have the powers of intellect and will, and so these are not necessary to understand it; but it cannot be an animal if it does not have the vegetative powers of nutrition, growth, and reproduction, as well as the physico-chemical components on which these in turn are based. And finally, the human being, shown as SF_h farthest on the right, requires everything on the left to carry out its life functions. The human substance is at once human, and animal, and plant, and inorganic. The human soul, as Aquinas explains it, includes virtually within itself an animal soul, a plant soul, and the form of an inorganic substance—and so it contains all their powers as power parts.[7] Through them it is able to energize its many bodily parts, the organs and components of which the human body is composed.

I stated earlier that this diagram comes the closest one can get to providing a picture of the human soul, so let me now spell out what is meant by that. Note that apart from the letters and the boxes on the diagram we have also included circular lines to create the impression of a field radiating out from protomatter (PM). That field may

7. ST I, q. 76, a. 3, c.

now be thought of as an energizing or enlivening field, and indeed as an analogue to the soul itself, for the soul is what energizes and enlivens the body. It is shown there in static fashion—complete, extending from PM to embrace the powers farthest to the right, intellect and will. But it may also be viewed in dynamic fashion, as a field beginning at PM and gradually expanding out and bringing with it the various powers shown on the diagram. I explain such a process to the nursing graduates on the analogy of the development of the parts of the human body. The body begins with what is little more than a complex protein molecule like DNA, then becomes a primitive organism capable of only nourishment and growth, then develops organs that enable it to sense and to move, and finally becomes an infant with a nervous system and a brain capable one day of rational activity. As the organs develop, the soul enlivens them with the powers necessary to activate the functions of plant life, animal life, and finally human life. That is the way St. Thomas conceived of our physical origins. The human seed, in his view, is first informed by a plant soul with its powers, then this is replaced by an animal soul with its powers, and finally God creates a human soul endowed with all those powers in eminent fashion, and a new human person thus enters His kingdom.[8] One can see now why his account of human origins is referred to as delayed hominization.

I have often asked nursing graduates if they see any evidence of the reverse process happening at the end of human life, of the energizing field contracting, as it were, withdrawing the soul's powers as the various organs atrophy or otherwise become incapable of supporting vital functions. Many say yes. For it appears that it is not uncommon for elderly or comatose patients first to lose their power to think clearly, then their powers to perceive or to remember and even begin to show signs of a demented state, then merely to subsist in what is called a persistent vegetative state, and finally to perform life functions only when connected to an external machine. If this truly happens it could be a case of the psychic dehominization described at the beginning of this essay.

To complete this discussion of nature and substantial form I must finally talk briefly about a strange type of nature which, as opposed to the stable natures just treated, may be called a transient nature.

8. St. Thomas goes into detail on this process in four places: *In II Sent.* d. 18, q. 2, aa. 1 and 3 (Mandonnet, pp. 457–72); SCG II, chaps. 86–89; *De potentia*, q. 3, aa. 9–12 (Marietti, pp. 63–78); and ST I, q. 118. All of these texts are analyzed by Michael A. Taylor in "Human Generation in the Thought of Thomas Aquinas: A Case Study on the Role of Biological Fact in Theological Science" (S.T.D.diss., The Catholic University of America, 1981).

This is what some medievals spoke of as an *ens viale,* "a being on the way." St. Thomas did not have an extensive knowledge of such entities, instanced in his day as seeds or *semina,* which quite obviously are on the way to becoming plants and animals.[9] Now one of the great discoveries of modern science, in my view, is its uncovering a vast number of transient entities in the world of nature. I refer to the world of elementary particles, most of which have a very transitory existence. Practically all are radioactive, with an extremely short half-life; others are charged particles, whose charge makes them open-ended, as it were, ready to become something else at the first opportunity. These particles are undoubtedly real in some way. Do they also have natures? Can we speak of the nature of a proton, a neutron, and so on? On the basis of our diagram we would say yes: the four basic forces are operative in the subatomic realm as in the atomic, and the same proto-matter or mass-energy is available for their coming-to-be and passing away. But if they have natures, these are not stable natures like those discussed thus far. Their organizing form is not a stabilizing form in the sense used here, and yet for the brief period of their existence it is a specifying form, an SF_t, with the subscript t standing for transient, a nature that enjoys in most cases but a fleeting existence, yet is still a part of the physical universe.

CREATION AND EVOLUTION

Thus far I have talked of matter and form, of material and formal causality, but have not yet discussed the efficient causes whereby natural processes are activated. A convenient way of entering this topic is a second diagram (Fig. 2), which combines Thomistic theology with modern science to give a concordist view of the origin of the universe.[10] I say this because it associates God's creative act at the beginning of time with the "big-bang" theory of cosmic evolution.

9. St. Thomas does not appear to have used the expression "ens viale" in his published writings, for it is not listed in the *Index Thomisticus.* Yet there is no doubt that he employed the concept. Note, for example, the passage in ST I, q. 119, a. 1, ad 3, where he refers to the "humidum nutrimentale" as "quod nondum habet perfectam naturam speciei, sed est *in via,* ut sanguis et hujusmodi" (emphasis added). Again, in SCG II, chap. 89, after first noting that in the generation of animals and men, culminating as it does in a "forma perfectissima," there are "plures formae et generationes intermediae," he goes on to state that "intermedia non habent speciem completam, sed sunt *in via* ad speciem; et ideo non generantur ut permaneant, sed ut per ea ad ultimum generatum perveniatur" (emphasis added).

10. I have used a schema similar to this and provided a fuller explanation of it in "Nature and Human Nature as the Norm in Medical Ethics," *Catholic Perspectives on Medical Morals,* ed. Edmund D. Pellegrino et al. (Dordrecht: Kluwer Academic Publishers, 1989), 25–53, esp. 36–40.

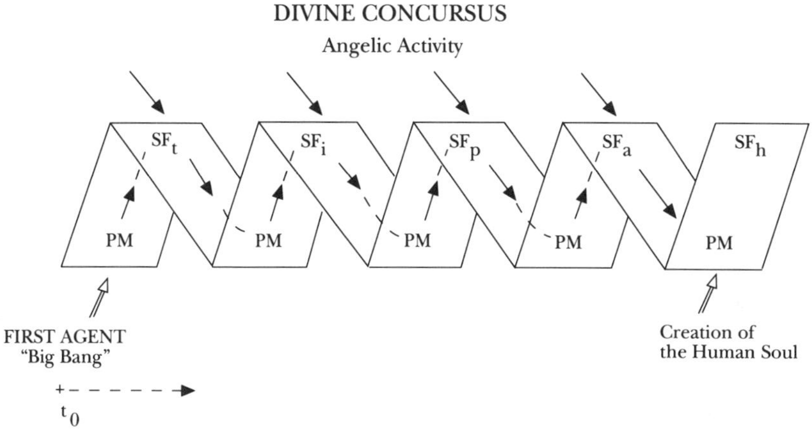

DIVINE CONCURSUS
Angelic Activity

FIG. 2. A CONCORDIST VIEW OF CREATION AND EVOLUTION

As can be seen on the diagram, time t_0 began some ten to twenty billion years ago with the production by God, *ex nihilo*, of the primordial mass-energy of which the universe is now composed. Simultaneous with this, God as First Agent also initiated the "big bang," a cosmic explosion whose vestiges are still discernible at the edges of our expanding universe. If we are to believe scientific accounts, what happened immediately after this went as follows: a very brief period, much less than a second by our reckoning, of fundamental particle activity at very high energies; then a longer period for the formation of chemical elements and compounds, from which stars and planets were formed some five billion years ago; then periods of biogenesis during which were formed, at least on the planet Earth, the plants and animals now inhabiting its surface; and finally the period of hominization, the culmination of biogenesis, when *homo sapiens* made a first appearance.

Note, now, a remarkable correlation that exists between Figure 2 and Figure 1. All one has to do is insert transient natures at the beginning of the second diagram, to take care of elementary particles, and one finds precisely the same sequence of natures or substantial forms as in the first. The second starts with SF_t, followed by SF_i, SF_p, SF_a, and SF_h, in that order, precisely the order shown in Fig. 1. It has been said that ontogeny recapitulates phylogeny, that the individual human arises from nature in much the same way as the human species itself came to be. Should we now say that phylogeny recapitulates cosmogony, that the human species came to be in the same way as the cosmos itself, along with the rest of God's creation? Not quite. And when we understand why not we will have a good insight into St. Thomas's view of the hominization process.

There are many observations one could make about Figure 2, but for purposes here we are interested mainly in efficient causality, the agent cause or causes responsible for cosmic evolution. Note that God's creative action at the beginning of time is represented on the diagram by an arrow with a double shaft. Coming off from this is a dashed line, weaving its way, as it were, continuing the impulse of God's creative action through protomatter to all the substantial forms in succession, in each case educing a new substantial form from the potency of matter, but stopping abruptly at the last box, that showing matter informed by the human soul. According to St. Thomas, God is the Author of Nature and his causal action is present in every activity that takes place in our universe. "Deus operatur in omni operante," "God is operative in every creaturely action."[11] But Aquinas would distinguish God's creative act at the beginning of time from his co-action or concourse with other causal agents throughout time. He called the latter action the divine *concursus,* shown by the additional arrows giving input along the top of the diagram. St. Thomas is also known as the Angelic Doctor, mainly because he had an angelic mind, but perhaps because he also had great regard for the angels. He thought he had sufficient scriptural evidence to attribute to them a significant role in the governance of the universe.[12] So, along with the divine *concursus,* we show a place for angelic activity, guiding the course of cosmic evolution, as it were, to bring it to the stage where *homo sapiens* would first appear.

Here it is time to raise a crucial question. Where, in Aquinas's view, do substantial forms come from? A few sentences back I mentioned a process of eduction, saying that the weaving causal action shown in Figure 2 "educes" new substantial forms from the potency of matter. This is Thomas's famous doctrine of the *eductio formae de potentia materiae,* "the eduction of a form from the potency of matter."[13] His teaching maintains that all natural forms, the human soul excluded, are already precontained in the potentialities of protomatter, and so require only the action of a suitable agent to bring them forth into

11. ST I, q. 105, a. 5, c.
12. ST I, q. 100. For a detailed discussion of how St. Thomas saw the angels as movers of the heavenly bodies, and how his teaching in this respect differed from that of Albertus Magnus and Robert Kilwardby, see James A. Weisheipl, "The Celestial Movers in Medieval Physics," *The Thomist* 24 (1961): 286–326, esp. 319–26.
13. ST I, q. 90, a. 2, ad 2.

being. We can illustrate this simply using the analogy of the sculptor. Consider Michelangelo and his sculpting the statue of David preserved today in Florence. Where did the form of David exist before it was chiseled out of marble by Michelangelo? We could focus on the exemplary cause and say that the form of David pre-existed in the mind of the sculptor himself. But we could also focus on the material cause, the block of marble, and say that David's form was resting in there all along, simply waiting to be led forth, educed, liberated from the matter by Michelangelo's chisel. In a proportionate way, Aquinas would say that natural substantial forms are resident in protomatter, their exemplars already present in the divine mind, awaiting only the proper agent to confer on them actual existence.

This is true, as has been said, of all natural forms, the human soul excluded. Because of this, apart from the divine *concursus,* no direct intervention by God in the universe throughout all of time has been indicated until the moment of man's appearance. It is then that God creates again, producing the human soul from nothing and infusing it into matter that has been specially prepared for its reception. Precisely because it is itself an immaterial or spiritual soul, one endowed with powers of intellect and will that transcend any material organ, the substantial form of man cannot be precontained in matter the way David's form could be precontained in the marble from which it was hewn. It must come to be directly from the hand of God, so to speak. That is why God's creative action is shown a second time, now on the right of Figure 2, again by an arrow with a double shaft to indicate His direct creation of the human soul. Note again that at the last rhombus in the diagram there is a break in the single line of causation: the natural process of cosmic evolution can bring organisms to a level just below that of thought and volition, but it cannot progress to the final stage. God himself must complete the process, producing *ex nihilo* the human soul, tailored to match the ultimate disposition of matter as this has been prepared, over billions of years, for its reception. And that creative act, according to Catholic teaching, would be repeated each time throughout the centuries that a new human person has come into existence, with its matter being likewise disposed, through the procreative action of the human parents, to receive an individual, incommunicable, and immortal soul.

At the risk of losing readers who are confused rather than helped by symbols, I now present formula (1), which synthesizes the information contained in Figure 2 in a more compact form.

$$o \Rightarrow SF_t \rightarrow SF_i \rightarrow SF_p \rightarrow SF_a \Rightarrow SF_h \qquad (1)$$

Instead of the rhombic boxes arranged like a pantograph, the formula displays only the succession of substantial forms that run along their top; the protomatter component is always the same and so can be left out. The arrows with the double shafts represent God's creative action, first originating from o or "nothing" at the beginning of time and then again at the instant of hominization. Arrows with single shafts represent the eduction of a form from the potentiality of protomatter, in the eduction process already explained. This shorthand will be helpful for diagramming how hominization occurs, as we are about to see.

INDIVIDUATION

We are now finally in position to discuss individuation, the process whereby in natural generation an individual member of any natural species comes into being. The principle of individuation, according to Thomistic teaching, is given in the cryptic formula "materia signata quantitate," "matter signed with quantity."[14] The basic idea is that in natural generation a new individual is produced from pre-existing matter, from protomatter that is so disposed by a previous form or by the action of agents that it is capable of supporting a new substantial form. By being "disposed" Aquinas means having sufficient quantity or quantitative parts of its matter, and that these are suitably arranged or disposed that one or more individuals with that form will emerge from the generative process. As a concrete illustration, consider formula (2), familiar to many readers from their study of elementary chemistry:

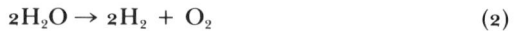

$$2H_2O \rightarrow 2H_2 + O_2 \tag{2}$$

This says to the chemist that two molecules of water break down, say, under electrolysis, into two diatomic molecules of hydrogen and one diatomic molecule of oxygen. Its bearing on the problem of individuation may be seen by considering the two hydrogen molecules that result from the breakdown. Each has the same nature, and yet one is distinct from the other. What makes the two distinct? In light of the principle of individuation, matter signed with quantity, one can say that the electrolysis so alters the quantity of the water molecules that it is impossible for these to break down, for example, into one molecule each of hydrogen and oxygen. The matter of H_2O is so "signed" by its quantity that the only way mass-energy requirements can be satis-

14. Cf. *In V Metaph.*, lect. 8, n. 876 (Marietti, p. 236); *In De Trinitate*, q. 4, a. 2, ad 2 and ad 4 (Decker, p. 144).

fied is by the eduction from protomatter of two hydrogen natures, each with a different but equal mass-energy, along with one oxygen nature. A biologist might say that the hydrogen molecules are "twins," identical twins, and if so, this type of twinning seem connatural to many chemical processes.

Before taking up the more interesting biological examples that the twinning terminology suggests, let us look briefly at formula (3), which describes a more complex breakdown taken from nuclear chemistry:

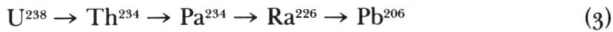

$$U^{238} \rightarrow Th^{234} \rightarrow Pa^{234} \rightarrow Ra^{226} \rightarrow Pb^{206} \tag{3}$$

Probably less familiar to many, this diagrams the natural radioactive transformation of one element into another, what is referred to as the uranium series whereby uranium breaks down into lead. The elements shown, with their atomic numbers, are respectively uranium, thorium, protactinium, radium, and lead. According to formula (3), one nature or atom of uranium breaks down successively into a single nature or atom of thorium, then of protactinium, then of radium, and finally of lead. What quantitative dispositions would serve to explain this? The nuclear chemist would say that there is a basic instability in the heaviest nucleus of the atoms in the series, that of uranium, and this results in changes in the nuclei and electronic structures of the atoms that emerge successively during its radioactive breakdown. These changes must always satisfy the quantitative dispositions (essentially mass-energy requirements) of the protomatter, with the result that the natures are educed from its potency in the order shown.

Notice that in the radioactive example I have slipped in a problem. Are radioactive elements examples of stable natures, the way I have described them, or are they examples of transient natures, like the elementary particles and the seeds already mentioned? I bracket that question here, since I discuss possible answers to it elsewhere.[15] So let us move instead to biological generation, where seeds or *entia vialia* seem to be clearly involved, and where transient natures must enter explicitly into our discussion. Here too a nucleus is involved, only now it is not the nucleus of an atom but the nucleus of a cell—a much more complicated situation that opens up a wider range of possibilities.

To begin, let us update St. Thomas's medieval view of plant generation by proposing the model embodied in formula (4):

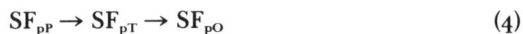

$$SF_{pP} \rightarrow SF_{pT} \rightarrow SF_{pO} \tag{4}$$

15. In "Nature and Human Nature," 42–44.

Here the subscript pP refers to the parent plant, the subscript pT refers to the transient plant-like nature of the seed during its development, and the subscript pO refers to the offspring, numerically different from pP but pertaining to the same species. The agency involved in the first transition, from SF_{pP} to SF_{pT}, is a natural agency associated with the powers of plant life shown in Fig. 1. Chemical materials are absorbed by the parent organism through the powers of nutrition, growth, and reproduction to form the genetic materials contained in the seed. Then, after separation from the parent, a form of life persists in the seed. This begins its own internal development through an incipient plant-like form, SF_{pT}, which St. Thomas referred to as an "active force" (*vis activa*) that gives it a plant nature "according to first act" (*secundum actum primum*) though it is not yet a form in the full sense.[16] This suffices to draw nourishment to the incipient organism and direct its growth until its quantitative parts are sufficiently articulated to sustain a stable, individual plant nature of the species. At that point a new plant form, SF_{pO}, is educed from the potentiality of protomatter, and a new individual of that species has been produced.[17]

16. ST I, q. 118, a. 1, ad 3: ". . . illa vis activa quae est in semine, ex anima generantis derivata, est quasi quaedam motio ipsius animae generantis: nec est anima, aut pars animae, nisi in virtute; sicut in serra vel securi non est forma lecti, sed motio quaedam ad talem formam. Et ideo non oportet quod ista vis activa habeat aliquod organum in actu; sed fundatur in ipso spiritu incluso in semine, quod est spumosum, ut attestatur eius albedo." Also ad 4: ". . . in animalibus perfectis, quae generantur ex coitu, virtus activa est in semine maris, secundum Philosophum in libro *De generatione animalium* [Bk. 2, chaps. 3–4, 736a24ff.]; materia autem foetus est illud quod ministratur a femina. In qua quidem materia statim a principio est anima vegetabilis, non quidem secundum actum secundum, sed secundum actum primum, sicut anima sensitiva est in dormientibus. Cum autem incipit attrahere alimentum, tunc iam actu operatur. Huiusmodi igitur materia transmutatur a virtute quae est in semine maris, quousque perducatur in actum animae sensitivae: non ita quod ipsamet vis quae erat in semine, fiat anima sensitiva; quia sic idem esset generans et generatum; et hoc magis esset simile nutritiori et augmento, quam generationi, ut Philosophus dicut [*De generatione et corruptione*, Bk. 1, chap. 5, 321a9–29]. Postquam autem per virtutem principii activi quod erat in semine, producta est anima sensitiva in generato quantum ad aliquam partem eius principalem, tunc ille anima sensitiva prolis incipit operari ad complementum proprii corporis, per modum nutritionis et augmenti." See also the following note.

17. For details, see Taylor, "Human Generation," 273–326, for the passages in the *Summa* cited in the previous note. Apparently St. Thomas explained this process somewhat differently in each of the four places he discusses it, depending on the biological authority he was using at the time. Probably the fullest treatment is that in the *De potentia*, analyzed by Taylor on pp. 223–66, where Thomas makes more use of medical terminology deriving from Avicenna than in the other places. Two texts Taylor points out are particularly helpful: one on p. 237, n. 47, citing *De potentia*, n. 3, a. 9, ad 9; the other on p. 258, n. 103, citing *De potentia*, q. 3, a. 12. Here are these texts in the order mentioned:

"In generatione autem animalis apparent diversae formae substantiales, cum primo

The generation of a human individual is obviously more complex, but for St. Thomas it proceeds along analogous lines. Again, to update his medieval account, we may schematize the process as shown now in formula (5):

$$2SF_{hP} \rightarrow nSF_{pT} \rightarrow mSF_{aT} \Rightarrow 1SF_{hO} \qquad (5)$$

This formula is similar to (4) but definitely more complex. As before, the subscript hP refers to the human parent at the beginning of the process and the subscript hO to the human offspring at the end. Since human generation is bisexual, the process starts with two mature human souls or persons, one female and the other male, and it terminates in one human offspring, since we are not now considering the production of twins. The double-shaft on the last arrow shows that the soul of the offspring is created directly by God, although the organic materials suitable for the soul's reception have been pro-created by the parents. The intermediate stages are represented by two transient natures, one plant-like, represented by subscript pT, the other animal-like, represented by subscript aT. Notice that a small n and a small m have been used to number these types of genetic material. In the normal case and in our modern understanding, the process starts with two seeds ($n = 2$), an egg and a sperm cell, although there might be more than one sperm if multiple births were being discussed. They combine to form a unicellular zygote, but that cell quickly divides and subdivides to form a complex cell mass that grows and nourishes in a way analogous to plant life—hence the subscript pT. In later stages of development this embryonic human develops organs of sensation and movement and so manifests the characteristics

---

appareat sperma, et postea sanguis, et sic deinceps quousque sit forma hominis vel animalis. Et sic oportet quod huiusmodi generatio non sit simplex, sed continens in se plures generationes et corruptiones. Non enim potest esse quod una et eadem forma substantialis gradatim educatur in actum, ut ostensum est. Sic ergo per virtutem formativam, quae a principio est in semine, abiecta forma spermatis, inducitur alia forma; qua abiecta, iterum inducatur alia: et sic primo inducatur anima vegetabilis; deinde ea abiecta, inducatur anima sensibilis et vegetabilis simul; qua abiecta, inducatur non per virtutem praedictam sed a creante, anima quae simul est rationalis sensibilis et vegetabilis. Et sic dicendum est secundum hanc opinionem quod embrio antequam habeat animam rationalem, vivit et habet animam, qua abiecta, inducitur anima rationalis" (Marietti, p. 68).

"... secundum quod Philosophus probat in XV *de Animalibus*, semen non deciditur ab eo quod fuit actu pars, sed quod fuit superfluum ultimae digestionis; quod nondum erat ultima assimilatione assimilatum. Nulla autem corporis pars est actu per animam perfecta, nisi sit ultima assimilatione assimilata; unde semen ante decisionem nondum erat perfectum per animam, ita quod anima esset forma eius; erat tamen ibi aliqua virtus, secundum quam iam per actionem animae erat alteratum et deductum ad dispositionem propinquam ultimae assimilationi; unde et postquam decisum est, non est ibi anima, sed aliqua virtus animae" (Marietti, p. 77).

of animal life—hence the subscript aT. But notice now the m before SF_{aT}. Recent embryological studies have shown that the number m is not necessarily the same as the number n, whatever that may be, nor is it necessarily the 1 that precedes the individual human offspring, $1SF_{hO}$. The initial cell mass is apparently made up of pluripotential cells that are uncertain, if we may use that term, as to the number of organisms it will eventually produce. Twinning can take place during its development and, what is even more unusual, recombination can take place where splitting had previously occurred. Thus it is not always the case that $n = 2$ and $m = 1$, as one might expect. What starts out as apparently one organism might end up as two or more, and what starts out as two or more might end up as one.

This extraordinary finding, in my view, provides strong confirmation of St. Thomas's view that transient natures continue to inform the incipient organism for some time after the initial formation of the zygote. If God had created the human soul and infused it into the zygote at the moment of fertilization, then a stable individual of human nature would already have been formed. And, were another individual to be formed subsequent to that moment, this would be an instance of asexual generation, the production of one individual from another of the species—a type of generation found in lower forms but not proper to humans. The phenomenon of twinning and recombination therefore gives unexpected confirmation of St. Thomas's teaching that unstable natures, that is, transient natures, continue to inform the incipient organism until such time as the proper dispositions are at hand for the irreversible formation of an individual human being. Only at that moment does God create a new soul, a substantial form that has a transcendental order to the matter so prepared for it, and infuse this intellectual soul into such matter, with the result that a new human person finally comes into being.

COGITATION

With this we come to our final topic, cogitation, wherein we will treat in much briefer compass the reverse process, the depersonification of the human organism, what was referred to earlier as "psychic dehominization." We use the term "cogitation" to focus on the use the human intellect makes of the cogitative sense in its thought processes. The cogitative sense is one of the inner senses, pointed to on Figure 1 by an arrow going downward and to the left from the box labeled "intellect." This teaching, implicit in Aristotle but developed in detail by Aquinas, holds that it is impossible for the human being to indulge in cogitation, that is, actively to employ intellect and will, without reflecting on phantasms, on what modern psychologists call the percepts or concrete images associated with brain activity.[18] The teaching has been related to recent findings in neurophysiology by D. Alan Shewmon in an article entitled "The Metaphysics of Brain Death, Persistent Vegetative State, and Dementia."[19] Here we may skip the technical details; suffice it to say that Shewmon invokes principles very similar to the ones used throughout this essay to substantiate the suggestion made earlier about psychic dehominization. In fact, his entire analysis may be summed up in formula (6), which turns out to be almost the reverse of formula (1):

$$SF_h \rightarrow SF_{aT} \rightarrow SF_{pT} \rightarrow SF_i \qquad (6)$$

Shewmon's thesis is that human cogitation is so dependent on the brain that, if the areas of the brain that are used by the cogitative sense for its operations are impaired or removed, they will cease to be informed by the human soul, which will be replaced by an animal soul virtually contained within the human. As he states this possibility, the "death of *a person* can come about through destruction of only those parts of the brain which are necessary for the proper functioning of the intellect and will."[20] Thus, even though the human body appears unchanged on the surface, a substantial change would have taken place. The human soul, SF_h, would be replaced by a transient animal-like soul, SF_{aT}, corresponding to the state of dementia; then, if further deterioration takes place, the latter soul would be replaced by a transient plant-like soul, SF_{pT}, corresponding to what is called the persistent vegetative state; and finally, when life signs cease altogether, the body would corrupt completely to inorganic matter, SF_i, the "dust of the earth" from which it originally came.[21]

Earlier we referred to Mierczyslaw Krapiec's teachings on human death. Let us return to that now and couple it with Shewmon's analysis to propose a Thomistic exploration of what the last stages of human life might be like. A colleague of Pope John Paul II when the future pope was a philosophy professor, Krapiec combines St. Thomas's teachings with recent insights in phenomenology to discuss the personal experience of death. He begins with the terms mentioned earlier, making the distinction between death "accepted passively," that is, as

18. *In III De anima,* chap. 2 (Leonine, pp. 208–13); ST I, q. 86, a. 1, c.
19. *The Thomist* 49 (1985): 24–80. Further reflections on Shewmon's article will be found in Philip Smith, "Transient Natures at the Edges of Life: A Thomistic Exploration," *The Thomist* 54 (1990): 191–227.
20. Shewmon, "The Metaphysics of Brain Death," 59 (emphasis added).
21. Ibid., 58–61.

the decomposition of the human organism or the separation of the soul from the body, and death "understood actively," that is, as a real experience of the human spirit. This experience, he says, occurs precisely at the moment when the individual becomes fully capable of making a decision in relation to the whole of human life, at the very moment in which the human personality, understood in a dynamic, psychological sense, attains its complete fulfillment. Such a total actualization of the human spirit is the culmination of all the changeable acts performed during the course of life, and so it occurs beyond the point at which the individual can return to the temporal and changeable conditions of earthly existence. This active experience of death, Krapiec continues, cannot occur in conjunction with the coactivity of the brain; it is transtemporal, and so can occur only "in the sphere of spirit, as the spirit brings to an end the changeable states and changeable activity of its powers."[22]

Death, understood in this active sense, is for Krapiec the moment of making ultimate decisions; without such a moment, the human being would be a "thing" and not a person experiencing the most important stage of his or her development. He further proposes that, at the moment of active death, God stands concretely and intuitively before the human intellect, permitting a total confrontation of personal desires and decisions with concrete and infinite good, and thus brings to fulfillment every natural desire of the human will. He writes:

If, then, at the moment of the completion of the changeable way of existence, i.e., at the moment of death, a person would not solve the existential questions involved in the whole of human cognition, then the human being would be an unnatural being. The whole course of human nature as a human being, the pursuit of the discovery of the meaning of existence, would be a pursuit never fulfilled. But since changeable duration merely gives rise to the whole of this problematic without solving it, only in the moment of the completion of this duration can this pursuit be fulfilled, if at all. Thus, if we are not to claim that human life is an absurdity, we must say that only when God, as the ultimate reason of being, stands concretely and intuitively before the human intellect, is human life fulfilled. This is the final, full, cognitive act to which the whole of psychic life is ordered.[23]

Later he continues to explore this thought:

Without this appearance of God, human nature would not have a rational ontical structure, since the pursuit of nature would be objectless, and objectless pursuit is not a pursuit of nature. If, therefore, we want to treat human

22. *I-Man,* 177.
23. Ibid., 179.

nature rationally, then we cannot ignore natural inclinations. And if this is how the matter lies with human desire, then one ought to accept the fact that in the fulfillment of the human being's time, which is called death, God will stand before us in order to draw us to himself like a magnet, no longer through a world of changeable beings, but through his very self. The world of things and people prepares, enables, and suits us for this more intense natural desire of the human will. Only in this moment—if it happens at all— can there occur a total confrontation of human desires and decisions with concrete and infinite good, because in no other moment of human life is such a confrontation even possible.[24]

The clear implication of these passages, though not stated explicitly, is that the human soul at the moment of active death has passed beyond the earthly pale and subsists as an individual substance, already separated from the body with which it previously shared earthly existence.

Krapiec does not speculate about the moment of active death in relation to the pathological state of the human organism, other than to state that the personal experience of death is outside of time and so cannot occur in conjunction with any brain activity. Obviously he is thinking about the natural death of an elderly human being. But it is here that we may rejoin Shewmon's pathology of brain death to draw some further corollaries. According to St. Thomas's theory of knowledge, as we have noted, all human knowing in the state of union with the body occurs by reflection on phantasms, produced by the cogitative sense through the intermediary of various brain states. As long as the soul operates with phantasms it can make changes through its higher powers, intellect and will. Put otherwise, it can always "change its mind" and thus does not reach the point of ultimate decision to which Krapiec refers. Conversely, at the moment in time when phantasmal activity ceases, these changes are no longer possible; the natural mode of operation of the body-soul composite ceases, and the individual's rational life is over. If the intellect and will later function, they do so as powers of a separated substance and not as the operative powers of a natural body.[25] In other words, the person's truly human and changeable existence is terminated, and the human soul, precisely as human, ceases to have any proper function it can exercise in the body. The moment of active death, viewed passively, becomes the moment in which the human soul departs from, or is separated from, the body.

If this analysis is correct, and the body continues to manifest vital activities, in Shewmon's view it does so as a humanoid organism. The

24. Ibid., 181.
25. See St. Thomas's discussion of how such powers may be activated in ST I, q. 89.

body is specifically human, and thus should be classified under the human species, but it no longer possesses a stable human nature and will gradually decline and decay. Its life functions in this state, to use our terminology, are those of a transient nature, human in origin, but animal and vegetative in actual operation. There is therefore a succession of substantial forms in the humanoid organism, and the overall dying process may be referred to as one of dehominization. Obviously the transient natures that animate the organism in the interval between the death of the person and that of the entire body enjoy more stability than do elementary particles with their fleeting temporal existences. But despite their relative stability in some instances, these are not the stable forms of human nature that confer durability in being. They are but transitory entities directing the life of the organism during the final stages of its existence.

With this we have come to the end of our story. Let us conclude by posing two simple questions. The first is this: On the basis of Aquinas's legacy as described in this presentation, is Thomism *really* dead? Is it a fossilized, archaic body of teaching, of antiquarian interest only, of no possible application in our miracle age of science and technology?

The second question is closely related to this first. At the beginning of this essay we bemoaned the lack of contact, even in Catholic circles, between the speculative natural philosophy of man as taught by St. Thomas and practical norms in conformity with his principles that pertain to ethics or moral science. Do the matters discussed here, essentially those pertaining to a Thomistic philosophy of nature and of science, bear any relation to the moral problems now confronting secular society and the Church? I mean the problems of what to do at the beginning of life—contraception, "choice," *in vitro* fertilization, frozen embryos, surrogate motherhood, abortion directly or indirectly induced; or what to do at the end of life—with dementia or persistent vegetative states, "when to pull the plugs," as the nurses say. I think they have, that these are the areas where work needs most urgently to be done. And so let us make an additional point, one that borders on an appeal, not now to philosophers, but rather to students of philosophy. There has been enough metaphysical imperialism, enough ethical dialectics and casuistry, in Catholic philosophy. It is time to leave the stratosphere, to come down to earth, to the world of matter and form, to study Aquinas again at the level of the *Physics* and the *De anima*. That is where the action is, where the future is, and, one might add, where the hard work is. Students would be well advised to ponder this aspect of Aquinas's legacy when planning their own careers as philosophers for the twenty-first century.[26]

26. Note added in proof: Well over a year after this essay was delivered as a lecture the following article was published that contested the analysis of delayed hominization in the essay cited in n. 10 above: Stephen J. Heaney, "Aquinas and the Presence of the Human Rational Soul in the Early Embryo," *The Thomist* 56 (1992): 19–48. The article is worth consulting because it reviews the literature favoring delayed hominization and includes much, including yet more recent work, that has not been cited in our published material. Unfortunately Heaney himself illustrates precisely the type of metaphysical imperialism against which I inveigh in the closing paragraph of this essay. He concludes on the note that all of his adversaries (this author included) have concentrated too much on the "material conditions" for hominization, and presumably not enough on the ontological principles hominization requires. But he gets himself caught in a *petitio principii*, because all of the ontological arguments he offers simply presuppose that the human soul is already present in the embryo, precisely the point that is being contested. Does Heaney think that God, as the Author of Nature, dispenses with requisite "material conditions" when infusing the human soul into matter that might not be properly disposed, thus making of every conception a quasi-miracle? His own analysis of such conditions betrays an uneasiness with Thomistic natural philosophy as well as with recent physical science and human embryology. On the reconstruction he offers, moreover, he is forced to negate all of St. Thomas's texts favoring delayed hominization. To what end? Simply to sustain a position at which he has arrived on *a priori* grounds, one in no way consonant with the thought of the Angelic Doctor.

10

Henry of Ghent's "*De reductione artium ad theologiam*"

STEPHEN F. BROWN

The two chief critics of Thomas Aquinas in the late thirteenth century were Godfrey of Fontaines and Henry of Ghent. Godfrey frequently criticized Thomas from the side of Aristotle, Henry from the side of St. Augustine. In the present article we will examine the critique Henry of Ghent brought against Aquinas and other teachers at Paris in regard to the role of philosophy in the framework of Christian wisdom. Henry's attack on Aquinas was taken seriously enough by Thomas's early followers, principally John of Paris and William Peter of Godino, that the prologues to their commentaries on the *Sentences* of Peter Lombard are collections of questions written specifically against Henry.

In his *De reductione artium ad theologiam* St. Bonaventure very calmly explains how the manifold wisdom of God revealed in the Scriptures lies hidden in all knowledge and in the world of nature, how all forms of knowledge serve the study of the sacred writings, and, for that reason, how such study uses the language and examples that belong to all other domains of knowledge.[1] Henry of Ghent never wrote a treatise formally entitled *De reductione artium ad theologiam*, but if he had, it would have been a somewhat different work than Bonaventure's. We believe that the ground for such a claim may be found in Henry's *Summa*. There, in article 7, Henry argues why theology is the principal study among all the human sciences and how and why all other areas of knowledge are its handmaids. In effect, it is his *De reductione artium ad theologiam*.[2] But, whereas Bonaventure's treatise is

1. S. Bonaventura, *De reductione artium ad theologiam* (ed. Quaracchi, vol. 5), 328: "Et sic patet quomodo multiformis sapientia Dei, quae lucide traditur in sacra Scriptura, occultatur in omni cognitione et in omni natura. Patet etiam quomodo omnes cognitiones famulantur theologiae; et ideo ipsa assumit exempla et utitur vocabulis pertinentibus ad omne genus cognitionis."
2. Henricus de Gandavo, *Summa quaestionum ordinariarum*, a. 7, qq. 1–13 (Paris 1520), ff. 47r–63r.

a fresh representation of the position of Hugh of St. Victor, especially as found in his *Commentarium in Hierarchiam Coelestem Sancti Dionysii Areopagitae*,[3] Henry *argues* the case in the context of the new philosophical and theological challenges of the 1260s–1280s in Paris.[4]

Medieval Christian authors from the time of Peter Damian (d. 1072) had been troubled by the domineering tendencies of the human sciences when they were linked to the study of the Scriptures.[5] Peter warned that human learning should not arrogantly claim for itself the right of a teacher, but, like a handmaiden (*ancilla*), should offer her mistress a submissive service.[6] Frequently in the twelfth century the ancillary or serving character of the humanistic disciplines was underscored by Hugh of St. Victor, as we have mentioned, and also by Robert of Melun and John of Salisbury.[7] The proper role of the human disciplines was stressed even more in the letter *Ab Egyptiis* sent by Pope Gregory IX to the theologians of Paris in 1228, warning them, in the words of St. Paul, "not to be led astray by diverse and strange teachings" (Heb. 13:9) that put the head where the tail should be and the tail where the head should be (cf. Deut. 28:13–14); rather, they should force the handmaids to serve the queen.[8] In his *De reductione artium ad theologiam* Bonaventure continued this tradition and re-

3. On the influence of Hugh of St. Victor on St. Bonaventure's treatise see *De reductione*, 325, and Emma Thérèse Healy, *Saint Bonaventure's "De reductione artium ad theologiam"* (St. Bonaventure, N.Y.: The Franciscan Institute, 1955), 11–14. Cf. Hugo de Sancto Victore, *Commentarium in Hierarchiam Coelestem S. Dionysii Areopagitae*, Bk. 1, chap. 1 (PL 175, 923–28).

4. For an introduction to the changing philosophical and theological scene in the 1260s–1280s, see Fernand Van Steenberghen, *La Philosophie au XIIIe Siècle*, Philosophes médiévaux, vol. 9 (Louvain: Publications Universitaires and Paris: Béatrice-Nauwelaerts, 1966), 357–493.

5. On the use of the word "ancilla" in medieval literature, see Stephen F. Brown, "Key Terms in Medieval Theological Vocabulary," in *Méthodes et instruments du travail intellectual au moyen âge*, ed. Olga Weijers, Etudes sur le Vocabulaire intellectuel du Moyen Age, vol. 3 (Turnhout: Brepols, 1990), 93–96.

6. Petrus Damianus, *De divina omnipotentia* (PL 145, 603).

7. Hugo de Sancto Victore, *De sacramentis Christianae fidei*, prol., chap. 6 (PL 176, 185); Robertus Meledunensis, *Sententie*, praef., ed. R. M. Martin and R. M. Gallet, in *Oeuvres*, vol. 3, pt. 1 (Louvain: "Spicilegium Sacrum Lovaniense," 1947), 30; and Ioannes Saresberiensis, *Entheticus* (PL 199, 974). Petrus Abelardus, *Dialogus inter philosophum et Iudaeum* (PL 178, 1637), traces the word "ancilla" back to St. Jerome, *Epistolae*, ep. 70 (PL 22, 666): "Legerat in *Deuteronomio* Domini voce praeceptum mulieris captivae radendum caput, supercilia, omnes pilos, et ungues corporis amputandos, et sic eam habendam in coniugio. Quid ergo mirem, si et ego sapientiam saecularem propter eloquii venustatem, et membrorum pulchritudinem, de *ancilla* atque captiva Israelitidem facere cupio?"

8. *Enchiridion Symbolorum*, n. 442, ed. Heinrich Denzinger and Karl Rahner (Barcelona, Friburg, Rome: Herder, 1957), 206. Cf. Henricus A. Denifle and Aemilo Chatelain, *Chartularium Universitatis Parisiensis*, vol. 1, nn. 87 (Paris: Delalain, 1889), 143: "Cum sapientie sacre pagine relique scientie debeant famulari . . ."

presented in a stronger logical form the schema on the organization of the sciences given by Hugh. Henry of Ghent saw the need to go further and to argue the case for preserving this tradition.

As Aristotle's philosophical writings, together with the commentaries of Avicenna and Averroes, gradually turned the arts faculties of the universities into Aristotelian philosophy faculties,[9] late thirteenth-century authors became more and more concerned about making precise the relationship of Aristotelian philosophy to theology. This discussion frequently focused on the distinction between "ancilla" in the sense of "famulatus" in contrast to "ancilla" in the sense of "subalternatio." Already in England in 1253 Robert Kilwardby manifested the tension: "Non est hic continentia subalternationis, sed continentia principalitatis et famulatus est hic."[10] Henry of Ghent, in a much more debative Parisian atmosphere, was forceful in asserting the difference between *subalternatio* and *famulatus*: "The acts of assistance and service are altogether different from subalternation; and it is nonsensical to say that the act of assisting is a form of subalternation."[11] John of Paris, however, stressed their essential identity: *famulatus* and *subalternatio* both signify the relation of a superior and an inferior.[12] Henry, however, insisted that *subalternatio* does not further connote "service" the way that *famulatus* does. Both words underline the more noble status of Christian revelation. But, for Henry, this is not enough; *ancilla* must be tied to *famulatus* to insure the assisting role of philosophy as a servant of theology.

In *Summa* a. 7, q. 4, Henry spells out in exact detail what Aristotle meant by subalternation and employs the Philosopher's examples of different types of subalternation in the *Posterior Analytics* to exhaust the possible ways that one science may be subalternated to another.[13]

9. On the change within the arts faculty from a liberal arts faculty to an Aristotelian philosophy faculty, see Van Steenberghen, *La philosophie au XIIIe Siècle*, 357–426.

10. Robertus Kilwardby, *Quaestiones in librum primum Sententiarum*, q. 14, ed. J. Schneider (Munich: Verlag der Bayerischen Akademie der Wissenschaften, 1986), 35.

11. Henricus de Gandavo, *Summa*, a. 7, q. 5 (f. 54rH): "Subministratio enim et famulatus omnino aliud est a subalternatione; et est fatuum dicere quod subministratio sit aliquis modus subalternationis. Hoc enim nullus dicit nisi ignorans Philosophi determinationem circa scientiarum subalternationem."

12. Ioannes Parisiensis, *Reportatio in I Sent.*, prol., q. 3, ed. J.-P. Muller (Rome: Herder, 1961), p. 12: Et si dicatur, quod verum est, quod istae scientiae sibi invicem famulantur, ut ibidem dicit Philosophus, dico quod pro eodem habeo, quia non intelligo per istum famulatum aliquid aliud quam rationem subalternantis et subalternati." Cf. p. 11: "Dicendum quod nomine subalternantis et subalternati nihil aliud accipiendum est, nisi ratio superioris et inferioris."

13. Henricus de Gandavo, *Summa*, a. 7, q. 4 (f. 52rv), esp.: "Isti proculdubio sunt quattuor modi subalternationis, secundum determinationem Philosophi; nec sunt plures nec pauciores, nec alii ab istis."

In Henry's analysis of Aristotelian subalternation, its essential characteristic is that the subalternating science gives the "why" (*propter quid*) of that which the subalternated science gives the "that" (*quia*).[14] He well realizes that someone like Thomas Aquinas, and his followers, like John of Paris, might want to extend the meaning of the term "subalternation" to cover the case of theology's relationship to the knowledge of God and the blessed, where the latter have clear and manifest knowledge of principles, and theologians *in via* accept the same principles on divine authority and grasp them obscurely and only by faith. He wonders, however, whether this agrees with what Aristotle had meant by "subalternation." Certainly, Aristotle's examples in the *Posterior Analytics*, Henry contends, don't fit such a case. The Philosopher's examples are all instances of *propter quid* and *quia*, not of "clear" and "obscure."[15] That is the reason for Henry's conclusion: "Hoc est per se et essentiale, quod scientia subalternans dicit *propter quid* de quo subalternata dicit *quia*."[16]

The four examples of subordination that Aristotle gives in Book 1 of the *Posterior Analytics* represent, for Henry, the only four modes of subalternation that flow from the essential nature of subordination just presented. If subalternating and subalternated sciences consider the same object but differ because one considers its "why" (*propter quid*) while the other considers its "that" (*quia*), there are only four possible alternatives. If the two sciences consider the same absolute object but study one by examining its cause and the other by sense experience alone, then we have, in this case, Aristotle's example of how astronomy subalternates to itself naval science, or what he, in giving the example, calls *apparentia*. Both of these sciences consider the same absolute object, namely, the conjunction of certain stars as an indicator of future storms or future fair weather. The astronomer, however, knows the reason or cause *why* such a conjunction points to a particular kind of weather, while the sailor knows that it is a sign of the arrival of such weather, but only by experience. Two sciences, likewise, might study the same absolute object, but one takes a theo-

14. Ibid., q. 5 (f. 53vE): "In subalternatione enim, ut dictum est supra, hoc est per se et essentiale, quod scientia subalternans dicat propter quid de quo subalternata dicit quia."

15. Ibid. (f. 54rG): "Si vero illud appelletur subalternatio quando una scientia habet claram et apertam notitiam principiorum, cuius auctoritate altera scientia recipit eadem principia tamquam obscura et nota solumodo per fidem, scientiae divinae vel beatorum ista scientia subalternatur. Sed postquam notum fuerit de rebus et intelligamus quid dicere velimus, disputationem de nominibus particularibus relinquamus, et videat qui hoc poterit, utrum naturae subalternationis iuxta determinationem Philosophi congruat."

16. Cf. n. 14 above.

retical approach and looks for the reason or cause *why* something works, whereas the other science knows simply *that* it works and knows that this is so by having done it repeatedly. Here we have Aristotle's example of how mechanical science is subalternated to stereometry; the former knows *that* a certain way of constructing a building works, because it has been done often enough. Stereometry knows the principles involved in such construction and knows *why* it works.

Two sciences, however, can also deal with objects that are not absolutely the same, but one is a contracted or determined form of the absolute object, the way, for example, a line that is visual is a contracted or determined form of a line taken simply, or a number existing in sound is a contracted form of a number taken simply. Now if one of two sciences considers the absolute object while the other considers the object as contracted, then we have the type of subalternation that Aristotle attended to when he spoke of geometry as a subalternating science and optics as a subalternated science. Once again we must note, according to Henry, that geometry demonstrates the interrelationships of lines, whereas optics, taking these demonstrated truths of geometry as suppositions (*that* they are so), goes on to clarify how, according to these demonstrated proportions of lines, all that is seen is seen. In brief, geometry considers its objects as a *propter quid* science; optics does so as a *quia* science. Finally, the two sciences of arithmetic and music have a relationship of subalternation, for arithmetic considers the varying proportions among numbers and demonstrates these proportions. Music, on the other hand, takes these proportions of numbers demonstrated by arithmetic, supposing *that* they are true, and attempts to show how the harmony of sounds is in accord with these proportions.[17]

Having provided his analysis of subalternation, Henry moves in q. 5 to the position of St. Thomas that sacred doctrine is subalternated to the knowledge of God and the blessed. He quickly dismisses Thomas's claim by saying that "this position arises from a simplistic view and ignorance of the nature of subalternation."[18] Sticking to his strict analysis of Aristotle's positions, Henry notes that there is no *propter quid* knowledge except by way of discursive reason. God and the blessed do not know by discursive reason. Thus, they do not have *propter quid* knowledge, even though they do have *clearer* knowledge. Since subalternating sciences, according to Aristotle, must provide *propter quid* knowledge, the knowledge of God and the blessed can not

---

17. Henricus de Gandavo, *Summa*, a. 7, q. 4 (f. 52rv).
18. Ibid., q. 5 (f. 53vE).

be a subalternating type of science in relation to a subalternated science of theology or sacred doctrine.[19]

The principal debate, nonetheless, of a. 7 is not about the relation of theology as a human study to the knowledge of God and the blessed. It rather runs in another direction: how does theology relate to the other human disciplines and how do these human disciplines relate to theology?

In q. 4 Henry considers the first of these questions: How does theology relate to the other human disciplines?[20] It is important to keep in mind the four modes of subalternation he has found in Aristotle's examples in the *Posterior Analytics*. When one looks at the first two modes, it is easy to see that they do not exemplify any contribution coming from the subalternating science to the subalternated science. The astrologer knows why a certain conjunction of the stars points to foul or fair weather. Yet, his knowledge in no way plays a part in such predictions made by the sailor. The sailor makes his predictions solely on the basis of repeated experiences he has had or has learned. Likewise, an expert in stereometry knows why such and such a building precedure works. His knowledge, however, has nothing to do with the builders who construct such an edifice. They simply do it because frequent building has taught them that it works.

Thus, against St. Thomas once again, Henry declares that it is not essential to subalternation that the subalternated science uses something that has been determined in the subalternating science.[21] This is true for the third and fourth types of subalternation; but it is not essential to all forms of subalternation, as the consideration of the first and second modes indicates. The general or essential characteristic of subalternation, for Henry, is that the subalternating science deals with the "why" (*propter quid*) while the subalternated science deals with the "that" (*quia*). It is not necessary in every mode of subalternation that the inferior science use something that has been determined in the

19. Ibid. For Henry, the will of God is the *causa propter quid* of all things (cf. n. 24 below). God, however, does not know His will as the cause of all things by *propter quid* demonstration, even though He knows it most clearly.

20. Ibid., q. 4 (ff. 51v–53r).

21. Ibid. (f. 53rH): "Dicendum quod non est verum, secundum quod quidam credunt: quod hoc est generale in omni subalternatione, quod scientia subalternata utitur determinatis in subalternante. Hoc enim solum habet veritatem in tertio et quarto modo subalternationis, non autem in primo et secundo. Perspectiva enim utitur demonstratis in geometria et musica demonstratis in arithmetica sed navalis non demonstrato in astrologia utitur quia demonstratum est in illa (non enim novit nauta ex tali coniunctione stellarum sequi tempestatem aut tranquillitatem quia hoc supponit ipse esse probatum ab astrologo) sed quia hoc experientia multiplici collegit."

superior one. Neither does the subalternating science have to make any mention of the *proper* principles of the subalternated science. It is enough that the subalternating science consider such first principles as are necessary to explain the "why" (*propter quid*) of the proper principles of the subalternated science, *if it were applied to them*. Strictly speaking, even if the superior sciences considered such an application, this would still be irrelevant to the inferior sciences of the first and second modes of subalternation. It is sufficient in such cases of subalternation that the superior science devotes itself to the cause of those things that are supposed or are spoken of in the inferior science. The inferior or subalternated science does not have to borrow or receive the cause (*propter quid*) from the superior or subalternating one. In the first two modes of subalternation the inferior sciences operate on their own. In fact, Henry adds, it does not have any relevance to subalternation whether the superior science devotes itself to the cause (*propter quid*) by natural reason or, as in the case of theology, by revelation. The inferior or subalternated science works on its own turf, without consideration of what goes on in the territory of the superior or subalternating science.[22]

Henry's model for the relationship of theology to the human sciences is that of the first and second modes of subalternation given by Aristotle. It is not Thomas Aquinas's model which employs the examples from Aristotle's other forms of subalternation.[23] In accord with the first mode of subalternation, Henry declares, all the speculative and practical sciences are subalternated to theology. Principally they consider the proximate causes that can be gathered naturally from their effects, or they consider proximate human goals or ends, not ultimate ones, and they consider these things that exist in the world of experience and do not ask the ultimate "why" or "for what" (*propter quid*). They presume the existence of the things before them and do not ask the ultimate "why" of their existence. So they do not attend to the first principle, separate from these objects of experience, that freely produces them all for his own ultimate purposes.[24]

Henry's biblical parallel to his position is the story of Joseph at the

22. Ibid. (f. 53rHI).
23. E.g., ST I, q. 1, a. 2, c.; *In De Trinitate*, q. 2, a. 2 (Decker, pp. 85–90).
24. Henricus de Gandavo, *Summa*, a. 7, q. 4 (f. 52vF): "Ad cuius intellectum sciendum quod secundum dicta superius Philosophi in eis quae ad creaturas pertinent solummodo, causas proximas colligatas naturaliter suis effectibus principaliter considerant, quas supponunt dicentes solum de illis quia sunt, non autem ad primum omnium principium voluntarium ab omnibus separatum attendunt quae est causa propter quid aliorum omnium, quam considerat ista scientia, causalitatem omnium quae fiunt Deo ascribendo etiam super ea quae sunt prima et propria principia in singulis aliis supposita."

end of Genesis. Joseph had been sold into slavery by his jealous brothers. He had, however, risen to prestige and power in Egypt when his brothers arrived there starving from a plague-ridden Canaan. Joseph said to them: "So, it was not you who sent me here but God" (Gen. 45:8); and "As for you, you meant evil against me; but God meant it for good, to bring it about that many people should be kept alive, as they are today" (Gen. 50:20). For Henry, the other human disciplines live on one level, like Joseph's brothers, with their purposes; the human discipline of theology, however, lives on a separate level—looking to the ultimate purposes of God. It is because it deals with these ultimate causes and ends that theology is the *principal* science among all human theoretical and practical disciplines.[25] Because it studies the ultimate end of the other sciences, theology, as the principal science, judges the objects that belong to the less principal disciplines in terms of their ultimate end.[26] In judging the other sciences, theology evaluates them in the manner described by St. Augustine in his *De doctrina Christiana*: whatever is harmful in these sciences must be rejected; whatever is helpful should be accepted.[27] As Henry rephrases it: whatever is not in agreement with the rule of faith, no matter how it might appear to human wisdom, must be rejected; and whatever agrees with the rule of faith, no matter how much it goes against human wisdom, must be upheld.[28] The believer, especially one to whom the believed truths of theology have become intelligible, must judge all truths, both speculative and practical, when they have relevance to the articles of the faith.[29]

In q. 5 Henry moves to the second query: How do the other human disciplines relate to theology? His response to this question follows the final point in Bonaventure's summary of the thesis of the *De reductione artium ad theologiam*: "Patet etiam quomodo omnes cognitiones famulantur theologiae; et ideo ipsa assumit exempla et utitur vocabulis

25. Ibid. (f. 52vG): "Et per hoc, ut in sequentibus determinabitur, ista scientia est principalis super omnes scientias, et speculativas et activas."

26. Ibid., q. 5 (f. 54vI): "Et sic ordinat et regulat ea quae sunt aliarum scientiarum in finem eorum ultimum, quod ipsaemet facere non possunt. Sicut scientia militaris accipit instrumenta sua ab aliis artibus sibi subiectis, quibus utitur dirigendo eas in debitos fines, ut inferius amplius declarabitur."

27. S. Augustinus, *De doctrina Christiana*, 2, 42 (PL 34, 64).

28. Henricus de Gandavo, *Summa*, a. 7, q. 6 (f. 55rN): "Quaecunque enim eis quae fidei sunt consentanea in aliis scientiis, proculdubio vera sunt censenda; quaecunque vero repugnantia falsa sunt omnino iudicanda."

29. Ibid. (f. 55vP): "Homo igitur fidelis maxime cui credibilia huius scientiae facta sunt intelligibilia, iam spiritualis existens, ex hac scientia omnia tam in speculandis quam in agendis habet iudicare sufficienter ex hac scientia instructus, cum ipse in eis quae sunt huius scientiae e nemine iudicandus sit." On the proper knowledge of the other sciences that the theologian is not concerned with, see ibid. (f. a57rZ).

pertinentibus ad omne genus cognitionis."[30] For Henry, who is following a tradition already found in St. Bonaventure, the principal sources
of his thesis are mined from the *Synod of Pope Eugene* which urges that
"diligence be taken that masters and doctors be prepared who would
assiduously teach the study of letters and the teachings of the liberal
arts because in them the commandments are especially made manifest
and clear," and from the *Gloss on Leviticus* that urges: "Learn the arts,
so that through them, as an instrument, the divine scriptures may be
brought forth."[31] After Henry's time, in the era of Peter Aureoli's
Scriptum in I Sententiarum at Paris in 1317, Henry's approach to theology will become known formally as *declarative theology*. Effectively,
this means that the role of philosophy and the liberal arts is subor-
dinated to the Scriptures in such a way that their task is to manifest
or bring clarity to the truths of the faith by explanations of terms and
by examples or analogies that are most suitable to manifest a certain
understanding of the objects of Christian belief.[32]

There is, in a sense, a dependence of theology on philosophy and
the other sciences. It is not, however, a dependence whereby theology
gets its principles or starting points from such disciplines. This would
make of theology a purely human science. Rather, it is a dependence
of another type altogether. Theology starts with its own proper principles, the revealed truths found in the Scriptures. These truths, however, such as the trinity of persons in God, or the Incarnation of the
Word, are so far above human understanding that they cannot be
made manifest to human beings except with the help of things known
to us from the world of sense experience and proved in the other
sciences.[33] The theologian uses the human sciences to come to a
greater understanding of the more distant objects of faith revealed in
the Scriptures and to bring this understanding to others. His procedures parallel the procedures of metaphysicians who also deal with

30. Cf. n. 1 above.
31. Cf. Henricus de Gandavo, *Summa*, a. 7, q. 9 (f. 59vR).
32. Petrus Aureoli, *Scriptum in I Sententiarum*, Prol., sect. 1, q. 1, nn. 112–16, ed.
Eligius M. Buytaert, Text Series 3 (Louvain, Paderborn, St. Bonaventure, N.Y.: Franciscan Institute, 1953), 164–66.
33. Henricus de Gandavo, *Summa*, a. 7, q. 5 (f. 54rVI): "Propter defectum secundi
membri theologia non subalternatur alicui scientiae a qua sumit id de quo dicit quia,
alia propter quid, quia non assumit mendicando tamquam principia suae scientiae et
regulas suae conditionis. Immo habet principia propria superiora principiis omnium
aliarum scientiarum. Subalternata autem scientia mendicando principia sua accipit a
superiori scientia, quia nulla habet propria. Sed theologia assumit ab omnibus scientiis
eis principando et in usum suum ad declarandum ea quae ex suis principiis propriis
propter eorum elongationem a nobis manifesta esse non possunt nisi adminiculo nobis
cognitorum ex sensibilibus et probatis et manifestatis in aliis scientiis." Cf. q. 6 (f. 55v–
56rQ).

difficult truths. This should not be difficult for those in the philosophy faculties to understand: metaphysicians rightly claim that their science is superior to all the other purely human disciplines; still, they need to use physics and other particular disciplines, giving examples to make us understand what they are speaking about in metaphysics. Now, the human sciences help theology in other ways besides bringing understanding to truths that are distant from our prevailing sense experience. Besides assisting our understanding by bringing suitable analogies and other sensible illustrations to assist our understanding of the truths of the faith, theology also uses the purely human sciences to defend its truths against attackers, to show that the Christian faith often agrees with the teachings of great pagan thinkers of the past, and to prepare through philosophical instruction the road to the faith that fulfills the human quest for meaning.[34] Yet its chief internal contribution is to bring a greater understanding of the objects of Christian faith itself.

If the main contributions of the natural human sciences, according to Henry, are to defend the faith, to show the frequent accord of pagan writers with Christian faith, to attract people through secular writings to this faith, and to bring some understanding to its truths, does he allow these sciences any legitimacy outside of performing these functions? Is anything a valid object of study apart from its usefulness or service to theology? In other words, should Christians study any discipline if it does not lead to salvation? Also, if there are frequent accords between what is held by Christian faith and what was taught by the philosophers, how does he deal with the disaccords that sometimes occur?

The first of these problems is faced by Henry in q. 10. He answers it through a number of distinctions. Although every scientific study has as its final fulfillment the future vision of God—and no human discipline but theology deals with this ultimate goal of human life—there are still some sciences that have their own immediate proper and respected ends, distinct from man's ultimate end and also distinct from the theoretical knowledge they provide. Carpentry is immediately centered on building benches or tables; medicine attempts to preserve and restore bodily health; and politics tries to foster the peace of the city. Such sciences, for sure, can be learned without consideration of the assistance they might bring to theology, since they aim at the common benefit of men. Other sciences, however, are not

34. Ibid., q. 9 (f. 59rvR).

directed to a practical end distinct from the theoretical knowledge they provide. Philosophical sciences, for instance, are studied purely for the knowledge they offer. Each is necessarily ordained to a higher speculative discipline, since it itself does not attain man's ultimate end, the vision of God. Such studies are vain and marked by curiosity if they do not lead to the ultimate end of human existence. Some of them may be pursued without a direct or immediate link to theology. Logic or natural philosophy may be studied for the help they might provide in metaphysics. Yet, by direct or indirect approaches, all theoretical disciplines must serve the ultimate or principal discipline, theology, which alone is ordered to the future vision of God.[35]

Anyone who learns the philosophical sciences while establishing an end in these sciences themselves, just to know the nature of things, and not in a serving relationship to theology . . . , such people walk in the vanity of their own human understanding. . . . For the other sciences that do not have their own proper goals have not been given to man except to assist theology, and therefore it is useless to learn them except in order to serve this science. Neither is it allowable for them to learn these other sciences, because . . . those who love to pursue the philosophical sciences for their own sake cannot, or hardly can, avoid errors contrary to the true faith.[36]

In a criticism, most likely aimed at Siger of Brabant, Boethius of Dacia, and their followers, Henry concludes that it is altogether illicit to remain in the arts faculty simply to enjoy the knowledge gained in the liberal sciences and not directing the knowledge acquired from these disciplines to another purpose or use and especially the use of serving the science of theology.[37]

If, as Henry claims, those who love to pursue philosophy cannot, or hardly can, avoid errors against Christian faith, then how is the theologian to deal with the errors of the philosophers? Henry is quick to assert that there is no conflict between theological truth and philo-

---

35. Ibid., q. 10 (f. 6orB): "Dicendum ad hoc quod omnis humana scientia vitae huius ordinatur ad finem humanae vitae, quae est aperta Dei visio in futuro. Et ideo cum nulla aliarum unquam finem illum in se includat, necessarium est quod quaelibet illarum ordinetur ad aliquem finem alium a se, mediante quo ordinatur ad illum finem ultimum, ita quod non nisi in ordine ad illum finem ad quem immediate ordinatur debeat addisci; aliter enim frustra addisceretur et in vanum."

36. Ibid. (f. 6orB): "Qui enim philosophicas scientias discunt finem statuendo in ipsis propter scire naturas rerum, non in ordine ad usum istius scientiae, . . . isti sunt qui ambulant in vanitate sensus sui. . . . Aliae enim scientiae quae fines proprios non habent, re vera non sunt homini concessae nisi propter istam. Et ideo vanum est eas discere nisi in usum istius; nec licet, quia . . . qui philosophicis diligit insistere propter se non potest, vel vix potest errores evadere verae fidei contrarios."

37. Ibid. (f. 6orC): "Unde in scientiis liberalibus stare propter delectationem illius scire quod in eis invenitur, non ordinando scire acquisitum ex illis ad aliam utilitatem, et maxime in usum huius scientiae, omnino illicitum est."

sophical truth.[38] If there is a conflict, then it is due to the bad judgment of either philosophers or theologians, not due to philosophy or theology. Henry warns both philosophers and theologians to be careful of the manner in which they deal with their domains:

Wherefore, just as a rash theologian who is unacquainted with the things that belong to philosophy can consider many things to be false in the philosophical sciences which are in fact most true, and believes that this is the case on theological principles, and is mistaken, so, on the other hand, a rash philosopher can consider many things to be false in theology which are nonetheless most true, and believes that this is the case because of philosophical principles, and he also is mistaken. He can be mistaken on two counts: either he wrongly believes that his principles are true philosophical principles or he applies them beyond their scope in tearing down theological truths.[39]

Philosophers who argue against the resurrection of the body contend that the body is not capable of restoring itself and conclude that since it cannot restore itself the body is not capable of restoration. Their unstated principle then is that only if the body can restore itself is it capable of restoration, and this is false, Henry argues, since an omnipotent God can act beyond the limits of nature.[40] Likewise, Averroes

38. Ibid., q. 13 (f. 62rR): "Et quamvis ita sit, quaecunque tamen vera sunt iudicio huius scientiae falsa esse non possunt in recto iudicio naturalis rationis, si ad ea capienda posset naturalis ratio elevari, sicut econverso quaecunque vera sunt iudicio vero naturalis rationis in alia scientia, in recto iudicio huius scientiae falsa esse non possunt. . . . Unde, etsi quaedam quae in rei veritate vera sunt et vera iudicantur recto iudicio huius scientiae iudicio alterius sapientis, ut mundani, falsa esse dicuntur, hoc non contingit nisi per errorem iudicantis qui praesumit iudicare quae facultatem suam excedunt, in quibus omnino certum iudicium habere non potest."

39. Ibid. (f. 62vS): "Unde, sicut temerarius theologus ignorans ea quae sunt philosophiae multa potest reputare falsa in scientiis philosophicis quae tamen sunt verissima, et credere hoc se habere ex principiis theologicis, in quibus deceptus est, sic econtrario temerarius philosophus multa potest reputare esse falsa in hac scientia quae tamen sunt verissima, et credere hoc se habere ex principiis philosophicis, in quibus deceptus est, vel quae male ad vera theologica destruenda applicat."

40. Ibid. (f. 62vRS): "Ut si arguat aliquis quod 'natura non potest idem corporaliter reparare, ergo non potest fieri resurrectio mortuorum' male extendit principia vera philosophiae naturalis. Multa enim in materia naturali virtute superiori possunt fieri quae natura non potest facere, ut dictum est supra. Unde debet concludere 'ergo actione naturae non potest fieri resurrectio mortuorum' et ibi stare. Sed cum concludit quod a nulla alia virtute hoc potest fieri, philosophiam excedit, quia hoc ex principiis philosophiae non habet sed contrarium potius. Ex quo enim philosophia docet primum principium omnium esse potentiae infinitae, licet ignoret quomodo possit operari supra solitum cursum naturae, non debet negare quin ab aliqua virtute supernaturali hoc sit possibile fieri, cum scit esse aliquod agens infinitae virtutis. Nec etiam in philosophia debet asserere quod illud non possit fieri, quia ignorat quomodo fieri possit supra consuetum cursum naturae, ut demus Deum aliquid posse quod non fatemur investigare non posse, sicut dicit Augustinus in epistola ad Volusianum. Et forte si aliquid praesumant dicere quod extra cursum consuetum natura primum principium nihil posset agere, hoc re vera humana temeritas confingit, nec recta ratio ex principiis

oversteps the limits of his principles when he argues against the Trinity in his commentary on Book 12 of the *Metaphysics*. He extends the principle that every person is a substance beyond its domain of application.[41]

In correcting these false uses of philosophy, however, Henry does not side with the rash theologians. He argues that since these false arguments are based on errors of natural reason, either in regard to true principles of philosophy or to their overextended application, they can be refuted by the guidance of natural reason on its own part or by the help of supernatural illumination whereby supernatural realities are known.[42] Henry thus is not anti-philosophical. He does stress the distinction between philosophy and philosophic tradition, as he fosters the study of philosophy and attacks the uncritical following of a particular philosophic tradition. Philosophy, however, even though defended, is never permitted as an independent discipline. It must be competent, but its end always is its service to theology and to the ultimate supernatural end of human existence. It always must have a *reductio ad theologiam*.

---

philosophiae dictat." Note the parallel between Henry's argument here and proposition 17 (Mandonnet, p. 215) of the articles condemned at Paris in 1277. Article 17 reads: "Quod impossibile simpliciter non potest fieri a Deo, vel ab agente alio.—Error si de impossibili secundum naturam intelligatur."

41. Ibid. (f. 62vS): ". . . Sicut Commentator ille haereticus Averroes, super XII *Metaphysicae*, impossibile reputat Deum esse trinum et unum, quia, ut dicit, non possunt esse tres nisi in eis numeretur substantia, et non intellexit quid dixit."

42. See Henry's philosophical argument against those who oppose the resurrection of the body in n. 40 above.

Contributors

Oliva Blanchette is professor of philosophy at Boston College, where he has been teaching since 1964. He received his Ph.D. from Université Laval. He was dean of the School of Philosophy at Boston College from 1968 to 1973 and has been director of the Institute for Social Thought. His publications include *For a Fundamental Social Ethic* (1973), a translation of Maurice Blondel's *Action* (1984), *The Perfection of the Universe According to Aquinas* (1992), along with numerous articles in social philosophy, philosophy of history, philosophy of religion, and metaphysics. He is currently in the process of completing a book in metaphysics, provisionally entitled *A Reconstructive Essay in the Philosophy of Being*.

Stephen F. Brown is professor of theology and director of the Institute of Medieval Philosophy and Theology at Boston College. He received his Ph.D. in philosophy from the Université Catholique de Louvain in 1964, having written his dissertation under Fernand Van Steenberghen. He has been the editor or assistant editor for five volumes of the *Opera Philosophica et Theologica* of William of Ockham, has revised *Ockham: Philosophical Writings,* and has most recently translated, with introduction and commentary, the *Itinerarium mentis in Deum* of St. Bonaventure for Hackett Publishing Company. The author of more than twenty-five articles in medieval philosophy and theology, he has been president of the Society for Medieval and Renaissance Philosophy and is now vice-president of *La Société internationale pour l'étude de la philosophie médiévale*.

David M. Gallagher received his Ph.D. in philosophy from The Catholic University of America in 1988. He is presently assistant professor of philosophy at The Catholic University of America. He has published several articles in the area of Thomistic moral philosophy. He spent the 1993–94 year as a visiting researcher at the Thomas-Institut at the University of Cologne with a grant from the Hanns Seidel Foundation.

Jorge J. E. Gracia, Distinguished Professor of Philosophy at the State University of New York at Buffalo, received his Ph.D. from the University of Toronto. He has been a National Endowment for the Humanities and Canada Council Fellow, and has been president of the Society for Medieval and Renaissance Philosophy, the International Federation of Latin American and Caribbean Studies, and the Society for Iberian and Latin American Thought. He is the editor of two volumes on metaphysics and contemporary Latin American philosophy of the *Encyclopedia Iberoamericana de Filosofía.* He has authored three books: *Introduction to the Problem of Individuation in the Early Middle Ages* (1984), *Individuality: An Essay on the Foundations of Metaphysics* (1988) (winner of the 1992 John N. Findlay Award in Metaphysics), and *Philosophy and Its History: Issues in Philosophical Historiography* (1992). Additionally he has published two translations with commentaries: *Suárez on Individuation* (1982) and *The Metaphysics of Good and Evil according to Suárez* (1989); edited twelve other books; published more than one hundred articles on metaphysics, historiography, medieval philosophy, and Latin American thought; and serves as editorial consultant to more than a dozen journals.

John P. Hittinger was a research associate at the Maritain Center, University of Notre Dame, from 1990–93. He received his Ph.D. from The Catholic University of America. He has taught at Benedictine College in Atchison, Kansas, and at the College of St. Francis, where he is presently a professor of philosophy. He has published articles on the philosophy of Jacques Maritain and John Locke. He is interested in the application of philosophy to issues of public policy, and is active in the American Public Philosophy Institute and the Religion and Public Life Ramsey Colloquium.

Alejandro Llano, Ordinary Professor of Philosophy at the University of Navarra (Pamplona, Spain) since 1977, received his Ph.D. from the University of Valencia. Besides his work on German Idealism, he has studied ontology and theory of knowledge in Aristotle and Thomas Aquinas, bringing them into dialogue with problems of contemporary logical and linguistic analysis. He has also dealt with problems of political philosophy and the philosophy of culture. In addition to numerous articles in European and American journals, he has published the following books: *Fenómeno y trascendencia en Kant* (1973); *Etica y política en la sociedad democrática* (1981); *Ciencia y Cultura al servicio del hombre* (1982); *Gnoseología* (1982, 3d ed., 1991); *Metafísica y Lenguaje* (1984); *El futuro de la libertad* (1985); *La nueva sensibilidad* (1988, 2d ed., 1989; English translation: *The New Sensibility*, 1991); *El humanismo en la Empresa* (1991). In 1976 he obtained the Chair of Metaphysics at the Autónoma University of Madrid, and was visiting professor at The Catholic University of America in 1990. Since 1991 he has been the President of the University of Navarra.

Edward P. Mahoney, professor of philosophy at Duke University, joined his faculty in 1965. He received a Ph.D. from Columbia University in philosophy in 1966. He has been a Fulbright teaching fellow at the University of Rome and a visiting professor at UCLA and The Catholic University of America. A former Guggenheim Fellow, he has also held fellowships from the Danforth Foundation and the National Endowment for the Humanities. He edited *Philosophy and Humanism* (1976) and *Medieval Aspects of Renaissance Learning* (rev. ed., 1992) and has also served as a co-editor of *Renaissance Quarterly*. He has published a wide range of studies on psychological theories, conceptions of *scientia naturalis*, schemes of metaphysical hierarchy, and the impact of the Greek Commentators during the medieval and Renaissance periods. Several of his studies have focused on the influence of medieval philosophers like Albert, Thomas, Scotus, and Jandun during the Renaissance.

Gregory Martin Reichberg is assistant professor of philosophy at The Catholic University of America. After predoctoral studies in France at the University of Toulouse and the Centre Indépendant de Recherche Philosophique, he received his Ph.D. in philosophy from Emory University in 1990. He has published articles on Thomistic epistemology, philosophical issues in theology, and the philosophy of science.

Kenneth L. Schmitz is Professor Emeritus of Philosophy and Fellow of Trinity College in the University of Toronto, where he received his Ph.D. in philosophy in 1952. The recipient of Humboldt grants and a Canada Council Research Grant, he has also been President of the Hegel Society of America, the Metaphysical Society of America, and the American Catholic Philosophical Association. His numerous publications have focused on the philosophies of Kant and Hegel, the philosophy of religion, aesthetics, and philosophical issues in theology. His McGivney Lectures on the philosophical anthropology of Karol Wojtyla will be published by The Catholic University of America Press (forthcoming). In 1992 he was awarded the Aquinas Medal by the American Catholic Philosophical Association.

William A. Wallace, O.P., is Professor Emeritus of Philosophy and History at The Catholic University of America, where he taught from 1963 until his retirement in 1988. He received the Ph.D. in philosophy in 1959 from the University of Fribourg in Switzerland, and in addition holds four honorary doctorates from American institutions. Recipient of many grants from the National Endowment for the Humanities and the National Science Foundation, he has been president of the American Catholic Philosophical Association, which awarded him the Aquinas Medal in 1983. He has published fifteen books and over one hundred articles in journals or chapters in books edited by others. One of the principal editors of the *New Catholic Encyclopedia* and a long-time editor of *The Thomist,* he served as Director General of the Leonine Commission from 1976 to 1987. Apart from Thomism, his main intellectual interest has been the history and philosophy of science, where he has done pioneering research on Galileo's early Latin notebooks.

Works Cited

Abelard, Peter. *Logica nostrorum petitioni sociorum.* Edited by B. Geyer. *Beiträge zur Geschichte der Philosophie des Mittelalters* 21 (1933): 505–88.

Aertsen, Jan. "The Convertability of Being and Good in St. Thomas Aquinas." *The New Scholasticism* 59 (1985): 449–70.

Anawati, Georges C. "Saint Thomas d'Aquin et la Métaphysique d'Avicenne." In *St. Thomas Aquinas 1274–1974: Commemorative Studies* (2 vols.), vol. 1, 449–65. Toronto: Pontifical Institute of Mediaeval Studies, 1974.

Anderson, James. *An Introduction to the Metaphysics of St. Thomas Aquinas.* Chicago: Regnery Gateway, 1953.

Augustine, Saint. *De doctrina Christiana.* PL 34.

Averroes. *Commentarium Magnum in Aristotelis De Anima Libros.* Corpus Commentariorum Averrois in Aristotelem, Versionum Latinarum, vol. 6, pt. 1. Cambridge: Medieval Academy of America, 1953.

Avicenna. *Metaphysica.* In *Opera philosophica.* Venice, 1508. Reprint. Louvain: Bibliothèque S.J., 1961.

Bärthlein, Karl. "Untersuchungen zur aristotelischen Modaltheorie." *Archiv für Geschichte der Philosophie* 45 (1963): 43–67.

Bazán, Bernardo Carlos. *Siger de Brabant: Quaestiones in tertium De anima, De anima intellectiva, De aeternitate mundi.* Philosophes médiévaux, vol. 13. Louvain: Publications Universitaires and Paris: Béatrice-Nauwelaerts, 1972.

———. "La dialogue philosophique entre Siger de Brabant et Thomas d'Aquin." *Revue philosophique de Louvain* 72 (1974): 53–155.

———. "Averroes y Sigerio de Brabante: La noción de 'intellectum speculativum'." In *Actas del V Congreso Internacional de Filosofía Medieval*, vol. 1, 541–49. Madrid, 1979.

———. "*Intellectum Speculativum*: Averroes, Thomas Aquinas, and Siger of Brabant on the Intelligible Object." *Journal of the History of Philosophy* 19 (1981): 425–46.

Beach, John. "Another Look at the Thomism of Etienne Gilson." *The New Scholasticism* 50 (1981): 522–28.

Benested, Brian. "Rights, Virtue and the Common Good." *Crisis* 1 (December 1983): 28–32.

Blumenberg, Hans. *The Legitimacy of the Modern Age.* Translated by Robert W. Wallace. Cambridge: MIT Press, 1985.

Blythe, James M. "The Mixed Constitution and the Distinction Between Regal and Political Power in the Work of Thomas Aquinas." *Journal of the History of Ideas* 47 (1986): 547–65.

Bobic, Joseph. *Aquinas On Being and Essence: A Translation and Interpretation.* Notre Dame: University of Notre Dame Press, 1965.

Boehner, Philotheus. "Historical Notes on the Concept of Truth in Scholasticism." In *Collected Articles on Ockham*, edited by Eligius M. Buytaert, 175–99. St. Bonaventure, N.Y.: The Franciscan Institute, 1958.

Boethius. *In Isagogen Porphyrii commenta*. Edited by S. Brandt. Corpus scriptorum ecclesiasticorum latinorum, vol. 48. Vienna: Tempsky, 1906. Reprint, New York: Johnson, 1966.

Bonaventure, Saint. *De reductione artium ad theologiam. Doctoris Seraphici S. Bonaventurae . . . Opera Omnia*, vol. 5. Quaracchi, 1882–1902.

Brown, Stephen F. "Key Terms in Medieval Theological Vocabulary." In *Méthodes et instruments du travail intellectual au moyen âge*, edited by O. Weijers, 93–96. Études sur le Vocabulaire intellectuel du Moyen Age, vol. 3. Turnhout: Brepols, 1990.

Carlo, William. *The Ultimate Reducibility of Essence to Existence in Existential Metaphysics*. The Hague: Martinus Nijhoff, 1966.

Chenu, Marie-Dominique. *Toward Understanding Saint Thomas*. Translated and edited by A.-M. Landry and D. Hughes. Chicago: Henry Regnery Co., 1964.

Clark, Ralph W. "Saint Thomas Aquinas' Theory of Universals." *The Monist* 58 (1974): 163–72.

Clarke, Francis P. "St. Thomas on 'Universals'." *The Journal of Philosophy* 59 (1962): 720–25.

Clarke, W. Norris. "The Limitation of Act by Potency: Aristotelianism or Neoplatonism." *The New Scholasticism* 26 (1952): 167–94.

———. "The Meaning of Participation in St. Thomas Aquinas." *Proceedings of the American Catholic Philosophical Association* 26 (1952): 147–57.

Code, Lorraine. *Epistemic Responsibility*. Hanover, N.H.: University Press of New England, 1987.

Collins, James. "History in the Defence of Metaphysics." *The Review of Metaphysics* 2, no. 8 (1948): 105–25.

Cromp, Germaine. "Les sources de l'abstraction de l'intellect agent dans la 'Somme de théologie' de Thomas d'Aquin." Ph.D. diss., l'Université de Montréal, 1980.

Davidson, Herbert A. *Alfarabi, Avicenna, and Averroes on Intellect: Their Cosmologies, Theories of the Active Intellect, and Theories of Human Intellect*. Oxford: Oxford University Press, 1992.

De Finance, Joseph. *Être et agir dans la philosophie de Saint Thomas*. 3d ed. Rome: Presses de l'Université Gregorienne, 1965.

de Tocqueville, Alexis. *Democracy in America*. Edited by J. P. Mayer and translated by George Lawrence. New York: Doubleday, 1969.

Denifle, Henricus A., and Aemilo Chatelain. *Chartularium Universitatis Parisiensis*. 2 vols. Paris: Ex typis fratrum Delalain, 1889.

Denzinger, Heinrich, and Karl Rahner, eds. *Enchiridion Symbolorum*. Barcelona, Friburg, Rome: Herder, 1957.

Dilthey, Wilhelm. *Introduction to the Human Sciences*. In *Selected Works*. Edited by Rudolf A. Makkreel and Frithjof Rodi, vol. 1. Princeton: Princeton University Press, 1989.

Dondaine, H.-F. "Préface," *Compendium theologiae seu Brevis compilatio theologiae ad fratrem Raynaldum*. In *Sancti Thomae de Aquino opera omnia*, vol. 42. Rome: Commissio Leonina, 1979.

Donohoo, Larry. "The Nature of Desire: St. Thomas Aquinas's Primary Account of Desire." S.T.L. diss., Dominican House of Studies, Washington, D.C., 1988.

Ducoin, G. "Saint Thomas, Commentateur d'Aristote." *Archives de Philosophie* 20 (1957): 240–71, 392–445.

Ermatinger, Charles J. "The Coalescent Soul in Post-Thomistic Debate." Ph.D. diss., Saint Louis University, 1963.

———. "Giles of Rome and Anthony of Parma in an Anonymous Question on the Intellect." *Manuscripta* 17 (1973): 91–114.

Evans, Joseph W. "Jacques Maritain and the Problem of Pluralism in Political Life." In *Jacques Maritain: The Man and His Achievement*, edited by Joseph W. Evans, 215–36. New York: Sheed and Ward, 1963.

Fabro, Cornelio. *La nozione metafisica di partecipazione secondo S. Tommaso d'Aquino.* Milan: Societá Editrice 'Vita e Pensiero,' 1939. 3d ed., Turin: Societá Editrice Internazionale, 1963.

———. *Partecipazione e causalitá secondo S. Tommaso d'Aquino.* Turin: Societá Editrice Internazionale, 1960.

———. *Participation et causalité selon S. Thomas d'Aquin.* Louvain: Publications Universitaires and Paris: Béatrice-Nauwelaerts, 1961.

Ficino, Marsilio. *Opera omnia.* Basel, 1576. Reprint, Turin: Bottega d'Erasmo, 1962.

Finnis, John. *Natural Law and Natural Rights.* New York: Oxford University Press, 1978.

Flasch, Kurt. *Aufklärung im Mittelalter? Die Verurteilung von 1277.* Mainz: Dieterich, 1989.

Forest, Aimé. *La structure métaphysique du concret selon saint Thomas d'Aquin.* Paris: J. Vrin, 1932.

Fortin, Ernest. "The New Rights Theory and the Natural Law." *Review of Politics* 44 (1982): 590–612.

———. "Thomas Aquinas." In *History of Political Philosophy*, edited by Leo Strauss and Joseph Cropsey, 248–75. 3d ed., Chicago: University of Chicago Press, 1987.

Gallagher, David. "Aquinas on Moral Action: Interior and Exterior Act." *Proceedings of the American Catholic Philosophical Association* 64 (1990): 118–29.

Gardet, Louis. "Saint Thomas et ses Prédécesseurs Arabes." In *St. Thomas Aquinas 1274–1974: Commemorative Studies* (2 vols.), vol. 1, 419–48. Toronto: Pontifical Institute of Mediaeval Studies, 1974.

Gauthier, René A. "Introduction historique." In *Saint Thomas d'Aquin: Contra Gentiles, Livre premier.* Paris: P. Lethielleux, 1961.

———. "Quelques questions à propos du commentaire de St. Thomas sur le 'De anima'." *Angelicum* 51 (1974): 419–72.

———. "Préface." *Sentencia libri De anima. Sancti Thomae de Aquino opera omnia,* vol. 45, pt. 1. Rome: Commissio Leonina, 1984.

Geiger, Louis-Bertrand. *La participation dans la philosophie de saint Thomas d'Aquin.* 2d ed. Paris: J. Vrin, 1953.

———. "Abstraction et séparation d'après S. Thomas *In de Trinitate* q. 5, a. 3." *Revue des sciences philosophiques et théologiques* 31 (1947): 3–40.

Gilson, Etienne. *L'etre et l'essence.* Paris: J. Vrin, 1948. 2d rev. ed., 1962.

———. *Being and Some Philosophers.* Toronto: Pontifical Institute of Mediaeval Studies, 1949. 2d rev. ed., 1952.

———. *The Christian Philosophy of St. Thomas Aquinas.* Translated by L. K. Shook. New York: Random House, 1956.

———. Review of *Le retour à la scolastique* by Gonzague Truc. *Revue Philosophique de la France et de l'Etranger* 88 (1919): 322–24.

————. "Compagnons de route." In *Etienne Gilson: philosophe de la chrétienté*, edited by Jacques Maritain, 275–95. Collection Recontres, vol. 30. Paris: Editions du Cerf, 1949.

Gómez Cabranes, Leonor. *El poder y lo posible: Sus sentidos en Aristóteles*. Pamplona: EUNSA, 1989.

Gorce, Matthieu-Maxime. *L'essor de la pensée au moyen âge: Albert le Grand— Thomas d'Aquin*. Paris: Libraire Letouzey et Ané, 1933.

Grabmann, Martin. "Scientific Cognition of Truth: Its Characteristic Genius in the Doctrine of St. Thomas Aquinas." *The New Scholasticism* 13 (1939): 1–30.

Gracia, Jorge J. E. *Individuality: An Essay on the Foundations of Metaphysics*. Albany, N.Y.: State University of New York Press, 1988.

Hartshorne, Charles. *The Logic of Perfection and Other Essays in Neoclassical Metaphysics*. La Salle, Ill.: Open Court, 1962.

Healy, Emma T. *Saint Bonaventure's "De reductione artium ad theologiam."* St. Bonaventure, N.Y.: The Franciscan Institute, 1955.

Heaney, Stephen J. "Aquinas and the Presence of the Human Rational Soul in the Early Embryo." *The Thomist* 56 (1992): 19–48.

Heidegger, Martin. *Aristoteles, Metaphysik IX 1–3*. Gesamtausgabe, vol. 33. Frankfurt am Main: Vittorio Klostermann, 1981.

Henle, Robert J. *Saint Thomas and Platonism: A Study of the Plato and Platonici Texts in the Writings of Saint Thomas*. The Hague: Martinus Nijhoff, 1956.

Henry of Ghent. *Summa quaestionum ordinarium*. Paris, 1520.

Hintikka, Jaakko. *Time and Necessity*. Oxford: Clarendon, 1973.

Hintikka, Jaakko, Unto Remes, and Simo Knuuttila. *Aristotle on Modality and Determinism*. Acta Philosophica Fennica, vol. 29, no. 1. Amsterdam: North Holland, 1977.

Hittinger, John P. "Maritain and America." *This World* 3 (Fall 1982): 113–23.

————. "Maritain and the Intellectuals." *This World* 5 (1983): 164–68.

————. Review of *Theology of Freedom*, by John Cooper. *Crisis* 4 (December 1986): 32–33.

————. Review of *Natural Law and the Rights of Man*, by Jacques Maritain. *Crisis* 5 (July/August 1987): 51–52.

————. "Approaches to Democratic Equality." In *Freedom in the Modern World*, edited by M. Torre, 237–52. Notre Dame: American Maritain/Notre Dame Press, 1989.

————. "Three Philosophies of Human Rights." In *Towards a National Morality*, edited by W. B. Ball. San Francisco: Ignatius Press, 1992.

Hugo of St. Victor. *Commentarium in Hierarchiam Coelestem S. Dionysii Areopagitae*. PL 175.

————. *De sacramentis Christianae fidei*. PL 176.

Hugo, John. "Intelligence and Character: A Thomistic View." *The New Scholasticism* 11 (1937): 58–68.

Inagaki, B. Ryosuke. "Thomas Aquinas and the Problem of Universals: A Re-Examination." In *Studies in Philosophy and the History of Philosophy*, vol. 4, edited by John K. Ryan, 174–90. Washington, D.C.: The Catholic University of America Press, 1969.

Inciarte, Fernando. "El problema de la verdad en la filosofía actual y en Santo Tomás." In *Veritas et Sapientia*, edited by Juan J. R. Rosado and Pedro Rodriguez, 43–49. Pamplona: EUNSA, 1975.

Jacobi, Klaus. "Aussagen über Ereignisse: Modal- und zeitlogische Analysen in der mittelalterischen Logik." *Anuario Filosófico* 16, no. 1 (1983): 89–117.

Jerome, Saint. *Epistolae.* PL 22.

John, Helen James. "The Emergence of the Act of Existing in Recent Thomism." *International Philosophical Quarterly* 2 (1962): 595–620.

John of Paris. *Commentarium in libros Sententiarum.* Edited by J.-P. Muller. Rome: Herder, 1961.

John of Salisbury. *Entheticus.* PL 199.

———. *Metalogicon.* Edited by C. C. I. Webb. Oxford: Clarendon, 1929.

Kainz, Howard P. "The Multiplicity and Individuality of Intellects: A Reexamination of St. Thomas' Reaction to Averroes." *Divus Thomas* (Piacenza) 74 (1971): 155–79.

Kayser, John R. "Aquinas's 'Regimen Bene Commixtum' and the Medieval Critique of Classical Republicanism." *Thomist* 46 (1982): 195–220.

Kenny, Anthony. *Aquinas on Mind.* London and New York: Routledge, 1993.

Klünker, Wolf-Urich, and Bruno Sandkühler. *Menschliche Seele und Kosmischer Geist. Siger von Brabant in der Auseinandersetzung mit Thomas von Aquin.* Stuttgart: Verlag Freies Geistesleben, 1988.

Knuuttila, Simo. "Varieties of Natural Necessity in Medieval Thought." In *Estudios de Historia de la Lógica,* edited by Ignacio Angelelli and Angel d'Ors, 307–8. Pamplona: Eunate, 1990.

———, ed. *Reforging the Great Chain of Being: Studies of the History of Modal Theories.* Dordrecht: Reidel, 1980.

Koyzis, David T. "Yves R. Simon's Contribution to a Structural Political Pluralism." In *Freedom in the Modern World,* edited by M. Torre, 131–40. Notre Dame: American Maritain/Notre Dame Press, 1989.

Krapiec, Mierczyslaw A. *I-Man: An Outline of Philosophical Anthropology.* Translated by Marie Lescoe et al., and edited by Francis J. Lescoe and Roger B. Duncan. New Britain, Conn.: Mariel Publications, 1985.

Kuksewicz, Zdzislaw. *De Siger de Brabant à Jacques de Plaisance: La théorie de l'intellect chez les averroïstes latins des XIIIᵉ et XIVᵉ siècles.* Wroclaw: Ossolineum, 1968.

Künzle, Pius. *Das Verhältnis der Seele zu ihren Potenzen. Problemgeschichtliche Untersuchungen von Augustin bis und mit Thomas von Aquin.* Freiburg: Universitätsverlag Schweiz, 1956.

Lakebrink, Bernhard. *Hegels dialektische Ontologie und die Thomistische Analektik.* Ratingen: A. Hehn, 1968.

Lee, Patrick. "St. Thomas and Avicenna on the Agent Intellect." *The Thomist* 45 (1981): 41–61.

Little, Arthur. *The Platonic Heritage of Thomism.* Dublin: Golden Eagle Books, 1949.

Lomba, Joaquín. "El principio de individuación en Averroes." *Revista de filosofía* 22 (1963): 299–324.

Lovejoy, Arthur O. *The Great Chain of Being: A Study of the History of an Idea.* Cambridge: Harvard University Press, 1936.

MacIntyre, Alasdair. *After Virtue.* 2d ed. Notre Dame: University of Notre Dame Press, 1984.

MacLellan, Thomas M. "The Moral Virtues and the Speculative Life." *Laval Théologique et Philosophique* 12 (1956): 175–232.

Mahoney, Edward P. "Themistius and the Agent Intellect in James of Viterbo and Other Thirteenth Century Philosophers (Saint Thomas, Siger of Brabant and Henry Bate)." *Augustiniana* 23 (1973): 422–67.

———. "Saint Thomas and Siger of Brabant Revisited." *The Review of Metaphysics* 27 (1974): 531–53.

———. "Saint Thomas and the School of Padua at the End of the Fifteenth Century." *Proceedings of the American Catholic Philosophical Association* 48 (1974): 277–85.

———. "Agostino Nifo and St. Thomas Aquinas." *Memorie domenicane* n.s. 7 (1976): 195–220.

———. "Antonio Trombetta and Agostino Nifo on Averroes and Intelligible Species: A Philosophical Dispute at the University of Padua." In *Storia e cultura al Santo di Padova fra il XII e il XX secolo*, edited by A. Poppi, 289–301. Vicenza: N. Pozza, 1976.

———. "Sense, Intellect and Imagination in Albert, Thomas, and Siger." In *The Cambridge History of Later Medieval Philosophy*, edited by N. Kretzmann, A. Kenny, and J. Pinborg, 602–22. Cambridge: Cambridge University Press, 1982.

———. "Themes and Problems in the Psychology of John of Jandun." In *Studies in Medieval Philosophy*, edited by J. F. Wippel, 273–88. Studies in Philosophy and the History of Philosophy, vol. 17. Washington, D.C.: The Catholic University of America Press, 1987.

Marcel, Raymond. *Marsile Ficin (1433–1499)*. Paris: Les Belles Lettres, 1958.

———. *Marsile Ficin: Théologie platonicienne de l'immortalité des âmes.* 3 vols. Paris: Societé d'edition "Les Belles Lettres," 1964–70.

Maritain, Jacques. *Ransoming the Time*. Translated by Harry Lorin Binesse. New York: Scribner's, 1941.

———. *Existence and the Existent*. New York: Pantheon, 1948.

———. *Man and the State*. Chicago: University of Chicago Press, 1951.

———. *Christianity and Democracy* and *The Rights of Man and Natural Law*. Translated by Doris C. Anson. San Francisco: Ignatius Press, 1986.

———. "The Human Person and Society." In *Scholasticism and Politics*, edited and translated by Mortimer J. Adler, 61–90. New York: Doubleday, 1940.

Marlasca, Antonio, ed. *Les quaestiones super librum 'De causis' de Siger de Brabant. Edition critique*. Philosophes médiévaux, vol. 12. Louvain: Publications Universitaires and Paris: Béatrice-Nauwelaerts, 1972.

Mazzarella, Pasquale. "La critica di San Tommaso all' 'Averroismo gnoseologico'." *Rivista di filosofia neo-scolastica* 66 (1974): 246–83.

McCoy, Charles N. R. *The Structure of Political Thought*. New York: McGraw-Hill, 1963.

McInerny, Ralph. *Boethius and Aquinas*. Washington, D.C.: The Catholic University of America Press, 1990.

Michalos, Alex C. "The Morality of Cognitive Decision Making." In *Action Theory*, edited by M. Brand and D. Walton, 325–40. Dordrecht: D. Reidel, 1976.

Nardi, Bruno. *Tommaso d'Aquino: Trattato sull'unità dell'intelletto contro gli averroisti*. Florence: Sansoni, 1947.

———. "Note per una storia dell'averroismo latino, III: Egidio romano e l'averroismo." *Rivista di storia della filosofia* 3 (1948): 8–29.

Nédoncelle, Maurice. "Remarques sur la réfutation des averroistes par saint Thomas." *Rivista di filosofia neo-scolastica* 66 (1974): 284–92.

Noonan, John T. "The Existentialism of Etienne Gilson." *The New Scholasticism* 24 (1950): 417–38.

Ottaviano, Carmelo. *Tommaso d'Aquino: Saggio contro la dottrina averroistica dell'unità dell'intelletto.* Lanciano: Carabba, 1930.

Owens, Joseph. *Aquinas on Being and Thing.* Niagara: Niagara University Press, 1981.

———. *An Interpretation of Existence.* 2d ed. Houston: Center for Thomistic Studies, 1985.

———. "Common Nature: A Point of Comparison Between Thomistic and Scotistic Metaphysics." *Mediaeval Studies* 19 (1957): 1–14.

———. "Aquinas as Aristotelian Commentator." In *St. Thomas Aquinas 1274–1974: Commemorative Studies,* edited by E. Gilson (2 vols.), vol. 1, 213–38. Toronto: Pontifical Institute of Mediaeval Studies, 1974.

———. "Aquinas: Intimacy and Contingency of Existence." *American Catholic Philosophical Quarterly* 64 (1990): 261–64.

Parsons, Wilfrid. "Saint Thomas Aquinas and Popular Sovereignty." *Thought* 16 (1941): 473–92.

Peter Aureoli. *Scriptum in I Sententiarum.* Edited by E. M. Buytaert. Text Series 3. Louvain, Paderborn, St. Bonaventure, N.Y.: The Franciscan Institute, 1953.

———. *Dialogus inter philosophum et Iudaeum.* PL 178.

Peter Damian. *De divina omnipotentia.* PL 145.

Phelan, Gerald B. "The Being of Creatures." *Proceedings of the American Catholic Philosophical Association* 31 (1957): 118–25.

Popper, Karl R. *Objective Knowledge: An Evolutionary Approach.* Oxford: Clarendon Press, 1979.

Poppi, Antonino. *Saggi sul pensiero inedito di Pietro Pomponazzi.* Padua: Antenore, 1970.

———. *La filosofia nello studio francescano del Santo a Padova.* Padua: Antenore, 1989.

Prantl, Carl. *Geschichte der Logik im Abendlande.* 4 vols. Leipzig: S. Hirzel, 1855–70. Reprint, Graz: Akademische Druck-U. Verlagsanstalt, 1955.

Quevedo, Amalia. *Ens per accidens: Contingencia y determinación en Aristóteles.* Pamplona: EUNSA, 1989.

Quine, W. V. *From a Logical Point of View.* Cambridge: Harvard University Press, 1961.

Robert of Melun. *Sententie.* In *Oeuvres de Robert de Melun,* vol. 3, pt. 1. Edited by R. M. Martin and R. M. Gallet. Louvain: "Spicilegium, Sacrum lovaniense," 1947.

Robert Kilwardby. *Quaestiones in librum primum Sententiarum.* Edited by J. Schneider. Munich: Verlag der Bayerischen Akademie der Wissenschaften, 1986.

Rommen, Heinrich A. *The State in Catholic Thought.* St. Louis: Herder, 1947.

Salman, Dominique H. "Albert le Grand et l'averroisme latin." *Revue des sciences philosophiques et théologiques* 24 (1935): 38–65.

Sandel, Michael. *Liberalism and the Limits of Justice.* Cambridge: Cambridge University Press, 1982.

Schall, James V. "Metaphysics, Theology, and Political Theory." *Political Science Reviewer* 11 (Fall 1981): 1–26.

Schiller, Friedrich. *On the Aesthetic Education of Man.* Edited by E. M. Wilkinson and L. A. Willoughby. Oxford: Oxford University Press, 1967.

Schmitz, Kenneth. *What Has Clio to Do with Athena? Etienne Gilson: Historian and Philosopher.* Toronto: Pontifical Institute of Mediaeval Studies, 1987.

———. "Enriching the Copula." *The Review of Metaphysics* 27 (1974): 492–512.

———. "From Anarchy to Principles: Deconstruction and the Resources of Christian Philosophy." *Communio* 16 (1989): 69–88.

———. "Postmodern or Modern-plus?" *Communio* 17 (1990): 152–66.

Segura, Carmen. "La dimensión reflexiva de la verdad en Tomás de Aquino." *Anuario Filosófico* 15, no. 2 (1982): 271–79.

Shewmon, Alan. "The Metaphysics of Brain Death, Persistent Vegetative State and Dementia." *The Thomist* 49 (1985): 24–80.

Sigmund, Paul. *Natural Law in Political Thought.* Cambridge, Mass.: Winthrop Press, 1971.

———. "Maritain on Politics." In *Understanding Maritain: Philosopher and Friend,* edited by Deal W. Hudson and Matthew J. Mancini, 153–55. Macon, Ga.: Mercer University Press, 1987.

Simmons, Edward. "In Defence of Total Abstraction." *The New Scholasticism* 29 (1955): 427–40.

Simon, Yves R. *Philosophy of Democratic Government.* Chicago: University of Chicago Press, 1951.

———. "Beyond the Crisis of Liberalism." In *Essays in Thomism,* edited by Robert E. Brennan, 261–86. New York: Sheed and Ward, 1942.

———. "Thomism and Democracy." In *Science, Philosophy and Religion,* edited by Louis Finkelstein and Lyman Bryson, 258–72. New York: The Conference on Science, Philosophy and Religion in Their Relation to the Democratic Way of Life, 1942.

———. "The Doctrinal Issue Between the Church and Democracy." In *The Catholic Church in World Affairs,* edited by Waldemar Gurian and M. A. Fitzsimons, 87–114. Notre Dame: University of Notre Dame Press, 1954.

Smith, Philip. "Transient Natures at the Edges of Life: A Thomistic Exploration." *The Thomist* 54 (1990): 191–227.

Strauss, Leo. *Natural Right and History.* Chicago: University of Chicago Press, 1952.

———. *What is Political Philosophy?* New York: Free Press, 1959.

Stump, Eleonore, and Norman Kretzmann. "Being and Goodness." In *Divine and Human Action: Essays in the Metaphysics of Theism,* edited by T. Morris, 281–312. Ithaca, N.Y.: Cornell University Press, 1988.

Taylor, Michael A. "Human Generation in the Thought of Thomas Aquinas: A Case Study on the Role of Biological Fact in Theological Science." S.T.D. diss., The Catholic University of America, 1981.

Tuck, Richard. *Natural Rights Theories: Their Origin and Development.* Cambridge: Cambridge University Press, 1979.

Tweedale, Martin M. *Abailard on Universals.* Amsterdam: North-Holland Publishing Co., 1976.

Ugarte Corcuera, Francisco. "Estudio sobre la esencia." *Sapientia* 36 (1987): 171–94, 255–62.

Ushida, Noriko. *Étude comparative de la psychologie d'Aristote, d'Avicenne et de St. Thomas d'Aquin.* Studies in the Humanities and Social Relations, vol. 11. Tokyo: Keio Institute of Cultural and Linguistic Studies, 1968.

Van Steenberghen, Fernand. *Siger de Brabant d'après ses oeuvres inédites*, II: *Siger dans l'histoire de l'aristotelisme*. Les philosophes belges, vol. 13. Louvain: Éditions de l'Institut supérieur de philosophie, 1942.

———. *La philosophie au XIIIe siècle*. Philosophes médiévaux, vol. 9. Louvain: Publications Universitaires and Paris: Béatrice-Nauwelaerts, 1966.

———. *Maître Siger de Brabant*. Philosophes médiévaux, vol. 21. Louvain: Publications Universitaires and Paris: Vander-Oyez, 1977.

———. *Thomas Aquinas and Radical Aristotelianism*. Translated by D. J. O'Meara et al. Washington, D.C.: The Catholic University of America Press, 1980.

Vansteenkiste, C. M. Joris. "Avicenna-citaten bij S. Thomas." *Tijdschrift voor Philosophie* 15 (1953): 457–507.

Veatch, Henry. *Human Rights: Fact or Fancy*. Baton Rouge: Louisiana State University Press, 1985.

———. *Swimming against the Current in Contemporary Philosophy*. Studies in Philosophy and the History of Philosophy, vol. 20. Washington, D.C.: The Catholic University of America Press, 1990.

Verbeke, Gerard. *D'Aristote à Thomas d'Aquin. Antécédents de la pensée moderne. Recueil d'articles*. Ancient and Medieval Philosophy: De Wulf-Mansion Centre, series 1, vol. 8. Leuven: University Press, 1990.

———. "Thémistius et le 'De unitate intellectus' de saint Thomas." In *Thémistius: Commentaire sur le Traité de l'âme d'Aristote, Traduction de Guillaume de Moerbeke*, edited by G. Verbeke, xxxix–lxii. Corpus Latinum Commentariorum in Aristotelem Graecorum, vol. 1. Louvain: Publications Universitaires, 1957.

———. "L'unité de l'homme: Saint Thomas contre Averroes." *Revue philosophique de Louvain* 58 (1960): 220–49.

Vinati, J. "In opusculum Divi Thomae Aquinatis *De unitate intellectus contra Averroistas*." *Divus Thomas* (Piacenza) 6 (1885): 447–49.

von Wright, Georg Henrik. *The Varieties of Goodness*. New York: Routledge & Kegan Paul, 1963.

Walgrave, J. H. "Tertia via." In *Quinque sunt viae: actes du Symposium sur les cinq voies de la Somme theologique, Rolduc, 1979*, edited by L. Elders, 65–74. Rome: Libreria Editrice Vaticana, 1980.

Wallace, William. *From a Realist Point of View: Essays on the Philosophy of Science*. 2d ed. Lanham, Md.: University Press of America, 1983.

———. "Nature as Animating: The Soul in the Human Sciences." *The Thomist* 49 (1985): 612–48.

———. "Nature and Human Nature as the Norm in Medical Ethics." In *Catholic Perspectives on Medical Morals*, edited by Edmund D. Pellegrino et al., 23–53. Dordrecht: Kluwer Academic Publishers, 1989.

Wéber, Édouard-Henri. *La controverse de 1270 a l'Université de Paris et son retentissement sur la pensée de S. Thomas d'Aquin*. Bibliothèque thomiste, vol. 40. Paris: J. Vrin, 1970.

Weisheipl, James A. *Friar Thomas d'Aquino: His Life, Thought and Work*. With *Corrigenda* and *Addenda*. Washington, D.C.: The Catholic University of America Press, 1983.

———. "The Celestial Movers in Medieval Physics." *The Thomist* 24 (1961): 286–326.

———. "The Concept of Nature: Avicenna and Aquinas." In *Thomistic Papers*

I, edited by Victor B. Brezik, 65–87. Houston: Center for Thomistic Studies, 1984.

William, Mary. "The Relationships of the Intellectual Virtue of Science and Moral Virtue." *The New Scholasticism* 36 (1962): 475–505.

Wippel, John F. *Metaphysical Themes in Thomas Aquinas.* Washington, D.C.: The Catholic University of America Press, 1984.

———. "The Condemnation of 1270 and 1277 at Paris." *The Journal of Medieval and Renaissance Studies* 7 (1977): 169–201.

———. "Truth in Thomas Aquinas." *The Review of Metaphysics* 43 (1990): 295–326, 543–76.

Wolfe, Christopher, and John Hittinger, eds. *Liberalism at the Crossroads: An Introduction to Contemporary Liberal Political Theory and Its Critics.* Lanham, Md.: Rowman and Littlefield, 1994.

Woods, Martin T. "The Reduction of Essence in the Thought of Thomas Aquinas and Edmund Husserl." *The Thomist* 53 (1989): 443–60.

Zagar, Janko. "Aquinas and the Social Teaching of the Catholic Church." *The Thomist* 38 (1974): 826–55.

Zedler, Beatrice H., trans. *Saint Thomas Aquinas: On the Unity of the Intellect against the Averroists.* Medieval Philosophical Texts in Translation, no. 19. Milwaukee: Marquette University Press, 1968.

Zimmerman, Albert. "Dante hatte doch Recht." *Philosophisches Jahrbuch* 75 (1967–68): 206–17.

Index

Abelard: universals only in mind, 23

Abstract and concrete: modes of speech about God, 126–29; comparative perfection of, 127–30

Abstraction: in grasping being, 8–9; and universality of concepts, 22, 65, 103; of nature from existence, 31–34

Act: as adapted to *esse*, 6

Act and potency: in *esse*-essence composition, 6, 13–15; and perfection, 42–43, 108–12; in moral exercise of human qualities, 57–58; in God, 114–15, 125–26

Action. *See* Operation; Voluntary

Actus essendi: and *ens*, 4, 10; as source of perfection, 43; grades of participation in, 135. See also *Esse*

Agent intellect: particular in individual souls, 64–65, 96; in judgment, 78; unity of, 85, 88, 99; superfluous for separated intellect, 101

Akrasia: rule of reason lacking in, 53

Alexander of Aphrodisias, 88

Algazel, 104

Analogy: of being, 137–38; of kinds of possibility, 137–38

Ancilla theologiae: human sciences as, 195–200; as *famulatus* vs. as *subalternatio*, 196

Angels: in governance of universe, 182

Anselm, St., 125, 130

Appetites: ruled by reason, 150–51

Aristocracy: in best regime, 166–67

Aristotle: on universals, 21, 29; on the good, 38, 41; doctrine of analogy, 57; *De anima*, as read by Aquinas, 95–97, 101; perfection in, 110–12; infinity in, 112–15; notion of possibility in, 135–44; on truth of future contingents, 142–44; arguments for democracy, 151–52; subalternation in, 196–200; *Categories*, 21, 29; *De Anima*, 95–97, 101; *Metaphysics*, 113, 135–37, 139, 141–42; *Nicomachean Ethics*, 38–40, 41; *On Interpretation*, 142–44; *Physics*, 114, 117; *Politics*, 151–52; *Posterior Analytics*, 196–200; *Sophistical Refutations*, 140–41

Assent: chosen vs. natural, 76–78

Assumptions: abandoned in philosophy, 16–17, 35–36

Augustine, St., 5, 201

Authority: theories of its source, 153–56; as condition for subsidiarity, 158

Autonomy. *See* Subsidiarity

Averroes: on separated intellect, 63–64, 83–106; misread Aristotle, 88, 93, 95, 96; misread Themistius, 104; criticized by Henry of Ghent, 204–5

Averroists: truth not a value for, 70; no responsibility for knowing, 72

Avicenna: as source of Aquinas' Platonism, 6; existence in, 11, 25–26, 34; problem of universals in, 24–27; species neither one nor many, 25; single agent intellect in, 88

Bärthlein, K., 138

Basic forces: and Aquinas' four elements, 177; in subatomic realm, 180

Becoming: and perfection, 108–10, 115, 126; Hartshorne's metaphysics of, 125, 127

Being: characterized by universality, 3–4; grasped by judgment of *separatio*, 8–9; convertible with one in Boethius, 22; as accidental in Avicenna, 25–26; categories as modes of, 40–41; same as good *secundum rem*, 41–42, 43; and perfection, 42–43, 108–9, 135; *simpliciter* vs. *secundum quid*, 46; the will's act as, 55; of morally good action, 59–60; as first object of intellect, 69; kinds within the analogy of, 137–38; in things vs. in propositions, 137–38, 141–44. See also *Actus Essendi*; *Ens*; *Esse*

Bellarmine, Robert, 155, 156

Similitudo: intelligible species as, 91
Simon, Yves: on democracy as best regime, 150–72; on universal suffrage,
151–53; on authority from the people,
154–56; on consent of governed, 155–
56; on democracy and subsidiarity,
157–58; on human rights, 159–61; on
rights and nominalism, 160, 165, 170;
as unthomisitic, 163, 165, 167–72; his
democratic spirit, 168–71; his approach to Aquinas, 172
Simple apprehension: unable to grasp
being, 8–9
Sin. *See* Fault
Singulars. *See* Universals
Soul. *See* Human soul; Powers of soul
Species: and perfection of universe, 119,
122–25; evolution of, 122–25; result
from form, 176–77. *See also* Intelligible species
Specification. *See* Exercise and specification
Speculative reason: commanded by practical judgment, 73; applied to act by
will, 75–78; as subject of moral virtue,
80
Spinoza, 147
Stephen Tempier, Bishop, 93
Strauss, Leo, 170, 171
Studiositas: and good use of intellect, 81
Suarez, 155, 156
Subalternation: and philosophy as *ancilla
theologiae*, 195–200; in Henry of
Ghent, 196–200; in Aquinas, 197,
198; as theology's relation to human
sciences, 197, 198, 199–200
Subjectivism: avoided by Averroists, 64
Subsidiarity: defined, 157; and democracy, 157–59, 164; requires authority,
158; checks state power, 158; and
egalitarianism, 161
Subsistere: same as *esse* for Boethius, 20
Substantial change: in human generation, 178–79; in cosmic evolution,
180–83; and individuation, 184–88; in
brain death, 188–89, 192
Substantial form: in natural substances,
176–80; and specific natures, 176–77;
correlate of protomatter, 176–77; four
kinds of, 176–77; as stable, 176–77; as
transient, 179–80; creation of, 182;
eduction of from matter, 182–83
Sufficient reason, principle of: in medieval philosophy, 132
Summa contra gentiles : vs. unity of possible intellect, 87; on order in universe,

120; on possibility and potentiality,
141
Summa theologiae: on the good, 42–47;
moral action in, 47–49; on nature of
truth, 66–70; on knowing as moral,
71–78, 80–82; vs. unity of possible intellect, 88–89; on infinity in matter
and form, 115; on perfection of universe, 120, 133–35; on *tertia via*, 132,
147–48; on transmission of authority,
154–55, 162–64; on subsidiarity, 157–
58; on best regime, 166–67
Supercompletion: of God, 129
Synod of Pope Eugene, 202

Teleology: in cognition, 70
Telos (teleion, teleiosis): and boundary, 68,
111, 113–14; and perfection, 110–11,
113, 116; translations for, 111; as
completion, 113–14
Tertia via: and principle of plenitude,
132, 147–48
Themistius: as read by Aquinas, 85, 93,
96, 104; paraphrases on *De anima*, 93,
96; plurality of souls in, 104
Theology: use of philosophy for, 202–3
Theophrastus, 85
Thomas Aquinas: thought of permeated
by metaphysics, 3, 37; able to reformulate philosophical problems, 17, 27–
28, 35; treats morality in knowing, 61;
defended Aristotle, 106; and theory of
evolution, 122–25; as angelic doctor,
182
Thomism: as a tradition, xii–xiv; perennial *qua* Aristotelian, 2–3; and contemporary moral issues, 192–93
Thomistic metaphysics: why of present
interest, 1–2; centrality of being in, 1–
15; as neglecting study of nature, 2–3,
192; emphasis on universality, 3–4; in
twentieth century, 3–10; recovery of
the concrete, 4–10; distinct from Aristotle's, 5–6; emphasis on participation,
5–6; emphasis on existential act (*esse*),
6–10; emphasis on *separatio*, 8–9
Thomistic political philosophy: few
sources for in Aquinas, 149; and J.
Maritain, 149–72; and Y. Simon, 149–
72; contemporary rhetoric of, 170–71
Tradition: use of, ix–xiii; as a teacher,
ix–xi
Transcendentals. *See* Good; Being;
Convertibility
Transient natures: as *"ens viale,"* 175,
180; described, 179–80; in cosmic

DATE DUE

NOV 10 1994			
			Printed in USA